Open Slavic Linguistics

Editors: Berit Gehrke, Denisa Lenertová, Roland Meyer, Radek Šimík & Luka Szucsich

In this series:

1. Lenertová, Denisa, Roland Meyer, Radek Šimík & Luka Szucsich (Eds.). Advances in formal Slavic linguistics 2016.

2. Wiland, Bartosz. The spell-out algorithm and lexicalization patterns: Slavic verbs and complementizers.

ISSN: 2627-8332

The spell-out algorithm and lexicalization patterns

Slavic verbs and complementizers

Bartosz Wiland

Wiland, Bartosz. 2019. *The spell-out algorithm and lexicalization patterns: Slavic verbs and complementizers* (Open Slavic Linguistics 2). Berlin: Language Science Press.

This title can be downloaded at:
http://langsci-press.org/catalog/book/242
© 2019, Bartosz Wiland
Published under the Creative Commons Attribution 4.0 Licence (CC BY 4.0):
http://creativecommons.org/licenses/by/4.0/
ISBN: 978-3-96110-160-3 (Digital)
       978-3-96110-177-1 (Hardcover)

ISSN: 2627-8332
DOI:10.5281/zenodo.2636394
Source code available from www.github.com/langsci/242
Collaborative reading: paperhive.org/documents/remote?type=langsci&id=242

Cover and concept of design: Ulrike Harbort
Fonts: Linux Libertine, Libertinus Math, Arimo, DejaVu Sans Mono
Typesetting software: XƎLATEX

Language Science Press
Unter den Linden 6
10099 Berlin, Germany
langsci-press.org

Storage and cataloguing done by FU Berlin

Dedicated to the memory of Morris Halle, who introduced me to the problems of Slavic morphology, some of which this book aims to resolve.

Contents

Acknowledgments   v

Abbreviations and symbols   vii

1 Introduction   1

2 The spell-out mechanism in Nanosyntax   5
    2.1 Introduction 5
    2.2 Two problems of lexicalization 5
    2.3 What we already know about how lexicalization works 7
       2.3.1 Phrasal spell-out 8
       2.3.2 Shortest Move and linearization 12
       2.3.3 *ABA as a consequence of the Superset Principle 14
       2.3.4 The spell-out procedure in Starke (2018) 16
       2.3.5 Pointers 24
    2.4 Summary of the current state of the spell-out procedure 25
    2.5 Spell-out resulting in the reduction in the number of morphemes   26
       2.5.1 The problem 26
       2.5.2 Backtracking 29
       2.5.3 Subextraction 30
       2.5.4 Verb stem alternation 35
    2.6 Summary and roadmap 37

3 Deriving the verb stem alternation   39
    3.1 Introduction 39
    3.2 Background: The verb stem in Czech and Polish 40
       3.2.1 Verb stem morphology 40
       3.2.2 Thematic suffixes 41
    3.3 Degree achievements vs. semelfactives 45
       3.3.1 Adjectival vs. nominal roots 45
       3.3.2 Get vs. Give 47
       3.3.3 Light verb theory of -n 49
       3.3.4 -Ou as layers of the VP structure 52

Contents

3.4	Properties of the alternation	57
	3.4.1 Perfective stems	57
	3.4.2 Argument structure preservation	60
3.5	Representation	61
3.6	Spelling out -*aj* stems with subextraction	65
	3.6.1 Deriving the reduction	65
	3.6.2 Pointers	69
3.7	Subextract vs. backtracking	71
	3.7.1 Structures that shrink in the middle	71
	3.7.2 Shrinking at the root?	73
3.8	Remaining issues	75
	3.8.1 -*N-ou* drop	75
	3.8.2 -*Aj* on top of -*n*	77
3.9	Concluding remarks	78

4 Resolving a morphological containment problem — 81

4.1	Introduction	81
4.2	Syncretisms with the declarative complementizer	82
	4.2.1 Paradigm	82
	4.2.2 Analysis in Baunaz & Lander (2017; 2018a)	84
4.3	An ordering paradox with the demonstrative	89
4.4	Low indefinite demonstratives	90
	4.4.1 Severing spatial deixis from definiteness	90
	4.4.2 Lexicalization in Polish and in Russian	98
4.5	High definite demonstratives	103
4.6	Summary	106

5 Beyond Slavic: Sorting out a Latvian paradigm — 109

5.1	Introduction	109
5.2	Latvian demonstratives	110
5.3	Refining the pronominal base	113
5.4	Proximal *šis* and medial *tas*	118
5.5	Deriving the three readings of *kas*	122
5.6	Place -*ur* as a pronominal superstructure in *kur*	125
5.7	Caseless complementizer *ka*	131
5.8	Multi-dimensional morphological paradigms as homeomorphic singleton projection lines in syntax	133
5.9	Summary	137

6	**An apparent *ABA violation in Basaá**		**139**
	6.1	Introduction: an ABA paradigm	139
		6.1.1 Excursus on the Rel-cell in Swiss German	140
		6.1.2 Back to the Basaá paradigm	141
	6.2	Basaá demonstratives	142
	6.3	Non-wh-relatives in Basaá	144
	6.4	Resumptive relative clauses	148
	6.5	Summary	149
7	**Overview**		**151**
	7.1	Summary	151
	7.2	Loose ends	152

References	**153**
Index	**169**
Name index	169
Language index	173
Subject index	175

Acknowledgments

This book grew out of an interest in what initially seemed to be a couple of unrelated puzzles in the grammars of certain Slavic languages and Latvian. As the work on each of them progressed, it became clearer and clearer that they in fact all boil down to the way the syn-sem representations specific to each domain under the investigation become realized as morphology. This work presents the puzzles and the steps taken to bring us at least minimally closer to finding explanations for them.

Parts of the material discussed in this work were presented at colloquia held at the Department of Slavic at Humboldt University in Berlin in May 2017 and at the Institute of Linguistics at the University of Wuppertal in May 2018, as well as at the Olomouc Linguistics Colloquium (Olinco) held at Palacký University in Olomouc in June 2018, and at the *Exploring Nanosyntax* session at the annual LSA meeting held in New York in January 2019. I am indebted to the participants of these meetings for feedback and discussions. None of the material presented in this book has been published elsewhere, but an earlier report outlining the research on the demonstratives in Slavic and in Basaá which is developed here has been posted at LingBuzz as part of an unpublished collection of squibs in a festschrift for Michal Starke (Wiland 2018c).

Special thanks to Pavel Caha for a discussion and comments, which helped me bring the solutions reported here to their final shape. I have also benefited from questions and comments from Michal Starke, Lucie Taraldsen Medová, Radek Šimík, Anders Holmberg, Tobias Scheer, Dorota Klimek-Jankowska, Richard Holaj, Nicole Nau, Tatjana Navicka, and Jacek Witkoś. I am also indebted to two reviewers and the editors of the Open Slavic Linguistics series, especially Radek Šimík, for their excellent work. Suffice it to say, I am solely responsible for the statements made in this work.

Last but not least I would like to thank Sebastian Nordhoff and Felix Kopecky of Language Science Press for their support with the X₃LATEX skeleton.

This work has been supported by the Polish National Center for Science (NCN), grant no. 2016/2/B/HS2/00619 (Opus 11).

Poznań, 2nd March 2019   Bartosz Wiland

Abbreviations and symbols

ACC	accusative	N	light verb suffix -*n*/noun
AJ	theme vowel -*aj*	NEU	neuter
AUG	augment	NOM	nominative
COMP	complementizer	OP	operator
D	determiner	OU	theme vowel -*ou*
DAT	dative	OV	theme vowel -*ov*
DEIX	deixis	PART	participle
DEF	definiteness, definite	PFV	perfective aspect
DEG.ACH	degree achievement	PL	plural
DEM	demonstrative	PRT	particle
DIST	distal	PRES	present or non-past tense
FEM	feminine	PRON	pronoun
FSEQ	functional sequence	PROX	proximal
GEN	genitive	PST	past tense
GET	light verb Get	REL	relativizer
GIVE	light verb Give	SBJ	subject
I	theme vowel -*i*	SEMEL	semelfactive
INDEF	indefinite	SG	singular
INF	infinitive	SM	subject marker
INST	instrumental	WH	wh-pronoun
INV	invariant	⇔	relation between features and their exponence
ITER	iterative		
LOC	locative	⇒	result of spell-out
MED	medial	⤳	leads to
MSC	masculine		

1 Introduction

The aim of this book is two-fold. The first goal is to explain a curious instance of analytic vs. fusional realization of grammatical categories that we find in a semelfactive-iterative alternation in Czech and Polish verbs. Namely, a semelfactive verb stem as in the Czech *kop-n-ou-t* 'give a kick' alternates with an iterative verb stem as in *kop-a-t* 'kick repeatedly', which is a regular alternation between these two categories in both languages. The iterative *-aj* stem is morphologically less complex than the semelfactive stem formed with the *-n-ou* sequence, which is paradoxical given an analysis of iteratives as categories whose syn-sem representation is more complex than semelfactives.

The second goal is empirically unrelated to the verb stem alternation and, instead, focuses on categories related to the declarative complementizer, such as demonstrative, interrogative, and relative pronouns. Namely, the aim in this domain is to sort out those patterns in morphological paradigms with the complementizer which are in certain ways unexpected. The problems in such paradigms include an unexpected morphological containment (in Russian), a degree of morphological complexity (in Latvian), and a so-called ABA pattern of syncretic alignment (in Basaá), which we do not expect to find if syncretism is restricted to adjacent cells in a paradigm (cf. Bobaljik 2012).

The reason why morphological alternations inside the Czech and Polish verbs and morphological containment in the domain of Russian and some other complementizers are addressed in one book is that, I argue, both kinds of problems boil down to the way syntactic (hierarchical) representations become lexicalized (realized as linear representations). More specifically, the approach to lexicalization taken up in this work is informed by research on syntactic representations in the last quarter of a century, which shows that syntactic structures are maximally fine-grained, the result that is sometimes described as "one grammatical feature per one syntactic head". This result has led to a situation where syntactic representations are in principle submorphemic, in the sense that a lexical item, as for instance represented by α in (1), corresponds to more than one syntactic head in a phrase marker, a strand of research that has become known as Nanosyntax (Starke 2009, among others).

1 Introduction

(1)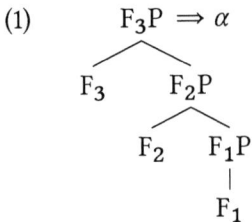

A scenario whereby a set of terminal nodes in syntax can be realized by a single lexical item has led both to the change in the way we should think about syntax and lexicon and to the change in the methodology of explaining morphosyntactic problems. The relation between syntax and lexical items (words and morphemes) comes out as a relation between a fine-grained mental representation of grammatical features (illustrated in (1) as an ordered sequence of F_n) and their linguistic exponents (α in 1). This architecture immediately excludes the existence of any kind of a pre-syntactic lexicon, not even the one which stores abstract morphemes, as these are created only in the process of realizing grammatical features (cf. Starke 2009: 1).

This set-up requires a spell-out formula which applies to phrasal rather than to terminal nodes, a procedure recently detailed in Starke (2018). This work investigates the limits of such a procedure in resolving the selected empirical problems in the domain of Slavic verbs and declarative complementizers. The overarching goal of the book is, thus, modest in the sense that it argues that we can get a better understanding of these empirical problems if we consider them from the perspective of the way the spell-out mechanism applies to the sequences of syntactic heads that make up the investigated grammatical categories. One novelty that this book brings to the table, however, is the addition of subextraction to the list of spell-out driven operation. The list of operations that has been argued in the literature to facilitate spell-out already includes successive cyclic movement and complement movement so extending this list by the third type of phrasal movement comes out as a legitimate step to consider.

The logical organization of the book is as follows. First, in Chapter 2, I provide an overview of the spell-out mechanism in Nanosyntax with a particular attention to the operations that allow us to predict if realizing a syntactic subtree as a morpheme is going to come out as a suffix or a "pre-" element, that is a prefix, a preposition, a particle, etc. In Chapter 3, I move on to discussing the alternation between semelfactive and iterative verbs in Czech and Polish, which appears to result in the reduction in the number of morphemes. I explore the possibility to derive such a reduction with extending the list of spell-out driven operations with subextraction and I point out limitations of such an analysis and discuss a possible alternative. Subextraction as a spell-out driven movement, however, is considered only in the domain of Slavic verbs and is not further explored in the domain of the declarative complementizer and related grammatical categories in Russian (in Chapter 4), in what is logically the second part of the book. The discussion of this domain is followed by a comparative look at the similar problem with these categories in Latvian (Baltic) in Chapter 5 and in Basaá (Bantu) in Chapter 6. The book ends with a summary and a list of loose ends that can be hopefully worked out in the future work.

2 The spell-out mechanism in Nanosyntax

2.1 Introduction

There are two separate problems that are associated with the term lexicalization. One is spell-out, that is the way in which syntactic representations become realized as morphemes. The other is the positions in which these morphemes appear with respect to other morphemes. The positional problem is sometimes referred to as the prefix vs. suffix opposition, which is a little misleading since the issue not only involves the predictions we can make about the placement of morphemes (the "before or after the stem" problem), but also the predictions we can make about the amount of affixes a particular syntactic representation is going to be realized by.[1]

In order to illustrate these two problems, let us walk through cross-linguistically attested patterns of genitivite marking on nouns. The choice to use genitive marking as an illustration of two major problems of lexicalization is motivated by the fact that it is a fairly familiar and well-described domain in the literature. Once the problems of spell-out and morpheme order are presented using genitive marking, the discussion in the remaining chapters will move to the domains of Slavic verbs and declarative complementizers.

2.2 Two problems of lexicalization

The first pattern of genitive case marking is found in Slavic languages, where the nominal root is followed by a single suffix, as shown on the example of the Polish noun *win-a* 'of wine'.

(1) Polish
     win-a
     wine-GEN
     'of wine'

---

[1] See DiSciullo (2005: 135–138, 154–156) and Kayne (2017) for some recent attempts to derive the prefix vs. suffix distinction from independent properties of grammar.

2 The spell-out mechanism in Nanosyntax

The second pattern is found in languages like Balkan Romani, where the genitive case is realized as two separate suffixes on the nominal root, as in (2).

(2) Balkan Romani (Friedman 1991: 57 as cited in Caha 2011b)
 čhav-és-koro
 boy-ACC-GEN
 'of boy'

Let us take note of the fact that the suffix -és is an accusative marker, as in čhav-és 'boy-ACC', while *čhav-koro is ill-formed.[2]

The third pattern of the lexicalization of genitive case is attested in English, where the genitive is realized as a pre-nominal *of*, as in *of wine*. A pre-nominal genitive is also attested as a bound morpheme for instance in Maybrat (West Papuan):

(3) Maybrat (Dol 1999: 97)
 amah ro-Petrus
 house GEN-Petrus
 'Petrus' house'

For our purposes, we will treat prepositional and prefixal marking as variants of a more general "pre-" distribution, as opposed to a "post-" distribution (suffixes and postpositions).

To sum it up, while Polish, Romani, and English realize genitive case as morphemes, they differ with respect to their amount and placement. This brings us to the following questions that pertain to the core of the lexicalization problem:

---

[2] The containment of accusative marker -és within a complex genitive marker -és-koro falls within a broader class of morphological containment of cases attested also in Ingush (Nichols 1994), Estonian (Blevins 2008), Kazakh (Plakendorf 2007), or Classical Armenian (Schmitt 1981; Caha 2013) and in a list of languages given in Plank (1999), including Finnish, Karelian, and Chukchi, among others. In Slavic, case containment is generally rare but can nevertheless be attested, for instance in the Prizren-Timok dialect of Serbian (Caha 2011a) or the colloquial form of the Polish instrumental plural *ocz-y-ma* 'eyes', which contains the syncretic NOM=ACC suffix -y, as shown in:

(i) Polish
 a. ocz-y
 eye-NOM/ACC.PL
 b. ocz-y-ma
 eye-INST.PL

- What is the source of these differences?
- Can we predict whether a language X will lexicalize genitive case – or any other grammatical features – as one or more morphemes?
- If so, then can we predict if these morphemes are going to be linearized as pre- or post-positional elements?

A strand of research that has provided methodology to answer these questions is Nanosyntax, a theory of the syntax-lexicon interface whose premise is that both the feature structure of morphemes as well as their amount and placement are the two results of the way syntactic representations are spelled out (Starke 2009; 2014b).

If we break down the existing methodology of Nanosyntax, we find two distinct notions that help us answer the questions listed above, namely (i) phrasal spell-out and (ii) the spell-out algorithm. Phrasal spell-out, the idea that a lexical item corresponds to a phrasal node in a syntactic tree, tells us how syntactic representations become realized as morphemes. The spell-out algorithm, in turn, makes a statement about predicting the placement of morphemes with respect to other morphemes as well as their amount.

Let us discuss in what follows how both tools explain our three patterns of genitive marking on nouns.

2.3 What we already know about how lexicalization works

Nanosyntax (henceforth NS) is a late insertion theory of the architecture of grammar, which assumes a neo-constructionist view of argument structure, and whose major premise is that syntactic representation can be submorphemic. This view is consonant both with a growing body of work on the structuralization of lexical semantics (e.g. Borer 2005; Ramchand 2008) and the so-called strong cartographic thesis, whereby every grammatical feature is a head of its own projection in syntax (Cinque & Rizzi 2008: 50).[3] A common platform for neo-constructionist theories is a close correspondence between the mental lexicon and syntactically relevant features, to the effect that the association between the "syn" and "sem"

---

[3] The "one feature per one syntactic head" theorem is also shared by Kayne (2005), an approach which unlike NS does not assume that terminal nodes of syntactic trees can be smaller than morphemes.

of a lexical item is tight, though the specific nature of this association differs among the theories.[4]

2.3.1 Phrasal spell-out

What constitutes a fundamental difference between NS and other theories of the syntax-lexicon interface is the nature of the association between the syn-sem properties of a lexical item and its exponence. With this respect, a standard assumption of mainstream generative grammar about constraining spell-out only to terminal nodes of a syntactic representation is also part of Distributed Morphology (DM). In DM, an exponent of a lexical item, e.g. α in (4), realizes a terminal node with pre-packaged feature bundles, e.g. the $[F_1, F_2, F_3]$ bundle in the following illustration (Halle & Marantz 1993; 1994; Embick & Noyer 2007; Embick 2015).

(4) XP
     |
     X $\Rightarrow \alpha$
     $[F_1, F_2, F_3]$

Limiting the interface between syn-sem properties of lexical items and their exponents to terminal nodes initially looks attractive. However, it comes with the cost of assuming the existence of a separate module, which will combine individual features F_1, F_2, F_3 into feature sets that the terminal node in syntax is specified for. The spell-out of a featurally complex terminal node in syntax requires the existence of such a pre-syntactic compositional mechanism which construes the features into a set no matter if the set is ordered (a hierarchy) or not (a bundle). The substitution of feature bundles for feature hierarchies in DM, thus, does

---

[4]"Neo-constructionist theories" are understood here as theories of argument structure that by and large stem from Hale & Keyser's (1993; 2002) work on syntactic representations of lexical items and, as such, argue that the properties of verbal predicates are construed in syntax rather than in a generative lexicon. In constructionist approaches, the meaning of a lexical item, e.g. the minimal meaning of a verbal root, is both conventionally and partially idiosyncratically associated with pieces of a syntactic structure and argument positions (e.g. Goldberg 1995; 2006; Booij 2002; Jackendoff 2002; Goldberg & Jackendoff 2004). This contrasts with neo-constructionist theories, which rely on more refined syntactic representations that are associated with meaning. The latter position, thus, suggests that there is a more direct and predictable relation between syntactic representations and its interpretation (semantics) (e.g. Mateu 2002; Borer 2003; 2005; Ramchand 2008). See Levin & Rappaport Hovav (2005), Acedo Matellán (2010: 19–48), Ramchand (2013), Mateu (2014), Acquaviva et al. (to appear) for overviews of the differences between generative theories of lexical semantics.

2.3 What we already know about how lexicalization works

not automatically remove the necessity for a pre-syntactic construal mechanism from the theory.

NS makes an opposite claim: spell-out targets phrasal nodes, as illustrated in (5), where features F_1, F_2, and F_3 all project their own phrases in line with the "one feature per one head" thesis.[5]

(5)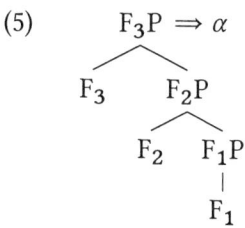

The upshot of such a scenario is that there is no need for a pre-syntactic mechanism of construal since complex feature structures are formed exclusively in syntax.

There are two immediate consequences resulting from such an alternative. One is that syntactic representations in NS are much more fine-grained when compared with representations postulated by theories of grammar that assume the existence of a pre-syntactic lexicon. The other is that the only building block of syntactic structures is an atomic privative feature rather than a morpheme, abstract (as in late insertion models like DM) or factual (as in lexicalist approaches).

An essential feature of all late insertion models is the nature of the matching mechanism between the feature set in a syntactic node with an exponent of a lexical item.

In DM, a lexical item can be *underspecified* with respect to the features in the node it spells out. For example, the exponent of a lexical item defined as in (6) can spell out the terminal node X of the tree in (4), which is specified for a larger set of features than the lexical item. (In the descriptions of lexical entries, let the symbol "⟺" indicate the association between the syn-sem structure of a lexical item and its exponence).

(6) Lexical entry
  $[\,F_1\,] \Longleftrightarrow \alpha$

If there exists another lexical item that meets the condition on insertion, such as the one in (7), the competition between α and β for lexicalizing the terminal node

---

[5] Phrasal spell-out has its origin in McCawley (1968). Outside NS, it has been applied to the analysis of pronouns in Weerman & Evers-Vermeul (2002) and Neeleman & Szendrői (2007).

X in (4) is resolved by the ELSEWHERE CONDITION, which Halle (1997) defines in terms of the greatest number of features in the terminal node that are matched by a lexical item.[6]

(7)   Lexical entry
      $[\, F_1, F_3 \,] \Leftrightarrow \beta$

Following the Elsewhere logic, the item β will win the competition for insertion with the item α.

A dissenting view is advanced by NS, which claims that lexical insertion is governed by the SUPERSET PRINCIPLE, defined as in (8), which submits that a lexical item (i.e. a lexically stored tree with grammatical features) can be *overspecified* with respect to the features in the syntactic node it spells out.[7]

(8)   Superset Principle (Starke 2009)
      An exponent of a lexical item is inserted into a syntactic node if its lexical entry has a subconstituent that matches that node.

On the strength of the Superset Principle, the exponent of a lexical item that is defined as in (9) will spell-out the superset as well as the subsets of the features that make up the syntactic tree in (5).

(9)   Lexical entry
      $[\, F_3 \,[\, F_2 \,[\, F_1 \,]]] \Leftrightarrow \alpha$

When a lexicon of a particular language contains multiple lexical items that are in competition for insertion into a node in syntax, the choice which one gets inserted is governed by the Elsewhere Principle defined as in the following:

(10) Elsewhere Principle
      Where several items meet the conditions for insertion, the item containing fewer features unspecified in the node must be chosen.

---

[6]This is one of a few approximations of the mechanism of insertion and competition resolution in DM. Halle (1997) unifies underspecification with the Elsewhere Condition into one Subset Principle, Bobaljik (2017) gives a more generic rule of insertion based on pairing a structural description of a lexical item with the features in a syntactic node, among some other versions of the same basic idea.

[7]See Caha (2018) for a comparison of lexical insertion in NS and DM and the results both mechanisms obtain in explaining the shapes of morphological paradigms.

2.3 What we already know about how lexicalization works

Thus, if a lexicon contains both lexical entries as in (9) and as in:

(11)   Lexical entry
        $[\,F_2\,[\,F_1\,]\,] \Leftrightarrow \beta$

then only the superstructure of our tree will be spelled out as α and its subsets will be spelled out as β, as shown in:

(12)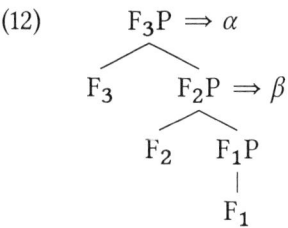

Note that on the strength of the Elsewhere Principle in (10), the AP subset of our tree in (12) is spelled out as β rather than α since the lexical item in (11) has only one feature that is unspecified in the F_1P node, feature F_2, while the lexical item in (9) has two such features, F_1 and F_2. In other words, the lexical item β is a better match for the syntactic node F_1P than the lexical item α.[8]

A central feature of the spell-out mechanism in NS is that it is attempted after each application of merge, without a delay. That is, in order to lexicalize the entire tree in (12), we attempt to spell-out each feature, F_1, F_2, and F_3 immediately upon their mergers in the phrase marker. The result is that a lexical entry that matches a bigger tree will always over-ride the entires that match its subconstituents, a principle sometimes referred to as CYCLIC OVER-RIDE.

In connection to the spell-outs of the representations in (5) and (12), let us also point out that the Superset Principle applies to an entire phrase marker. That is, features cannot be erased from a grammatical representation and at the end of a cycle every feature of a syntactic tree must be realized by a lexical item. Following Fábregas (2007), this restriction goes by the name EXHAUSTIVE LEXICALIZATION PRINCIPLE (see also Ramchand 2008, who formulates essentially the same idea working with a different empirical material than Fábregas 2007).

---

[8] The Elsewhere Principle is informally referred to in the literature on NS as "the minimize junk principle".

2 The spell-out mechanism in Nanosyntax

2.3.2 Shortest Move and linearization

The spell-out of a syntactic tree is not always going to result in over-ride. For example, the exponent of the following lexical entry

(13) $[\,F_4\,] \Leftrightarrow \gamma$

will not be inserted in the root node of the tree:

(14)
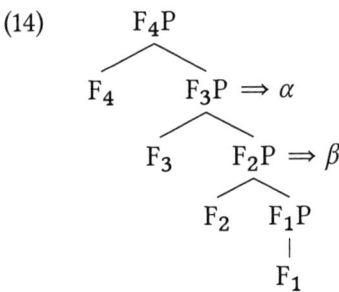

Due to the strict cyclicity of spell-out, F_4 must be spelled out before another feature is merged. Since it is impossible to spell out F_4 in the tree with γ "as is", a different possibility to spell it out is attempted: movement. As indicated in (15), the evacuation of F_3P will create the remnant constituent F_4P, which can then be spelled out as γ.

(15)
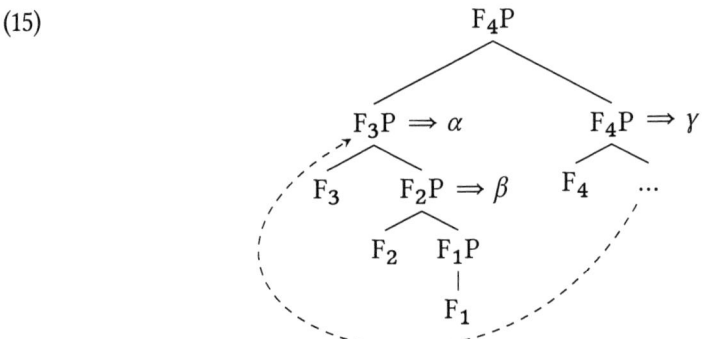

In Caha (2011b), the movement of the offending node is triggered by the shape of the lexical entry that a remnant constituent can match. For (15), this means that the structure of the lexically stored tree in (13) launches the evacuation of F_3P. A different rationale is given in Starke (2018), where movement operations are not triggered by shapes of existing lexical entries and instead take place as part of

2.3 What we already know about how lexicalization works

an ordered set of procedures that are launched whenever a syntactic tree with a newly merged feature F is not spelled out "as is". I will discuss the details of this spell-out procedure in the next section.

As indicated in (15), the evacuated node F_3P adjoins right above the node that is targeted by spell-out, the requirement sometimes referred to as SHORTEST MOVE. This movement takes place in agreement with the Extension Condition, whereby the output of merge must extend the tree at its root (Chomsky 1993). The evacuated F_3P creates a non-projecting sister node (a "specifier") to the node that is targeted by spell-out.

Such a structure is mapped onto a linear order of exponents in concert with a simplified version of the Linear Correspondence Axiom (Kayne 1994), whose traditional formulation is given in the following:

(16) Linear Correspondence Axiom (LCA, Kayne 1994)

If a non-terminal X asymmetrically c-commands a non-terminal Y, then all terminal nodes dominated by X will precede all terminal nodes dominated by Y.

The definition in (16) relies on the notion of asymmetric c-command, which distinguishes between categories and its segments, i.e. two directly connected nodes in a tree have the same label.

(17) Asymmetric c-command (Kayne 1994: 18)

X c-commands Y iff:
  a. X and Y are categories and
  b. no segment of X dominates Y and
  c. every category that dominates X dominates Y

This traditional formulation of the LCA relies on both non-terminal and terminal nodes but allows only terminal nodes to linearize. For example, the syntactic representation as in (18) will provide the following statement about the linear order of exponents: *x* precedes *y*.

(18)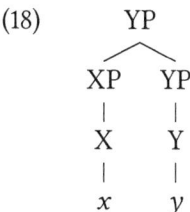

2 The spell-out mechanism in Nanosyntax

With lexical items spelling out only non-terminals, the linearization axiom must be modified. More precisely, it must be simplified to rely only on non-terminal nodes, as in the following formulation from Pantcheva (2011):

(19) Formulation of the LCA for phrasal spell-out (Pantcheva 2011: 135)

If a non-terminal X asymmetrically c-commands a non-terminal Y, then whatever spells out X precedes whatever spells out Y.

For the tree in (15), this means that the spell-out of F_3P as α and the spell-out of the lower segment of F_4P as γ will map onto the following sequence: α precedes γ.

2.3.3 *ABA as a consequence of the Superset Principle

A direct consequence of the Superset Principle that applies to a feature hierarchy rather than to a bundle is the so-called *ABA, which constrains the distribution of syncretic forms in paradigms. We can formulate it after Bobaljik (2007) as in (20).

(20) The *ABA generalization

In structured sequences (paradigms), a more complex structure and a less complex structure are not realized as form A, if structures that are in between them in terms of complexity are realized as form B.

The restriction of syncretic spans to adjacent cells of a paradigm informs us about structural contiguity of its categories and, thus, provides a major tool in discovering functional decomposition in grammar.

For example, let us consider Caha's (2009) decomposition of cases into sets of cumulatively ordered privative case-forming features K_n as in (21), where nominative corresponds to K_n, accusative to K_1+K_2, genitive to $K_1+K_2+K_3$, and so on. Due to the description of cases in terms of feature cumulation, (21) comes out as an exocentric representation in the sense that case phrases higher than NomP are construed by both their daughters. The representation of cases as a sequence of functional heads (fseq) follows from the observation that non-accidental case syncretism targets only adjacent cells of declension paradigms if they are arranged in the order predicted by the hierarchy in (21).[9]

---

[9] The term "non-accidental syncretism" should be understood here simply as identity of exponents which in certain environments become phonologically altered rather than any surface phonological form of a case marker. This is particularly important in the context of Slavic, where for example the exponent of the Polish nominative masculine suffix of the singular

2.3 What we already know about how lexicalization works

(21)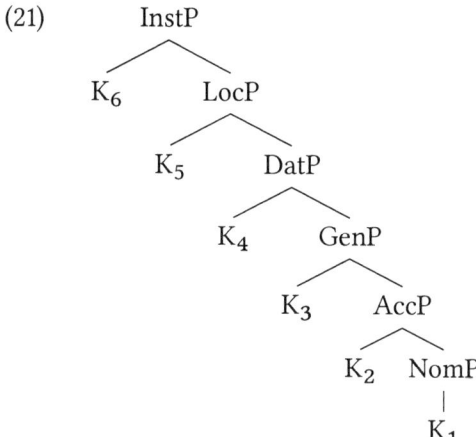

This is illustrated by the examples of case paradigms in Polish given in Table 2.1.

Table 2.1: Examples of attested case syncretisms in Polish

	'wine' NEU.SG	'sir/man' MSC.SG	'big' MSC.SG	'lamp' FEM.SG	'five' MSC
NOM	win-o	pan-U	duży-Ø	lamp-a	pięć-I
ACC	win-o	pan-a	duż-ego	lamp-ę	pięć-I
GEN	win-a	pan-a	duż-ego	lamp-y	pięci-u
DAT	win-u	pan-u	duż-emu	lampi-e	pięci-u
LOC	wini-e	pan-u	duży-m	lampi-e	pięci-u
INST	win-em	pan-em	duży-mi	lamp-ą	pięci-oma

In all the paradigms shown in the table, syncretic spans include only contiguous regions of the tree in (21), which indicates that the lexical entries for particular cases correspond to its constituents, as shown in (22) for the neuter singular noun *win* 'wine'.

---

nominal declension is a non-palatalizing [−ATR,+back,+round,+high] yer vowel *U* and the exponent of the numberless masculine suffix present in the declension of numerals such as *pięć* 'five' is a palatalizing [−ATR,−back,+round,+high] yer vowel *I*. Both yers are subject to deletion unless they lower to /e/ in a defined environment (see Gussmann 1980; Rubach 1984). Yers must not be confused with genuinely null exponents in Polish, such as the nominative masculine suffix of the singular adjectival declension shown on the example of *duży* 'big' in the third column in Table 2.1. See Wiland (2009: 35–38) and the references listed there for a more detailed illustration.

2 The spell-out mechanism in Nanosyntax

(22)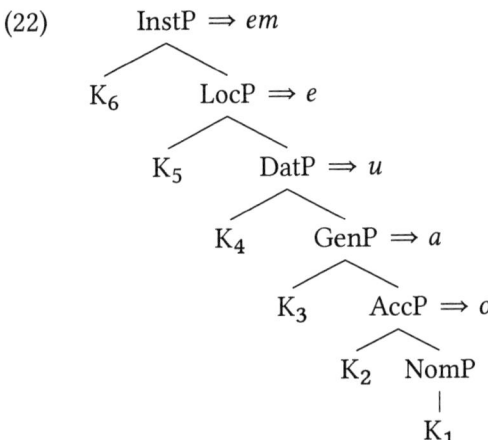

The Superset Principle explains the unattested ABA patterns in a straightforward way: since the lexical entry A is contained within the lexical entry B, it is impossible for A to lexicalize a structure bigger than B. For example, since the exponent -o in (22) spells out the accusative structure, which is contained in the genitive structure realized by -a, -o cannot spell out the structures that contain genitive at the same time.

Apart from an abundant work on the case fseq (e.g. Caha 2009; Zompí 2017; Starke 2017), sequences of syntactic projections have been deduced from syncretism falling as a consequence of the Superset Principle in the domain of Bantu class markers (Taraldsen 2010), spatial adpositions (Pantcheva 2011), aspectual prefixes in Polish (Wiland 2012), negation marking (De Clercq 2013; 2018), participles (Starke 2006; Taraldsen Medová & Wiland 2018a), and wh-pronouns in Germanic (Vangsnes 2013), among others. For some alternative accounts of syncretism see Stump (2001), Baerman et al. (2005), Burzio (2007), Müller (2008), or Bobaljik (2012), among others.

2.3.4 The spell-out procedure in Starke (2018)

To illustrate lexicalization patterns of genitive case features attested in Polish, Romani, and English, let us start with the lexical entries in (23), where the structure in (a) is a stand-in for the Polish accusative neuter of the singular declension and the NP in (b) is a stand-in for the nominal root *win* 'wine'.

(23)   Lexical entries in Polish
  a.   NP ⇔ *win* 'wine'
  b.   [K_2 [K_1]] ⇔ o

2.3 What we already know about how lexicalization works

The merger of the first feature of the case fseq on top of the NP root, the nominative-forming K_1, triggers spell-out in line with the theorem about a strictly cyclic character of merge and spell-out. However, K_1 in the tree on the left in (24) does not match any lexical entry in the Polish lexicon, which requires its spell-out to be attempted in a different way. For a moment, let us go with Caha's (2011b) idea that movement in syntax is driven by spell-out, which when applied to our case means that all we need to do to spell out K_1 is to evacuate the root *win* 'wine', as shown on the right side in (24).

(24) Merger and spell-out of nominative in Polish

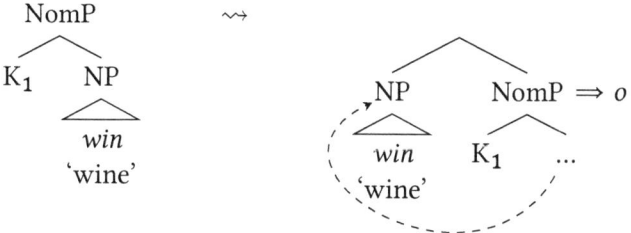

The constituent created in this way matches the lexical entry in (23b) and, on the strength of the Superset Principle, gets spelled out as *-o*, which comes out as the suffix on the root *win*.

The new cycle begins with the merger of next feature in the case fseq, the accusative-forming K_2, as in:

(25)

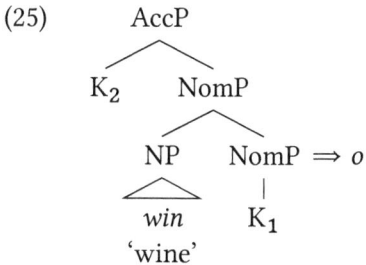

Such a structure cannot be spelled out as, again, it is not matched by any existing entry in the Polish lexicon. In contrast to Polish, a nominal root with a sequence of case features $K_2 > K_1$ merged on its top, can be spelled out right away in English, as shown in (26).

(26) Spell-out of the English syncretic root *wine*

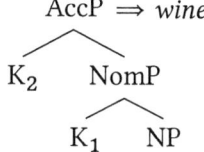

2 The spell-out mechanism in Nanosyntax

The in situ spell-out of the root *wine* together with NomP and AccP captures the fact that all nominative and accusative forms of English lexical nouns are syncretic with their roots.[10] Such a portmanteau spell-out is the basic option in which features can be realized as morphology as it does not require any movement operation to facilitate lexicalization. Let us, thus, call this option STAY.

In contrast to English, it is clear that neither NomP nor AccP is spelled out by STAY in the Polish accusative form *win-o* 'wine-ACC', as the spell-out of K_2 in the tree that looks like in (25) would over-ride the earlier spell-outs of both the NP root *win* 'wine' and the nominative suffix *-o*, to the effect that we would have a single portmanteau morpheme in their place, counter fact.

Since STAY fails, the next familiar possibility to spell-out K_2 is to attempt movement. Let us, thus, call this option MOVE. Unlike in the case of the nominative-forming feature K_1, however, this time there are two movement possibilities: we can continue with the movement launched in the previous cycle, the SPEC-TO-SPEC movement of the NP *win*, or we can move the complement of K_2 (the SNOWBALLING of *win-o*). This is a vacuous choice in an approach to lexicalization as in Caha (2011b) where spell-out driven movement is teleological, in the sense that it targets those nodes whose evacuation will create a constituent matching an existing lexical entry.

An alternative to such a characterization of spell-out driven operations is a scenario where we have an unambiguous specification of how to spell-out a feature. This is the position taken up in Starke (2018), who submits that out of the two movement possibilities, spec-to-spec is the first option to try. As shown in (27), the movement of the root *win* lets K_2 spell-out as part of the accusative superstructure of *-o*, in line with the lexical entry in (23b).

(27) Spell-out of the Polish accusative *win-o* 'wine'

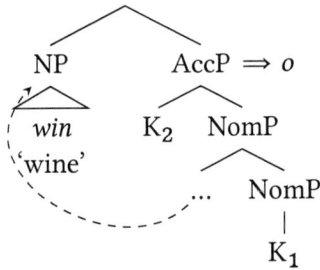

---

[10]There is no established distinction between closed and open class items in NS. While this constitutes a research question of its own, this issue does not have a bearing on the application of phrasal spell-out as long as open class items can be represented as syntactic phrases, the position recently made a case for, on different grounds, in Taraldsen Medová & Wiland (2018b) and Caha et al. (2019b).

2.3 What we already know about how lexicalization works

Consequently, the accusative *-o* surfaces as the suffix.

Given the lexical entries as in (28), spec-to-spec movement also facilitates the spell-out of K_2 in the Romani *čhav-és* 'boy'-ACC, as shown in (29).

(28)   Lexical entries in Balkan Romani
   a.   NP ⇔ *čhav* 'boy'
   b.   [K_2 [K_1]] ⇔ *és*

(29)   Spell-out of the Balkan Romani accusative *čhav-és* 'boy'

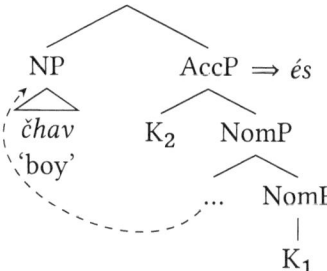

The merger of the next case feature in the fseq, the genitive-forming K_3 reveals that we need both spec-to-spec movement and complement movement to be listed in the spell-out algorithm. Whereas the first allows K_3 to spell-out in Polish, it does not in Romani. Assuming the lexical entry as in (30), a stand-in for genitive neuter, then successive-cyclic movement of *win* in Polish results in the genitive marker *-a* over-riding the earlier spell-out of the accusative *-o* and getting linearized as the suffix in *win-a* 'wine'. This derivation is shown in (31) below.

(30)   Lexical entry in Polish
   [K_3 [K_2 [K_1]]] ⇔ *a*

(31)   Spell-out of the Polish genitive *win-a* 'wine'

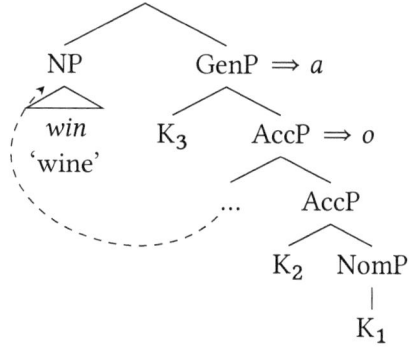

2 The spell-out mechanism in Nanosyntax

In contrast to the Polish genitive -a, the genitive marker -koro in Romani does not over-ride the accusative suffix -és but stacks as the second suffix. This indicates that the syn-sem structure realized by -koro includes only K_3, as in:

(32) Lexical entry in Romani

[K_3] ⇔ koro

This means that an attempt to spell this feature out by successive-cyclic movement of the root čhav as in (33) is not going to be successful, as the constituent formed by such a movement is not matched by any existing lexical entry.

(33)

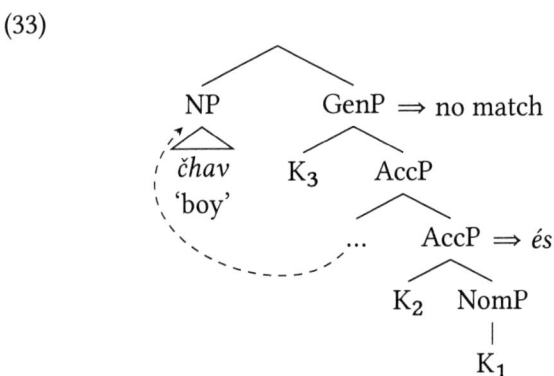

The failure to spell-out requires the derivation to backtrack by trying to move the complement of K_3. As shown in (34), the constituent created in this way is matched by the entry in (32) and -koro comes out as the external suffix.

(34) Spell-out of the Romani genitive čhav-és-koro 'boy'

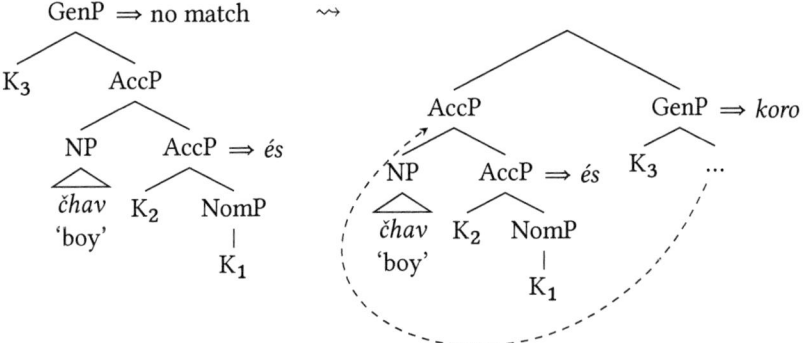

Two kinds of movements – spec-to-spec and snowballing – derive the genitive marking patterns attested in languages like Polish and Romani but they fail to

2.3 What we already know about how lexicalization works

derive the pre-nominal genitive marking in languages like English from the extension of the accusative structure, the AccP lexicalized as *wine*, by the merger of the next case feature in the fseq, K_3, as shown in (35).

(35) Merger and attempted spell-out of genitive by STAY in English

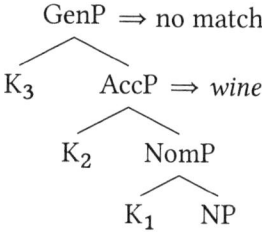

The lack of a specifier created by movement at the previous cycle in (35) leaves us with an attempt to spell out K_3 by snowballing, as in (36), which creates a structure that does not correspond to the prepositional *of*, either.

(36)

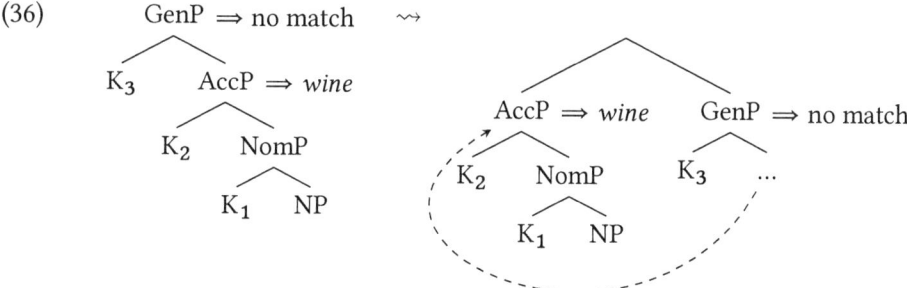

We are, thus, arriving at a situation where genitive cannot be spelled out by STAY but applying MOVE does not result in creating constituency which is matched by a lexical entry with K_3 either.

An immediate possibility is to assume the terminal node K_3 to lexicalize as *of*, which would make the correct prediction about *of* surfacing in front of *wine*. This is the way prepositional case marking is derived in Caha (2009; 2011b). However, the insertion of *of* directly into the terminal K_3 goes against the thesis that spell-out targets only phrasal nodes. Looking at the possibility of spell-out targeting both terminal and non-terminal nodes more globally, an empirical argument against "pre-" elements being inserted into terminal nodes is that they would have to comprise only specific markers, certainly not a situation we observe with a considerable subset of prefixes, particles, auxiliary verbs, or complementizers. For example, the English *with* is a syncretic marker of comitative and instrument,

2 The spell-out mechanism in Nanosyntax

that is a syncretic form of demonstrative pronoun, complementizer, and a relativizer, etc.

Maintaining the idea that spell-out targets only phrasal nodes in syntax, Starke (2018) proposes that the derivation backtracks to the previous cycle, at which point the last resort strategy kicks in: the merger of K_3 will take place in a parallel subtree and the spell-out of K_3 will be attempted upon merging the subtree with the mainline derivation.

In order to spawn the subderivation of the parallel case fseq, Starke (2018) states that what needs to be provided as the base is a nominal feature of the NP (literally, the N head in our representation). In line with the case fseq in (21), the first case feature to merge with the base feature N is the nominative-forming K_1, as shown in (37). Subsequently, the accusative feature K_2 is merged in the subderivation, which results in both derivations reaching the same size of the case fseq.[11]

(37) Subtree (left) parallel to the mainline derivation (right) in the formation of the English genitive

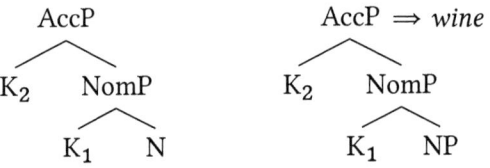

At this point the merger of the genitive-forming K_3 takes place in the subderivation, as shown in (38).

(38)

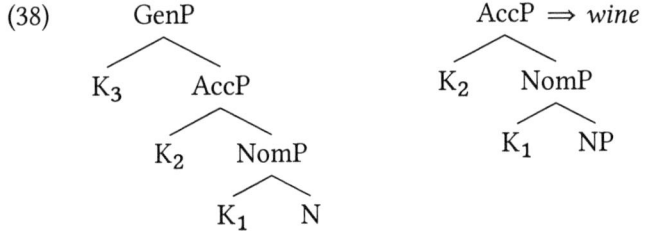

Once the genitive K_3 is merged in the subderivation, the resulting GenP-subtree is merged with the mainline and forms a complex left branch, as in (40). If the English lexicon contains the entry like in (39), then the left branch that contains

---

[11] Let us note that the subderivation up to the AccP size is not matched by any existing lexical item, as the sister node to K_1 is not a complex NP root, only an atomic nominal feature. The structure with K_1, K_2, and the singleton nominal feature N is not enough to be identified by any lexical entry in the English lexicon.

2.3 What we already know about how lexicalization works

K_3 is spelled out as *of*, which surfaces as a "pre-" element with respect to the accusative noun, as in *of wine*.

(39)   Lexical entry for the English genitive
       [K_3 [K_2 [K_1 N]]] ⟺ *of*

(40)   Merger and spell-out of the the English prepositional genitive *of*

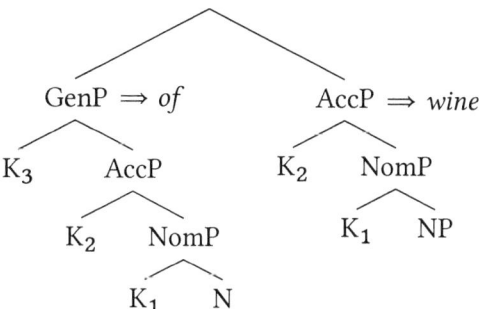

A comment about the last resort status of the left branch formation is in order. As Starke (2018) notes, launching the subderivation is a costly operation as it requires the growth of the two parallel trees to be coordinated up to the point of closing in the subderivation with the mainline. The formation of the left branch is hence kept as the final option in the spell-out algorithm.[12]

Deriving the patterns of morphological realization of a syntactic sequence is not the only result of the spell-out procedure that involves what we have called here MOVE and SUBDERIVE. Namely, these operations also allow us to define the distributional contrast between "pre-" elements (prefixes, prepositions, particles, complementizers, etc.) and "post-" elements (suffixes and postpositions) in a structural way. Namely, as Starke (2018) writes, "pre-" elements have a binary foot (e.g. the English *of*), whereas suffixes have a unary foot (e.g. the Romani *-és* or *-koro*). The binary foot of "pre-" elements is a result of SUBDERIVE, an operation spawned by the merger of two features; the unary foot of suffixes is a result of MOVE, with a proviso that spell-out driven movements do not leave a trace, which is confirmed by the observation that such movements do not show reconstruction or defective intervention effects.

---

[12] Let us recall that in line with the exhaustive lexicalization principle, a failure to spell out a feature results in derivation failure.

2 The spell-out mechanism in Nanosyntax

2.3.5 Pointers

A central feature of the spell-out procedure discussed so far is that lexical access takes place cyclically – after each merger of a feature in the phrase marker. Such a set up allows for an insertion of a lexical item which is sensitive to a lexical item that has been inserted at an earlier cycle. A tool in NS that facilitates a reference to lexical items inserted at previous cycles is called a POINTER, which is defined as in (41) (see also Taraldsen 2012; Caha & Pantcheva 2012; Starke 2014b; Vanden Wyngaerd 2018b; Caha et al. 2019a).

(41) A pointer is a node in a lexically stored tree that directs to a lexical entry.

A spell-out of syntactic feature that relies on a pointer is illustrated in (42), where the pointer node is indicated with an arrow.

(42) $F_3P \Rightarrow \alpha$
$\quad\quad\quad / \;\; \backslash$
$\quad\quad F_3 \;\; \beta$

Here, the lexical item α is inserted in the phrasal node which includes the feature F_3 and a constituent that has been spelled earlier out as a lexical item β. An essential difference between a lexical entry that involves a pointer and one that does not is that the first can spell out syntactic trees that can include only a subset of a structure that is realized by a different lexical item. For example, if the lexical entry for β is defined as in:

(43) $[F_2 [F_1]] \Leftrightarrow \beta$

and α is inserted into the node with the pointer to β in (42), this means that α can spell out the following syntactic trees:

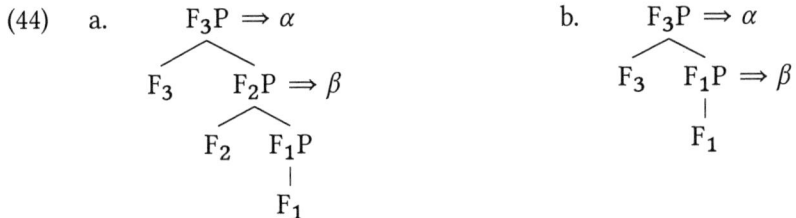

(44a) includes the superset structure of β and (44b) its subset. The pointer to the lexical entry of β, thus, allows α to spell-out a structure in (44b), which shrinks in the middle. This result is impossible to obtain under the Superset Principle if the lexical entry for α included a constituent $[F_3 [F_2 [F_1]]]$.

The pointer technology can explain suppletion. For example, while the productive formation of the English preterites includes the stem that is identical to the bare form of the verb, e.g. *want* and *want-ed*, a subset of the preterites is formed with a suppletive form of the verb, e.g. *give* and *gave*. This can be explained if the suppletive form of the preterite includes a pointer to the lexical entry of the bare verb. This is illustrated for *gave* in (45), where it spells out the phrasal node PastP which includes the preterite-forming feature Past and the pointer to *give*.

(45)   PastP ⇒ *gave*
          /⟶\
       Past *give*

The spell-out of PastP as *gave* will take place only if the node pointed to has been earlier spelled out as *give* (not as any other lexical item or constituent).

Other than explaining suppletive allomorphy, pointers have been used to explain idioms in Starke (2014b) as well as derive syncretic alignment in paradigms involving datives, locatives, and allatives in Caha & Pantcheva (2012) and in pronominal paradigms in Vanden Wyngaerd (2018b). I will return to pointers in Chapter 3 in an attempt to describe the lexical entry for the iterative affix in Czech and Polish.

2.4 Summary of the current state of the spell-out procedure

Let us synopsize the spell-out formula in Starke (2018), which is an unambiguous specification of how to lexicalize a grammatical feature, i.e. an algorithm for spell-out:

Step 1: STAY – add a feature F and spell-out (an in situ spell-out; derives the English NOM/ACC *wine*).

Step 2: SPEC-TO-SPEC – move the node merged in the previous cycle and spell out (derives the suffixal form of the Polish genitive *win-a* 'of wine').

Step 3: SNOWBALL – move the complement of the feature F and spell out (derives genitive marking in the Romani *čhav-és-koro* 'of boy').

Step 4: SUBDERIVE – remove F from the mainline derivation and build a phrase marker comprising F, merge it with the mainline derivation and spell out (results in merger of a complex left branch whose spell-out comes out as a "pre-" element on the stem; derives the English prepositional genitive marker *of*).

Such a procedure predicts that the lexicalization of a feature added to a derivation either keeps the same amount of morphemes (when the added feature is spelled out by the default STAY) or adds a morpheme (when it is spelled out by the remaining steps, MOVE SPEC-TO-SPEC, SNOWBALL, or SUBDERIVE).

2.5 Spell-out resulting in the reduction in the number of morphemes

2.5.1 The problem

So far we have discussed situations in which the addition of a feature to a syntactic representation leads either to the preservation or an increase in the number of morphemes at spell-out. For instance, the addition of the genitive-forming case feature K_3 to the AccP in Polish in example (31) resulted in the genitive suffix -*a* over-riding the accusative suffix -*o*, which preserved the same number of suffixes on the noun. In turn, the addition of K_3 to the AccP in Romani in example (34) and in English in example (40) resulted in the genitive case surfacing as an additional morpheme: the outer suffix in Romani and the prefix in English.

Let us now consider a situation where the addition of a feature to a syntactic representation gives a different result to the ones discussed so far, namely, instead of a preservation or an increase, it leads to a reduction in the number of morphemes at spell-out.

In order to illustrate such a scenario, let us suppose that an fseq in (46) is lexicalized by a *ROOT* and three affixes *X, Y, Z*, and that the span that ranges from F_1 up to F_5 in this fseq is lexicalized by a structure comprising three morphemes: *ROOT-X-Y*.

(46)
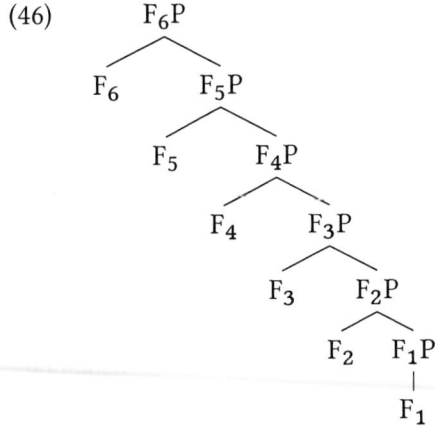

2.5 Spell-out resulting in the reduction in the number of morphemes

Such a result can be easily obtained with the following list of lexical entries:

(47)   a.   [F_3 [F_2 [F_1]]] $\Leftrightarrow$ ROOT
         b.   [F_4] $\Leftrightarrow$ X
         c.   [F_5] $\Leftrightarrow$ Y
         d.   [F_6 [F_5 [F_4 [F_3]]]] $\Leftrightarrow$ Z

With the spell-out procedure recapped in §2.4, *ROOT* will spell out the range of features from F_1 to F_3 by STAY, as shown in:

(48)
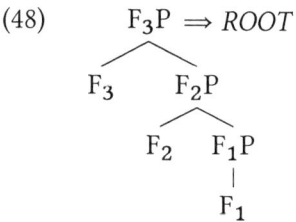

Next, the merger of F_4 will take place. The default option for spell-out, STAY, does not result in lexical insertion since there is no lexically stored tree listed in (47) that matches the syntactic structure that ranges from F_1 up to F_4, as indicated in:

(49)
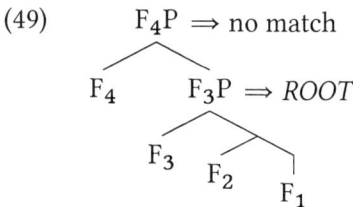

In this case, the movement of the previously spelled out constituent is attempted: F_3P *ROOT* moves on top of F_4P. This movement takes place in line with the Shortest Move condition, whereby the evacuated material has to adjoin right above the node where matching takes place. This step is shown in the following:

(50)
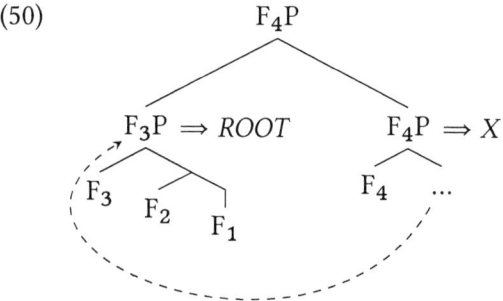

2 The spell-out mechanism in Nanosyntax

The remnant F_4P will spell-out as the suffix X, since it matches the lexically stored tree in (47b).

Next, the merger of F_5 will take place and the situation will repeat: following the evacuation of its complement node F_4P, the remnant F_5P will spell out as Y, as the constituent formed in this way matches the lexically stored tree in (47c). This is shown in the following:

(51)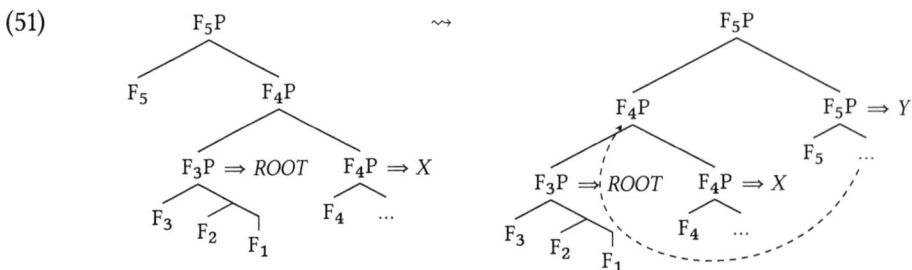

In this way, the Y morpheme will come out as the outer suffix in the tri-morphemic structure *ROOT-X-Y*.

Let us now suppose that along *ROOT-X-Y*, there is also a form *ROOT-Z*, which lexicalizes the span that ranges from F_1 up to F_6, that is a span of features which is minimally bigger than the one that is realized by *ROOT-X-Z*. The question now is: how can the addition of F_6 at the next cycle, shown in (52), result in the reduction in the number of suffixes on the *ROOT*: from *ROOT-X-Y* to *ROOT-Z*?

(52)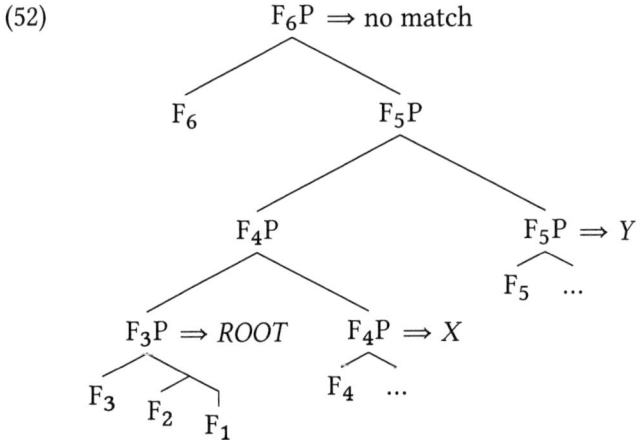

There are in principle two possible ways of deriving the reduction in the number of suffixes from *ROOT-X-Y* to *ROOT-Z*. One involves backtracking and trying an

2.5 Spell-out resulting in the reduction in the number of morphemes

alternative spell-out option (the option that kicks in whenever STAY is unsuccessful and evacuation of nodes spelled out earlier is required, see Pantcheva 2011: 160–168). The other one does not require backtracking and, instead, it involves adding subextraction to the list of spell-out driven movements. Let us outline both possibilities in turn.

2.5.2 Backtracking

The derivation in (52) with the added F_6 is not going to surface as *ROOT-Z* if we apply STAY, MOVE SPEC-TO-SPEC, or SNOWBALL, since none of these operations reduces the number of affixes. Instead, the reduction can be obtained if the derivation backtracks down to F_2P and, instead of spelling out F_3 by STAY as in (48), F_3 is spelled out following the movement of F_2P, which is realized as *ROOT* as a subset spell-out of the lexical entry in (47a) (on the strength of the Superset Principle in 8). As shown in (53), such an evacuation of F_2P will allow the F_3P remnant to be spelled out as *Z*, the subset of the lexical entry in (47d).

(53)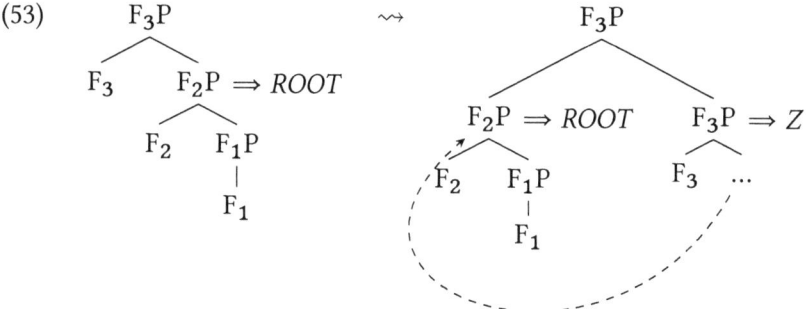

The remaining features F_4, F_5, and F_6 will all be spelled out by successive cyclic movement of F_2P *ROOT*. Such a movement will create intermediate specifier positions, whose sisters can all be spelled out as morpheme *Z* in line with the lexical entry in (47d).[13] This is illustrated in (54). Such a derivation involving backtracking down to F_2P results in the morphological structure *ROOT-Z*, a desired result.

A theoretical challenge for such an analysis is that it requires backtracking from F_6 all the way down to F_2P before SPEC-TO-SPEC movement of F_2P *ROOT*

---

[13] Let us bare in mind that on the strength of the Superset Principle, the remnants left by the evacuation of F_2P *ROOT* from F_3P up to F_5P will spell out as the subset and the remnant F_6P will spell out as a superset of the lexically stored tree in (47d).

2 The spell-out mechanism in Nanosyntax

can take place. This contrasts with how backtracking applies in the spell-out algorithm articulated in §2.4, where a failure to spell out feature F_n requires a return to the previous cycle F_{n-1} and trying a different spell-out option for F_n. In the situation outlined above, the reduction in the number of suffixes on the ROOT requires going back a few cycles before a different spell-out option can apply.

(54) Deriving reduction in the number of morphemes with backtracking

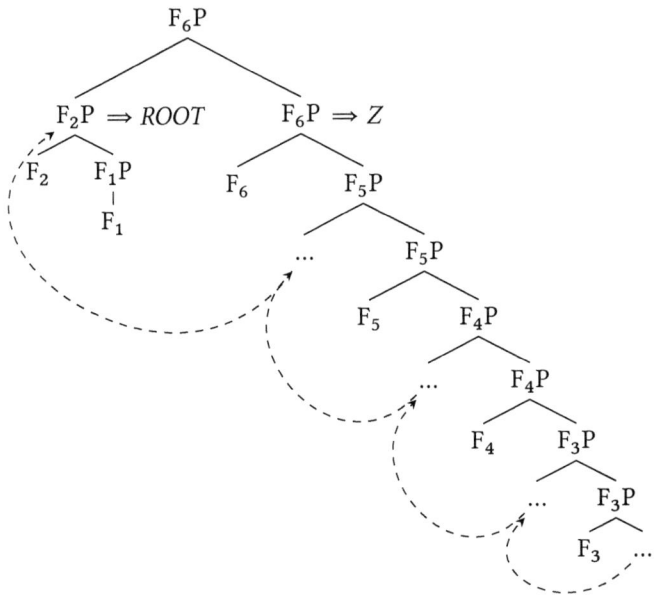

2.5.3 Subextraction

The other possibility of deriving the reduction in the number of suffixes from ROOT-X-Y to ROOT-Z is a subextraction of a previously spelled out constituent from the specifier node in which it is embedded. I will continue to refer to this type of spell-out procedure simply as SUBEXTRACT.

In order to illustrate this operation, let us return to (52), the cycle where the feature F_6 becomes merged on top of F_5P, the structure already spelled out as ROOT-X-Y. In such a representation, the subextraction of F_3P ROOT from F_4P (the specifier of F_5) will create a remnant constituent that comprises features F_4, F_5, and F_6, as shown in (55).

2.5 Spell-out resulting in the reduction in the number of morphemes

(55) Deriving reduction in the number of morphemes by SUBEXTRACT

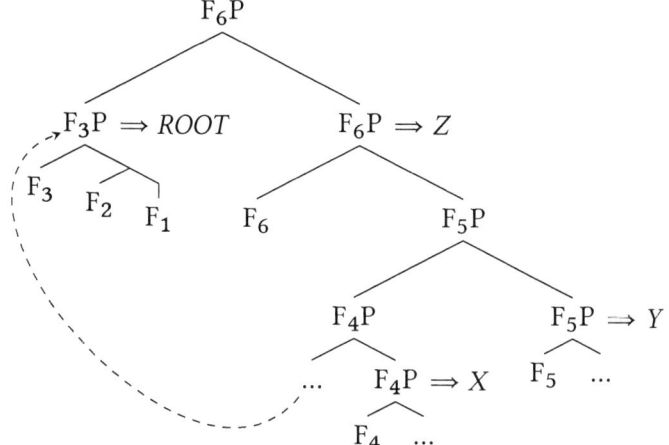

As indicated above, the remnant F_6P created in this way can be spelled out as Z if the lexical entry for this exponent is defined as in (56) rather than in (47d) (in other words, the lexically stored tree for the exponent Z must look different in the derivation of *ROOT-Z* obtained by backtracking and by SUBEXTRACT).

(56) Lexical entry for Z (2nd version, alternative to (47d))

[F_6 [[F_4][F_5]]] ⇔ Z

The insertion of Z into the remnant node F_6P in (55) will over-ride the earlier spell-outs of X and Y in a familiar way resulting in the morphological structure *ROOT-Z*, a desired result.

A theoretical challenge for such a solution is that a subextraction from a specifier that has been formed by movement at an earlier cycle violates the so-called FREEZING CONDITION, which can be formalized on the basis of Wexler & Culicover (1980) in the following way:[14]

(57) Freezing Condition

A moved constituent becomes an island for extraction.

---

[14] The formulation in (57) is in fact a paraphrase of Wexler & Culicover's (1980: 542) Generalized Freezing Principle, whose formulation as in (i) below has broader restrictions than extractions from raised phrases.

(i) Generalized Freezing Principle

A node is frozen if (a) its immediate structure is non-base, or (b) it has been raised.

The range of structures that are constrained by the protasis in (a) is irrelevant to the present discussion.

31

In (55), the evacuation of F_3P *ROOT* takes place from F_4P *ROOT-X*, a node that has become evacuated and remerged in a successful attempt to spell out F_5P (as Y). Assuming the Freezing Condition, the ban on extraction in the representation in (55) is not limited to F_3P *ROOT* but also to its sister node F_4P *X*. This issue is not merely theoretical in nature since the extraction of the right branch constituent, i.e. the one that corresponds to F_4P *X* in (55), is instantiated by the so-called CASE PEELING derivation argued for in Caha (2009: §4).

Peeling is argued in Caha (2009: §4) to derive case conversions, that is derivations where an NP argument changes its case depending on the syntactic position it occupies.[15] For example, case conversion in English is overtly visible in passivization involving pronouns, as in (58), where the accusative object *her* becomes the nominative *she* when it is raised to the subject position.

(58)   a.   The army promoted her.ACC to a higher rank.
        b.   She.NOM was promoted to a higher rank.

Case conversion between four different morphologically marked cases is observed in 'spray/load' alternations in Slavic. The alternations involving instrumental, genitive, accusative, and nominative case can be illustrated by the set of sentences with the Polish prefixed verb *za-ładować* 'load' in (59), where the case markers that participate in the conversion are bolded.

(59)   'Spray/load' alternation in Polish (Wiland 2018b: 241–242)

       a.   Jan   załadował ciężarówk-ę traw-ą
             Jan-NOM loaded   truck-ACC   grass-INST
             'Jan loaded the truck with grass.'

       b.   załadowa-nie traw-y   na ciężarówk-ę
             load-ING   grass-GEN on truck-ACC
             'the loading of the grass on the truck'

       c.   Jan   załadował traw-ę   na ciężarówk-ę
             Jan-NOM loaded   grass-ACC on truck-ACC
             lit. 'Jan loaded the grass onto the truck.'

       d.   Traw-a   został-a   załadowa-n-a   na ciężarówk-ę
             grass-NOM became-AGR loaded-PRT-AGR on truck-ACC
             'The grass was loaded on the truck.'

---

[15]The term "peeling" has its origin in Cardinaletti & Starke (1999: 195), who put forth a tripartition of pronouns into clitic < weak < strong. Such a hierarchy is based on structural containment that is described there in terms of peeling that applies to layers of syntactic structure: weak pronouns are "peeled" strong pronouns, and clitics are "peeled" weak pronouns.

2.5 Spell-out resulting in the reduction in the number of morphemes

This set shows the conversion between instrumental, genitive, accusative, and nominative marking on the Figure NP *traw-* 'grass', which is linked to the position in which the NP is licensed. Assuming the case fseq in (21), Caha argues that the case conversion is derived according to (60), where case-forming features K_n projected on top of the NP *traw-* 'grass' become stranded by the movements of their complement.

(60) Case peeling (Caha 2009: 142–145)

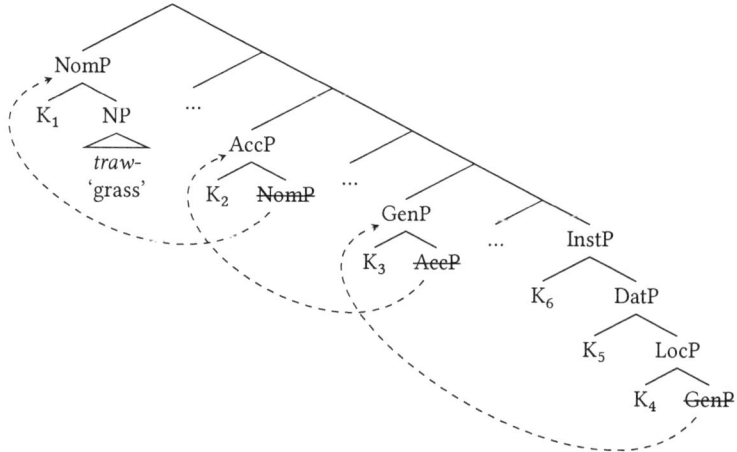

An argument for case peeling is based on the fact that the case conversions in both the passive transformation and the Polish 'spray/load' alternation involve a change that is constrained by the case fseq in (21): a bigger (containing) case converts into a smaller (contained) one, not vice versa. Caha (2009: 143–146) offers a detailed discussion of the role of case selectors in case peeling. In essence, the triggering mechanism for case peeling is the presence of selecting heads in the clause, which attract a matching case phrase – much in the spirit of the probe-goal system of Chomsky (2000), where the probe attracts a matching goal in its c-commanding domain. For instance, an accusative case selector such as a transitive V head will attract the AccP-layer from its c-commanding domain; a nominative case selector such as the T head will attract the NomP-layer from its c-commanding domain, and so on. The result is that in a single derivation, case-marked NPs will pass through multiple case positions. As acknowledged in Caha (2009: 146), such a view stands in opposition to most other theories of case derivation, including Chomsky (2000).

In the sense that both SUBEXTRACT illustrated in (55) and case peeling in (60) involve movement out of a moved node, the two violate the Freezing Condition defined as in (57). An instantaneous solution to this challenge, based on empirical evidence, is to abandon the description of freezing effects in terms of an all-out ban on extractions from a moved constituent.

Such a solution is motivated by the fact that, in parallel to evidence in favor of freezing properties of displacement, there is fairly strong evidence for the existence of well-formed extractions from fronted constituents. More precisely, on the one hand extractions have been argued to be blocked from adverbial phrases that have undergone locative inversion in English (Huybregts 1976), from extraposed PPs in English (Wexler & Culicover 1980), from phrases moved to SpecCP (Lasnik & Saito 1992 about English; Fanselow 1987; Grewendorf 1989; Müller 1998; 2010 about German), from phrases moved to SpecTP (Browning 1991; Collins 1994; Boeckx & Grohmann 2007 about English), from preposed constituents that feed remnant movement in German (Müller 1998), as well as from English topicalized PPs (Postal 1972) and DPs (Lasnik & Saito 1992), among others.[16]

On the other hand, examples of felicitous movements from moved constituents include extractions from pied-piped wh-phrases in Spanish (Torrego 1985), topicalization from subjects in German (Abels 2007), left-branch extraction of wh-words from fronted wh-phrases in Polish (Wiland 2010), and object extraction from fronted constituents leading to the non-canonical OVS order in Polish (Wiland 2016). Likewise, any movement out of an object phrase in canonical SOV languages is going to be an instance of anti-freezing under Kayne's 1994 Antisymmetry theory, whereby SOV orders are all derived by object raising from an underlying SVO structure. Yet, as pointed out in Corver (2017), extractions from objects in SOV languages are attested for instance in Dutch, as shown in the following, where the well-formed fronting of *wat* 'what' takes place from the preverbal object:

(61) Dutch (Corver 2017: 26)
  Wat$_i$ heb jij nog nooit [t$_i$ voor dingen] gezegd
  what have you yet never   for things   said
  'What kind of things haven't you ever said?'

There are at least two approaches to freezing that describe it in non-categorical terms: the feature-driven freezing (Boeckx 2008; Lohndal 2011) and Criterial Freezing (Rizzi 2006; 2007; Rizzi & Shlonsky 2007). The feature-driven approach submits that only A-movement for case checking will result in the moving NP becoming opaque for subextraction. Under this approach, case peeling – which is motivated by case selection (i.e. de facto checking) in Caha's work – should

---

[16]See Corver (2017) for a comprehensive overview of freezing effects.

2.5 Spell-out resulting in the reduction in the number of morphemes

be blocked. In turn, Criterial Freezing submits that while a moving constituent that targets a "criterial" (checking) position, becomes opaque to further movements. Subextraction from a constituent in such a position, however, is possible. As pointed out in Caha (2009: 146–147), Criterial Freezing not only renders case peeling to be licit but it also correctly predicts that NP-movement into a case position is terminated when a nominative position in the clause structure is reached. This is so since peeling involves a subextraction from a constituent merged in its selected position (e.g. movement of NomP from within AccP in 60) rather than cyclic movement of the same case layer through different positions in the clause (e.g. no second movement of AccP in lieu of NomP in 60).

Under non-categorical approaches to freezing effects, both peeling derivations and SUBEXTRACT are in principle admissible in grammar. More specifically, unlike case peeling that is predicted to be admissible under Criterial Freezing but not under the feature-driven analysis, subextractions are admissible under both. This is so since no movement leading to the representation in (55) targets a designated checking (or "criterial") position or is feature-driven. Instead, all these movements simply form a sister to the node that is targeted by spell-out at a given cycle – in the same way as spec-to-spec and snowballing movements do in the spell-out procedure.

2.5.4 Verb stem alternation

One domain where we find what looks to be a reduction in the number of morphemes is a semelfactive-iterative alternation in Czech and Polish, as shown in (62), where a morphologically more complex semelfactive (on the left) alternates with a less complex iterative (on the right).

(62) Czech
    a. kop-**n**-ou-t   – kop-**a**-t
        kick-N-OU$_{theme}$-INF   kick-AJ$_{theme}$-INF
        'give a kick'   'be giving kicks'
    b. štěk-**n**-ou-t   – štěk-**a**-t
        bark-N-OU$_{theme}$-INF   bark-AJ$_{theme}$-INF
        'give a bark'   'bark repeatedly'

(63) Polish
    a. kop-**n**-ą-ć   – kop-**a**-ć
        kick-N-OU$_{theme}$-INF   kick-AJ$_{theme}$-INF
        'give a kick'   'be giving kicks'

2 The spell-out mechanism in Nanosyntax

b. liz-n-ą-ć — liz-a-ć
lick-N-OU$_{theme}$-INF   lick-AJ$_{theme}$-INF
'give a lick'   'lick repeatedly'

For the present purposes, let us refer to verb stems on the left, which denote single-stage events, as semelfactives and to the verb stems on the right, which comprise the root and what is glossed here as the -aj theme, as iteratives.[17]

If we follow the analysis of iteratives as categories that in syn-sem terms are more complex than semelfactives (e.g. Smith 1997; Olsen 1997; Egg 2018), then the alternation in (62–63) comes out as puzzling since the iteratives are morphologically less complex than the semelfactives. Thus, if the iterative -aj stems are structurally bigger than semelfactive -n-ou stems, the spell-out of a feature added in their formation reduces the number of morphemes. This spell-out problem is outlined in the structural description below on the example of the stem kop-n-ou 'give a kick' of (62a) (where VP is a stand-in for a semelfactive verb stem and Asp is a stand-in for the feature extending a semelfactive stem into an iterative stem):

(64)

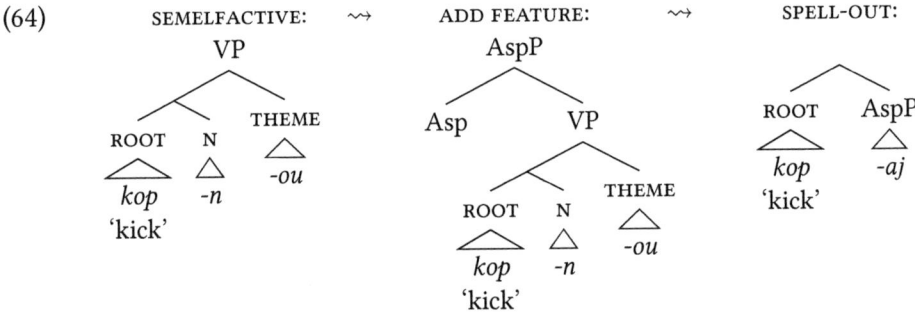

There are in principle two ways to achieve the reduction in the number of suffixes on the root, from the -n-ou sequence down to the single -aj: by backtracking or by SUBEXTRACT. I will consider both possibilities of deriving this reduction in detail in Chapter 3.

---

[17] The theme vowel -aj surfaces as /a/ before a suffix with a consonant in its onset such as the infinitival -t (Cz) / -ć (Pol) but also before the past participle suffix as in szczek-a-ł 'bark-AJ-PART'. This is due to a cyclic phonological truncation rule in Slavic, whereby glides become deleted before a consonant (see Jakobson 1948; Rubach 1984, among others):

(i) Glide truncation
     j, w → ∅ / _ C$_0$

What is indicated in the glosses in (62–63) and later in the text are underlying, "untruncated" exponents of theme vowels.

2.6 Summary and roadmap

In this introductory chapter, I have outlined an approach to the realization of syntactic trees (i.e. hierarchical feature structures) as morphological forms (i.e. linear sequences) based on phrasal spell-out and a strictly cyclic lexical access, the two key features of Nanosyntax. The strict cyclicity of lexical access means that every merger of a feature in a phrase marker is followed by an attempt to match it against the list of lexically stored trees and insert an exponent. If such an attempt is successful, the derivation either terminates (when no more features are merged) or advances to another cycle: the merger of another feature that is followed by an attempt to spell it out.

The spell-out procedure summarized in §2.4 involves an order list of procedures that kick in after the merger of a feature F, which comprise STAY, MOVE SPEC-TO-SPEC, SNOWBALL, and SUBDERIVE. In the next chapter, I consider the possibility of extending this list by subextraction, a natural candidate to be added to the two types of spell-out driven movements along spec-to-spec and snowballing. In particular, I will consider if what looks to be a reduction in the number of morphemes that we observe in the semelfactive-iterative alternation in Czech and Polish can be better captured by an analysis based on backtracking or by spell-out driven subextraction.

While Chapter 3 explores the possibility of explaining the alternation with subextraction, subsequent chapters focus exclusively on the application of the so-far established set of spell-out possibilities – the ones listed in §2.4 – and do not rely on extending this list with SUBEXTRACT.

In particular, Chapter 4 discusses the problem of morphological containment of the Russian demonstrative pronoun *to* in the structure of the declarative complementizer *č-to*. Such a morphological inclusion is paradoxical given the analysis of demonstrative pronouns in Baunaz & Lander (2017; 2018b) as categories that syntactically contain declarative complementizers. The resolution of this paradox is going to rely on accommodating demonstrative pronouns without definiteness marking such as the Russian *to* into a cross-categorial paradigm with complementizers and definiteness, analyzed as a separate category in the paradigm. The chapter also discusses how the application of the spell-out algorithm allows us to explain the differences in the morphological structures of the declarative complementizers in Russian and in Polish, another Slavic language without definiteness marking.

Chapters 5 and 6 extend the accommodation of non-definite demonstratives into the paradigm with the declarative complementizer to the languages from outside the Slavic group. Chapter 5 on Latvian deals with a similar type of morphological containment problem as the one observed in Russian. Unlike in Russian, however, the containment problem in Latvian concerns the complementizer *k-a*, which is morphologically less complex than the relativizer and the interrogative pronoun *k-a-s* 'what'. The latter are the categories that are syntactically smaller than the complementizer.

In turn, Chapter 6 resolves a problem with syncretic alignment in a paradigm Basaá, a Bantu language spoken in Cameroon. The Basaá paradigm appears to show syncretism between the demonstrative pronoun and the relativizer to the exclusion of the declarative complementizer. Given the organization of cells in a paradigm with these categories advanced in Baunaz & Lander (2017; 2018b), the Basaá paradigm is an instance of a *ABA violation. It is argued in the chapter that inspecting the syntax behind the offending cells in the paradigm, the *ABA violation in Basaá is only apparent.

Chapter 7 summarizes the results and points out the gaps in the analyses that remain to be closed in future work.

3 Deriving the verb stem alternation

3.1 Introduction

The domain which arguably exhibits the reduction in the number of morphemes is the alternation between semelfactive and iterative verb stems found in Czech and Polish, which is illustrated in the following:

(1) Czech
  a. kop-n-ou-t   – kop-a-t
     kick-N-OU$_{theme}$-INF   kick-AJ$_{theme}$-INF
     'give a kick'   'be giving kicks'
  b. štěk-n-ou-t   – štěk-a-t
     bark-N-OU$_{theme}$-INF   bark-AJ$_{theme}$-INF
     'give a bark'   'bark repeatedly'

(2) Polish
  a. kop-n-ą-ć   – kop-a-ć
     kick-N-OU$_{theme}$-INF   kick-AJ$_{theme}$-INF
     'give a kick'   'be giving kicks'
  b. liz-n-ą-ć   – liz-a-ć
     lick-N-OU$_{theme}$-INF   lick-AJ$_{theme}$-INF
     'give a lick'   'lick repeatedly'

The alternation involves a tri-morphemic semelfactive stem and a bi-morphemic iterative stem. The semelfactive stem, which can be roughly defined as one-time event, comprises a root, the *-n* suffix (with the light verb meaning Give), and a thematic suffix *-ou* (realized as *ou* in Czech and as a nasalized vowel *ą* in Polish). The corresponding bi-morphemic iterative stem, roughly defined as an event involving a repetition of a one-time event, comprises a root and the thematic suffix *-aj* (here realized simply as *a* due to a rule in Slavic phonology whereby a glide becomes truncated before a consonant).

    The fact that the iterative stem is morphologically less complex than a semelfactive is paradoxical given the account of iteratives as more complex in syn-sem

3 Deriving the verb stem alternation

terms than the second. If so, then the extension of structurally smaller semelfactives into bigger iteratives results in the reduction in the amount of morphemes. In what follows, I explore the possibility to derive this reduction by subextraction and compare it with an alternative analysis based on backtracking.

Let us begin with an overview of the structure of the Slavic verb stem and the properties of the alternation.

3.2 Background: The verb stem in Czech and Polish

3.2.1 Verb stem morphology

The morphological make-up of the verb in Slavic is to a large degree templatic, as shown below on the example of the Czech verb *dělat* 'do' in (3) and the Polish verb *zamykać* 'close' in (4).

(3)   (PREFIX) – ROOT – THEME – PARTICIPLE – AGR

    a.   u – děl – a – l   – a   (active: L-participle)
        PFV – do – AJ – PART – FEM.SG
        '(she) did'

    b.   u – děl – á – n   – o   (passive: N/T-participle)
        PFV – do – AJ – PART – NEU.SG
        '(it was) done'

(4)   (PREFIX) – ROOT – THEME – PARTICIPLE – AGR

    a.   za – myk – a – ł   – em   (active: L-participle)
        PFV – close – AJ – PART – 1SG.MSC
        '(I) closed'

    b.   za – myk – a – n   – y   (passive: N/T-participle)
        PFV – close – AJ – PART – MSC.SG
        '(being) closed'

The verb structure comprises a root, optionally preceded by lexical and/or aspectual prefix, which is followed by a thematic suffix (the so-called theme vowel), the participle morpheme (L in active non-present tense, and N/T in passive), and the subject agreement suffix.[1]

---

[1] Such a representation of the Slavic verb has its origin in Jakobson's (1948) analysis of the Russian conjugation, which has opened up the possibility to provide a structural description of the verb in all Slavic. For some alternative ways of classifying Slavic verbs into conjugation classes see e.g. Laskowski (1975), Townsend & Janda (1996), Czaykowska-Higgins (1988), Jabłońska (2007), and the references cited there.

3.2 Background: The verb stem in Czech and Polish

Before we take a look at the list of theme vowels in the structure of the Czech and Polish verb, a terminological distinction between roots and stems should be made clear. Unless specified differently in a particular context, I will refer to the "root" as an item understood pre-theoretically as in the following:

(5) A root is an open class lexical item that can form verbs, adjectives or nouns.

In line with this definition, a VERBAL ROOT is an open class lexical item that forms verbs, an ADJECTIVAL ROOT an open-class item that forms adjectives, and a NOMINAL ROOT an open class item that forms nouns. In turn, I will use the term 'verb stem' in the way that is common in the literature on the Slavic verb (and, in fact, often used in the context of verb morphology in general, too) as in the following:

(6) A verb stem is a (simplex or complex) morphological form that is subject to inflection.

This definition implies that a Slavic verb stem can in principle be morphologically more complex than a root, a situation that will be illustrated shortly.

3.2.2 Thematic suffixes

The thematic affixes in Slavic are verbalizers that come in between the root and the inflectional suffix (see e.g. Isačenko 1962; Halle 1963; Flier 1972; Lightner 1972 for Russian; Townsend & Janda 1996 and Komárek 2006 for Czech; Laskowski 1975; Grzegorczykowa & Puzynina 1979; Rubach 1984; Czaykowska-Higgins 1988 and Szpyra 1989 for Polish; Svenonius 2004a: 181–188 for a comprehensive overview). The list of themes in Czech and Polish is given in Table 3.1. Together with a root they merge with, thematic affixes form verb stems, which encode the verbal argument structure. The verbalizing property of thematic affixes is clear as we do not find them in present day Czech and Polish nouns or adjectives.

Whereas three theme vowels, the null theme, *-a*, and *-ov* produce a range of different aspectual and argument-structural classes of verb stems, the other theme vowels contribute to the properties of verb stems in a more predictable way.[2] For example, the null theme and the *-a* theme build both activity and process verbs

---

[2]Following the tradition of Slavic philology, largely shaped by the work done on Old Church Slavonic and modern Russian, Polish verb stems with the null theme vowel are sometimes referred to as consonantal stems rather than stems comprising a root and a null theme vowel (e.g. Rubach 1984; Czaykowska-Higgins 1988; Jabłońska 2007). The nature of such stems, however, is orthogonal to the following discussion of semelfactives.

3 Deriving the verb stem alternation

Table 3.1: Thematic affixes in Czech and Polish

thematic affix	Czech	Polish	gloss
∅	nés-∅-t	nie-∅-ść	carry
a	ps-á-t	pis-a-ć	write
ě/e	vid-ě-t	widzi-e-ć	see
aj	klek-a-t	klęk-a-ć	kneel
ej	kamen-e-t	kamieni-e-ć	become stone
ov	kup-ov-a-t	kup-ow-a-ć	buy
i	pros-i-t	pros-i-ć	ask
nou/ną	kop-nou-t	kop-ną-ć	kick

that belong to different argument-structural classes, e.g. the Czech transitive activity verbs *nés-∅-t* 'carry' or *ps-á-t* 'write', or the Polish unaccusative *paś-∅-ć* 'fall' or *u-mier-a-ć* 'die'.

The same holds true about the *-ov* theme, which also builds (broadly understood) activity stems, but there is a caveat about its distribution. Namely, one characteristic property of the *-a* theme is that it merges with verbal roots. Maintaining the approach to spell-out whereby every morpheme is a lexical realization of a phrasal constituent in syntax, we can represent a verbal root simply as the VP in the structure of *a*-stems as in the following:

(7)   [[VP root] -*a*]

The term verbal root, represented above as a morphological root (a particular lexical item) with the VP status in syntax, is descriptively understood in this context simply as an open-class lexical item that forms verbs but does not form adjectives or nouns. For example, neither the Czech root *pis-* 'write' nor the Polish root *mar-* 'die' can form adjectival or nominal stems. These and other roots can form adjectival participles and nominalizations, e.g. the Czech *ps-a-n-ý* 'written' or the Polish *u-mier-a-nie* 'dying'. These forms, however, are derived by suffixes that are all external to the verb stem, as indicated in (3–4). In order for nominal roots to form a verb stem with the *-a* theme they must be extended by the *-ov* suffix, which can be illustrated by the Polish examples such as *matk-a* 'mother-NOM.FEM' – *matk-ow-a-ć* 'to mother someone', *stół* 'table.NOM.MSC' – *stoł-ow-a-ć* 'to be eating out', *panik-a* 'panic-NOM.FEM' – *panik-ow-a-ć* 'to panic'. At the same time, the *-a* theme does not form verb stems by a direct merger with nominal roots, as in the unattested forms **matk-a-ć*, **stoł-a-ć*, **panik-a-ć*. This pattern

3.2 Background: The verb stem in Czech and Polish

is productive and holds in both Czech and Polish borrowings, as for instance *forward* – *forward-ov-a-t* 'to forward an email', *skype* – *skyp-ov-a-t* 'to skype', *biwak* 'bivouac.NOM.MSC' – *biwak-ow-a-ć* 'to bivouac', with bare nominal roots impossible to form -*a*-stems, as shown by the unattested **forward-a-t*, **skyp-a-t*, or **biwak-a-ć*. The resulting picture is that the merger of a nominal root with the -*ov* is a morphologically complex realization of the verbal root, as in (8), which makes such a structure fit to merge with the -*a* theme.

(8) [[_VP_ [_NP_ root] -*ov*] -*a*]

Hence, what is traditionally described as the -*ova* theme vowel in the literature on Slavic comes out as a sequence of two separate suffixes, -*ov* and -*a*, whose distribution can be best understood when considered jointly with the categories of roots they merge with.[3]

Unlike the null theme, the other thematic suffixes form verb stems whose synsem properties can be predicted more accurately.

For instance, the -*e* theme builds stative stems, e.g. the Czech *sed-ě-t* 'sit' *bol-e-t* 'hurt', or the Polish *leż-e-ć* 'lie (on a surface)', including what is sometimes classified as its subclass, namely verbs of perception and production of sounds, e.g. the Polish *słysz-e-ć* 'hear', *becz-e-ć* 'bleat', *rycz-e-ć* 'roar', *burcz-e-ć* 'growl', *brzęcz-e-ć* 'buzz', or *krzycz-e-ć* 'shout'. On top of that, -*e* can also form activity stems, e.g. the Czech *běž-e-t* 'run', *let-ě-t* 'fly', *sáz-e-t* 'plant'.

In turn, both -*aj* and -*i* themes build activity verbs. As stated earlier, the -*aj* theme forms iteratives, habituals and frequentives, while the -*i* theme builds a fairly wide range of transitives, e.g. the Polish *pal-i-ć* 'burn, smoke', *rob-i-ć* 'do', and reflexive verbs like the Czech *modl-i-t se* 'pray', among other activity verbs with different argument-structural properties. Notably, however, the -*i* theme is also a formative of "make X do Y" causatives such as the Czech *posad-i-t* 'make somebody sit', as in:

(9) Czech
 Petr posad-i-l dítě na židli.
 Petr.NOM sat-I-PART baby.NEU on chair.LOC
 'Petr sat the baby on the chair.'

The -*ej* theme builds a subset of the so-called degree achievements verbs, an aspectual category that can be approximately described as a change of state that

---

[3]This is not an exhaustive description of the -*ov* theme since it also can merge with a subset of adjectival roots. The -*ov-a* verb stems that are formed in this way are statives rather than activities, e.g. the Polish *chor-y* 'sick-ADJ.NOM.MSC' – *chor-ow-a-ć* 'be sick'.

3 Deriving the verb stem alternation

does not reach the endpoint (cf. Dowty 1979; Hay et al. 1999; Rothstein 2004), e.g. the Czech *šediv-ě-t* 'become grey', *kamen-ě-t* 'be turning into stone' or the Polish *łysi-e-ć* 'become bald', *rdzewi-e-ć* 'get rusty'.[4]

A large subset of degree achievement verbs is also formed by the *-n-ou* complex, which is analyzed in Taraldsen Medová & Wiland (2018b) as a sequence of two distinct morphemes only the second of which is a genuine theme vowel.[5] To a large extent, the list of roots forming degree achievements *-n-ou* stems is common to Czech and Polish, e.g. *bled-n-ou-t*/*bled-n-ą-ć* 'become pale', *hluch-n-ou-t*/*głuch-n-ą-ć* 'get deaf', *hořk-n-ou-t*/*gorzk-n-ą-ć* 'get bitter', *měk-n-ou-t*/*mięk-n-ą-ć* 'soften', *vad-n-ou-t*/*więd-n-ą-ć* 'wither', *mok-n-ou-t*/*mok-n-ą-ć* 'get wet', *hub-n-ou-t*/*chud-n-ą-ć* 'lose weight, get thinner', to name a few. Nevertheless, certain roots that form degree achievement *-n-ou* stems in Czech form degree achievement *-ej* stems in Polish, e.g. *hloup-n-ou-t* vs. *głupi-e-ć* 'get stupid', *hrub-n-ou-t* vs. *grubi-e-ć* 'get fat', *hloup-n-ou-t* vs. *głupi-e-ć* 'get stupid', *rud-n-ou-t* vs. *rudzi-e-ć* 'redden'.

Importantly, the *-n-ou* sequence forms also semelfactives, the category of verbs that can be approximately described as single-stage events. The list of roots forming semelfactive *-n-ou* stems also largely overlaps in Czech and Polish, e.g. *kop-n-ou-t*/*kop-n-ą-ć* 'give a kick', *kous-n-ou-t*/*kąs-n-ą-ć* 'give a bite', *štěk-n-ou-t*/*szczek-n-ą-ć* 'bark once', *dotk-n-ou-t*/*dotk-n-ą-ć* 'give a touch', *couv-n-ou-t*/*cof-n-ą-ć* 'move back once', *mrk-n-ou-t*/*mrug-n-ą-ć* 'wink once'. Despite the fact that the surface morphological forms of degree achievement and semelfactive verbs are identical, the internal structures of the morphemes they are made of are different. In the following section, I outline the description and analysis of these two verb stems given Taraldsen Medová & Wiland (2018b), which will serve as a starting point for the discussion of the semelfactive-iterative alternation, which involves the reduction in the number of morphemes.

---

[4]In the same way as in the case of the *-aj* theme, the final glide in *-ej* becomes deleted in front of a consonant of the following suffix due to the Glide Truncation rule given in footnote 17 in Chapter 2. The *-ej* suffix will surface in its entirety in non-past forms, e.g. the Polish *łysi-ej-emy* 'we are getting bald' or in imperatives, e.g. *łysi-ej* 'get bald'. These are also examples of environments that allow us to morphologically distinguish *-ej* from the theme vowel *-e*, which forms statives, as discussed above.

[5]The description of the thematic suffix as *-ou* is based on Czech. In Polish, the theme vowel *-ou* surfaces as a nasalized vowel *ą*, as in *marz-n-ą-ć* 'get cold'. Nasalization in Polish has been analyzed as a consequence of the presence of an underlying sequence of vowel and a nasal consonant in the coda, which suggests the Polish exponent is *-on* (cf. Gussmann 1980; Rubach 1984). Czaykowska-Higgins (1988) suggests a different analysis involving a nasal diphthong comprising a vowel and a nasal glide. Since this purely phonological difference is orthogonal to the syn-sem properties of the thematic suffix in the *-n-ou* sequence, I will continue to use the *-ou* notation in reference to both Czech and Polish.

3.3 Degree achievements vs. semelfactives

The major idea of Taraldsen Medová & Wiland (2018b) is that while both degree achievements and semelfactives comprise the root and the *-n-ou* sequence, all three morphemes exhibit different syn-sem properties in these categories.

3.3.1 Adjectival vs. nominal roots

The first contrast between these two verb classes targets the lexical category of the root. The root in degree achievement stems is adjectival (an adjective modulo the case suffix *-ý*) as for instance in the Czech *bled-ý* 'pale' – *bled-n-ou-t* 'get pale' (glossed in 10), *hluch-ý* 'deaf' – *hluch-n-ou-t* 'get deaf', *hořk-ý* 'bitter' – *hořk-n-ou-t* 'get bitter', or the Polish *blad-y* 'pale' – *bled-n-ą-ć* 'get pale', *chud-y* 'thin' – *chud-ną-ć* 'lose weight, get thinner'.

(10) Degree achievement (Czech)
 bled -n -ou -t
 pale$_{Adj}$ GET OU$_{theme}$ INF
 'get pale'

In turn, the semelfactive stems are all based on a nominal root (a noun modulo the case suffix), e.g. the Czech *kop* 'kick' – *kop-n-ou-t* 'give a kick' (glossed in 11), *písk* 'a whistle' – *písk-n-ou-t* 'whistle once', *vzlyk* 'a sob' – *vzlyk-n-ou-t* 'give a sob', or the Polish *pisk* 'a squeak' – *pisk-n-ą-ć* 'give a squeak', *krzyk* 'a scream' – *krzyk-n-ą-ć* 'scream once', *dotyk* 'a touch' – *dotk-n-ą-ć* 'touch once', etc.

(11) Semelfactive (Czech)
 kop -n -ou -t
 kick$_N$ GIVE OU$_{theme}$ INF
 '(give a) kick'

The formation of semelfactive *-n-ou* stems applies also to a subset of borrowed nominal roots, e.g. the Czech *klik* 'a click' – *klik-n-ou-t* 'to click once'.

There are a few important remarks that need to be made about the *-n-ou* semelfactives. First, only a subset of Czech and Polish nominal roots form such stems. For example, roots of such Polish nouns as *matk-a* 'mother-FEM.NOM', *stół* 'table.MSC.NOM', among many others, will not form *-n-ou* semelfactives, i.e. **matk-n-ą-ć*, **stoł-n-ą-ć* (these particular roots will forms *-ov-a* activities *matk-ov-a-ć*, *stoł-ov-a-ć*, as discussed in the previous section).

3 Deriving the verb stem alternation

Second, some other genuine *-n-ou* semelfactives, such as for instance the Czech *mrk-n-ou-t* 'give a wink' or the Polish *pac-n-ą-ć* 'give a smack' or *mach-n-ą-ć* 'wave once', do not have a simple noun formed only from the corresponding root with an added case suffix, i.e. the unattested *mrk, *pac, *mach.[6] The fact that the *-n-ou* stems based on nominal roots may not have a corresponding noun is not limited to semelfactives since examples of degree achievement verbs that do not have a corresponding adjective are also attested. For instance, the Czech degree achievement verb *plih-n-ou-t* 'get limp' or the Polish *więd-n-ą-ć* 'wither' do not have corresponding adjectives *plih-ý 'limp-ADJ.MSC.NOM', *więd-y 'wither-ADJ.MSC.NOM'. However, when prefixed, these roots still can still form adjectival L-participles, as in:

(12) a. z-plih-l-ý
     from-limp-PART-ADJ.MSC.NOM
     'limp'
   b. z-więd-ł-y
     from-wither-PART-ADJ.MSC.NOM
     'withered'

This contrast regarding the ability of nominal roots to form semelfactives indicates that there exists a syntactically sensitive typology of nominal roots which singles out eventive and countable nouns as candidates for the formation of semelfactive stems. Importantly, "eventive" and "countable" appear to be necessary but not sufficient features of nominal roots to qualify them as bases for the formation of semelfactive *-n-ou* stem. For instance, the Polish *opór* 'resistance' or *skarga* 'complaint' do not form such stems (*opor-n-ą-ć, *skarg-n-ą-ć) but both can form semelfactives in different ways. The first one forms a periphrastic semelfactive with the verb *dać* 'give' as in:

(13) dać   opór   władzy
     give.INF resistance.NOM authority.DAT
     'to give resistance to the authority'

The second one can merge with the activity theme *-i* and with the perfectivizing prefix *za-*, as in (14), which results in the formation of what Bacz (2012: 116) describes as an inchoative semelfactive, the one that marks the beginning of a new event or state. For the sake of explicitness, let us follow Klein (1994: §6.5) and

---

[6]Again, let us disregard nominalizations (the attested *mrknutí* 'winking', *pacanie* 'smacking', *machanie* 'waving') as even adjectival roots, like in the Polish *blad-y* 'pale-ADJ.NOM.MSC', can form nominalizations, e.g. *blednęcie* 'turning pale'.

3.3 Degree achievements vs. semelfactives

define perfectivity construed by prefixation with *za-* as location of the run time of the event denoted by the predicate within the time interval.[7]

(14) za-skarż-y-ć   decyzję
      PFV-complaint-I$_{theme}$-INF decision.ACC
      'to file a complaint against a decision'

Let us point out that the situation where a subset of nominal roots does not form semelfactive *-n-ou* stems does not have a bearing on the descriptive generalization that such stems are exclusively formed with nominal roots (in the same way as the situation where only a subset of adjectival roots form degree achievement *-n-ou* stems does not have a bearing on the generalization that such stems are only based on adjectival roots). This is also reflected by the fact that there exist a small group of *-n-ou* stems that are formed on what can be classified as verbal roots, in the sense that they only form verb stems rather than nouns or adjectives (other than nominalizations or adjectival participles), such as e.g. the Czech *ply-n-ou-t* 'flow, pass', *vi-n-ou-t* 'wind, wrap', *ž-n-ou-t* 'mow, cut', *tisk-n-ou-t* 'print', or the Polish *pły-n-ą-ć* 'swim', *ciąg-n-ą-ć* 'drag, pull', or *pło-n-ą-ć* 'burn'. The verbal status of such roots is also reflected by their ability to merge with typically verbal prefixes such as the completive *prze-*, as in the Polish *prze-płynąć* lit. 'complete a certain distance swimming' or the perfective *za-*, as in the Czech *za-vinout* 'swaddle', or the Polish *za-ciągnąć* 'pull onto', *za-płonąć* 'inflame' (cf. also (14), where *za-* merges with the verbal *i*-stem rather than with a nominal root as in the unattested **za-skarga*). All these stems that are based on verbal roots are activities rather than semelfactives or degree achievements, as predicted by the generalization about nominal and adjectival status of roots in the *-n-ou* stems.

3.3.2 Get vs. Give

The difference in the lexical category of roots the degree achievement and semelfactive stems are based on carries over to the readings of these categories. The reading of the degree achievements is described in Taraldsen Medová & Wiland (2018b) as the light verb Get applied to the property denoted by the adjectival root, which makes these categories essentially equivalent to English analytic degree achievements such as *get pale* or *get dark* (a subset of which also have synthetic

---

[7] See also Dickey & Janda (2009) for construing semelfactivity with perfectivizing prefixes in Russian, the point of departure in Bacz's (2012) analysis of semelfactives derived by prefixation in Polish. For a related discussion concerning perfectivization by prefixation in Polish see also Grzegorczykowa (1997) and Willim (2006: 187–189). For a related discussion of the interplay of perfectivizing function of verbal prefixes and theme vowels see Jabłońska (2004; 2007).

3 Deriving the verb stem alternation

variants, e.g. *darken, redden*, making it even more descriptively close to the ones in Czech and Polish).

In turn, the reading of the *-n-ou* semelfactives is described as the light verb Give applied to the (caseless) noun, a fairly close equivalent of English analytic semelfactives such as *give a kick, give a shout*, etc. The source of the light verb semantics that applies to the roots in both kinds of stems is argued there to be the *-n* morpheme, which leaves *-ou* to be a verbalizer, just like the other theme vowels are.

Even under the analysis of *-ou* as a verbalizing theme vowel that turns the 'Adj-root + Get' and the 'N-root + Give' complexes into, respectively, degree achievement and semelfactive verb stems, the *-ou* theme is not identical in both kinds of stems, either. This is due to the generalization inferred from a corpus study on Czech and Polish reported in Taraldsen Medová & Wiland (2018b) which states that degree achievement *-n-ou* verbs are all unaccusative, while semelfactive *-n-ou* verbs are either transitive/accusative or unergative.[8] Thus, under the assumption that argument-stuctural properties are associated with the verbal structure, this contrast is realized by the thematic suffix *-ou*. This is not to say that theme vowels, including *-ou*, are solely responsible for encoding the argument-structural properties of verb stems. As stated above, argument structure is a property of the stem in the sense that it depends on the combination of a theme vowel and a root. However, identifying different lexical categories of roots in different classes of stems opens up the possibility to understand the nature of the association between roots and theme vowels from the perspective of the argument structure in a more transparent way, the line of inquiry pursued in Jabłońska (2007).

The description of the syn-sem properties of both kinds of stems are summarized in Table 3.2. The fact that with adjectival roots the *-n* suffix contributes the Get-reading and with nominal roots it contributes the Give-reading as well as the fact that the *-ou* theme is present in unaccusative, transitives, and unergative *-n-ou* stems is analyzed as instances of syncretism.

---

[8]The reported diagnostic for distinguishing between unaccusatives and unergatives is the formation of adjectival passive participles, arguably the only reliable test for unaccusativity that can be applied to both Czech and Polish. Unaccusative verbs can form adjectival L-participles, while unergative and transitive verbs can form only N- or T-participles (cf. Cetnarowska 2002a, 2002b). For instance, unaccusatives like *vlhnout* 'get wet' (Cz) or *głuchnąć* 'get deaf' (Pol) can form L-based adjectival participles *z-vlh-l-ý* 'wet' or *o-głuch-ł-y* 'deaf', while unergative verbs like *dupnout* 'stamp' (Cz) or *cofnąć* 'move back (once)' (Pol) cannot: **dup-l-ý, *cof-ł-y*. For an account of this contrast see Taraldsen Medová & Wiland (2018a).

Table 3.2: Properties of degree achievement and semelfactive -n-ou stems in Czech and Polish in Taraldsen Medová & Wiland (2018b)

	root	light verb reading	argument structure
deg. achievement:	Adj	Get	unaccusative
semelfactive:	N	Give	accusative, unergative

3.3.3 Light verb theory of -n

More precisely, the analysis of the syn-sem structure of the -n affix in Czech and Polish follows the decomposition of the English lexical verb *give* into the sequence of light verbs involving "Give > Get" argued for in Richards (2001).

Richards (2001) considers English idioms which include the lexical *give*, like in (15), and shows that in such idioms the idiomatic part is smaller than *give DP*.

(15) a. The Count gives Mary the creeps.
 b. Mary gave John the sack.
 c. Mary gave Susan the boot.

Richards observes that the idiom is preserved with the lexical verb *get*, as in:

(16) a. Mary got the creeps.
 b. John got the sack.
 c. Susan got the boot.

This leads to a conclusion where the lexical structure of Get is a subset of Give.
Note also that *give*-idioms are broken with the *to*-dative variant:

(17) a. *The Count gives the creeps to Mary.
 b. *Mary gave the sack to John.
 c. *Mary gave the boot to Susan.

Richards (2001) takes this fact to indicate that double object constructions do not comprise a separate possessive functor (the abstract verb Have) and instead, the possessive is an integral component of a ditransitive *get*. As pointed out in Taraldsen Medová & Wiland (2018b: §4.2.3), the containment structure of the light "Give > Get" is not restricted only to the change-of-possession relation and is retained also with the change-of-state Get. We can see this on the example of the idioms that are preserved with the lexical verb *get*, as in:

3 Deriving the verb stem alternation

(18) a. Mary got sacked.
 b. Mary got booted.
 c. Mary got evil eyed (by John).

This fact is taken to indicate that the core component of Get-readings is the change itself: change-of-possession in the case of the English lexical verbs *get*, *give* and change-of-state in the case of the lexical *get* but not *give*. This makes the correct prediction about the status of the Get-readings in Czech and Polish degree achievements, which denote change-of-state, not change-of-possession.

Since we find both Get- and Give-readings in the combinations of roots with the *-n* suffix, this is taken to indicate that the light verb structure is realized synthetically in Czech and Polish by the *-n* morpheme, whose lexical entry can be minimally described as in:[9]

(19) Lexical entry for the light *-n* in Czech and Polish
 [Give [Get]] ⇔ *n*

The Get-subset of the structure realized by the *-n* morpheme is present in degree achievements, as illustrated on the example of *bled-n-ou-t* 'get pale', where it applies to the adjectival root, as shown in (20). More precisely, the change that is the core component of the Get-reading applies to the state denoted by the adjectival root, resulting in the perceived change-of-state.

(20) GetP
 ╱╲
 Get AdjP
  ╱╲
  bled
  'pale'

As shown in (21), following the spell-out motivated movement of the root node, GetP becomes lexicalized as *-n* on the strength of the Superset Principle and surfaces as the suffix.

---

[9] Minimally, since in the few activity *-n-ou* stems listed above which are based on verbal roots, such as *ply-n-ou-t* 'swim' (Cz), *vi-n-ou-t* 'wind, wrap' (Cz), *ciąg-n-ą-ć* 'drag, pull' (Pol), etc., we do not have the light Get- or Give-reading yet we do have the *-n* suffix. Unless verbal roots trigger semantic neutralization of Get and Give, a scenario I do not find immediate evidence for, this fact suggests that verbal roots such as *ply-*, *vi-*, *ciąg-*, etc. form activity *-n-ou* stems with the *-n* suffix whose superstructure syntactically contains the [Give [Get]] structure given in (19). The exhaustive description of the *-n* superstructure, however, will not have a bearing on the following analysis of the iterative alternation.

3.3 Degree achievements vs. semelfactives

(21) Partial spell-out of a degree achievement stem *bled-n* 'get pale'

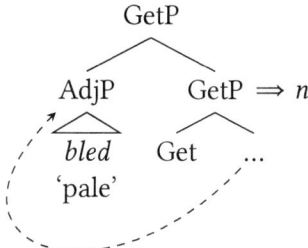

In turn, the superset of features listed in the lexical entry for *-ou* in (19) is present in semelfactives, the categories construed by the merger of the with the nominal root, as illustrated on the example of the Czech *kop-n-ou-t* 'give a kick' in (22). Unlike in degree achievements where the light Get applies to a state denoted by the adjectival root, in semelfactives, Get applies to an object of possession, which is denoted by the nominal root, a structure that projects into the GiveP after subsequent merger of the feature (see the discussion in Taraldsen Medová & Wiland 2018b: §4.2.3–4.3).[10]

(22)

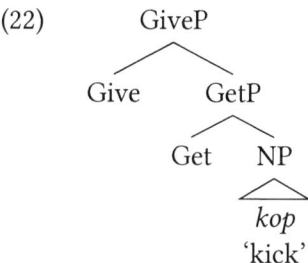

As shown in (23), the spell-out of GiveP takes place following two movements, the complement movement and the spec-to-spec movement at the next cycle, to the effect that *-n* comes out, again, as the suffix on the nominal root.

---

[10] Let us take note of the fact that the feature Give serves in the structure in (22) as a stand-in for a semantic feature that extends the GetP subset into GiveP. If we follow Dowty's (1979) description of the English lexical *give* as [Cause [Become [Have]]], our Give feature will correspond to a functor that introduces causation to a change-of-possession constituent GetP construed by the merger of Get and a nominal root, a feasible scenario which due to the purposes of this chapter I will not explore here further.

3 Deriving the verb stem alternation

(23) Partial spell-out of a semelfactive stem *kop-n* 'give a kick'

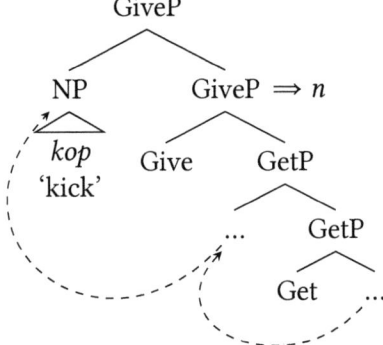

Let us also point out that the association of the Czech/Polish light *-n* morpheme with the English *give* and *get* is based not only on the proximity of the readings but also on valency identity between the synthetic forms of both kinds of stems in Slavic and the forms attested in English.

3.3.4 *-Ou* as layers of the VP structure

These argument-structural correlations are easily observed between the English periphrastic degree achievements like e.g. *get dumber, get soft, get blind*, etc., which correspond to the Czech/Polish synthetic unaccusative 'Adj-root *-n*' structures, as for instance in:

(24) Czech
      Petr   hloup-n-u-l.
      Petr.NOM stupid-GET-OU-PART.MSC.SG
      'Petr was getting more and more stupid.'

(25) Polish
      Kartofle   mięk-n-ą-∅   podczas gotowania.
      potatoes-NOM soft-GET-OU-PRES.3PL   during cooking
      'Potatoes soften during cooking.'

Likewise, the English causatives with the lexical *give* correspond to the causative 'N-root *-n*' structures. The second is particularly transparent in the narrow subset of Slavic periphrastic semelfactives which feature the lexical verb *dać* 'give' followed by an accusative direct object as for instance in (26a), a close equivalent of the synthetic *-n-ou* semelfactive in (26b).

(26) Polish
    a. Jan   dał kop-a   Karol-owi.
       Jan.NOM gave kick-ACC Karol-DAT
    b. Jan   kop-n-ą-ł   Karol-a.
       Jan.NOM kop-GIVE-OU-PART Karol-ACC
       'Jan gave Karol a kick.'

Of course, semelfactives that do not have periphrastic variants like *kopnąć/dać kopa* in (26) can be transitive/accusative, too, e.g. *bod-n-ou-t* 'stab' in (27a) or even double transitive, e.g. *skřip-n-ou-t* 'squeeze' in (27b):

(27) Czech (Taraldsen Medová & Wiland 2018b: ex. 82)
    a. Petr   bod-n-u-l   Karl-a.
       Petr.NOM stab-GIVE-OU-PART.MSC.SG Karl-ACC
       'Petr stabbed Karel (once).'
    b. Karel   skřip-n-u-l   Petr-ovi prst   do
       Karel-NOM squeeze-GIVE-OU-PART.MSC.SG Petr-DAT finger.ACC into
       dveř-í.
       door-GEN
       'Karel squeezed Petr's finger into the door.'

The other category of the Czech/Polish *-n-ou* semelfactives are unergatives, the equivalents of English semelfactives such as *sneeze* or *bark*, which denote a single stage event in sentences like in:

(28) a. The baby sneezed once at 8 o'clock.
     b. The dog suddenly barked at me.

In English, such verbs are usually homonymous with activities: iteratives as in (29a) and habituals as in (29b) (cf. Carlson 2012).

(29) a. The baby sneezed for a few minutes.
     b. The dog barked for several minutes (every Friday).

Contrary to English, the unergative *-n-ou* verbs such as the Polish *kich-n-ą-ć* 'sneeze (once)', *wark-n-ą-ć* 'gnarl (once)', *ziew-n-ą-ć* 'yawn' or the Czech *máv-n-ou-t* 'wave (once)', *syk-n-ou-t* 'hiss (once)', *dup-n-ou-t* 'stamp', etc. are unambiguously semelfactive.[11]

---

[11] As explained in footnote 8, the fact that these Czech and Polish verbs do not form adjectival L-passives confirms that they are unergatives rather than unaccusatives (cf. *kich-ł-y, *wark-ł-y, *ziew-ł-y, *máv-l-y, *syk-l-y, *dup-l-y, etc.).

3 Deriving the verb stem alternation

Dividing the -n-ou part of the stem into a sequence of the light -n and the genuine theme vowel -ou allows us to associate the argument-structural properties of degree achievement and semelfactive stems with their syntactic representations in a way which captures the fact that all theme vowels are verbalizers. However, since the degree achievement stems are unaccusative and the semelfactive stems are either transitive/accusative or unergative, representing the -ou theme as a simplex verbalizing head in syntax (such as the minimalist "little v") does not lead to predictions about the relation between the geometry of their syntactic representations and received argument structures.

The alternative is a representation of the -ou theme as a monotonically growing sequence of heads which realizes the "unergative > accusative > unaccusative" hierarchy. For the purposes of our discussion of the iterative alternation, let us represent the eventive verbal structure simply as an articulated VP, as in (30), where V_n heads indicate levels of embedding.[12]

(30)
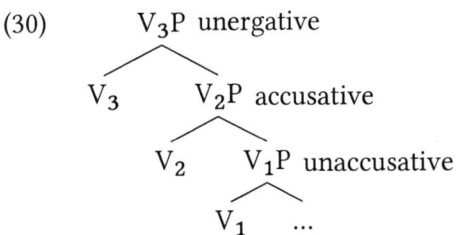

Such a representation reflects structural proximity between unergatives and accusatives based on the observation that external arguments of unergatives and accusatives are event initiators, which are introduced by higher heads than arguments of unaccusatives are (e.g. Levin & Rappaport Hovav 1995 and Ramchand 2008). In the domain of -n-ou stems, this sequence reflects the fact that a subset of semelfactives can be either unergative or accusative but never unaccusative, such as for instance the Polish *gwizd-n-ą-ć*. In (31a), it has a literal meaning 'whistle' when unergative and in (31b), where it occurs with an accusative object, it has a non-literal meaning 'steal'.

(31)   Polish (Taraldsen Medová & Wiland 2018b: ex. 89)
   a.   Jan   gwizd-n-ą-ł.
        Jan.NOM whistle-GIVE-OU-PART
        'Jan whistled (once).'

---

[12]This is an approximation of the representation of the argument structure discussed in Taraldsen Medová & Wiland (2018b), which is argued there to include case positions. Although important from the perspective of argument realization, the syntactic representation of the "unergative > accusative > unaccusative" hierarchy as in (30) is sufficient for present purposes.

3.3 Degree achievements vs. semelfactives

b. Jan gwizd-n-ą-ł kred-ę z klasy.
Jan.NOM whistle-GIVE-OU-PART chalk-ACC from classroom
'Jan has stolen the chalk from the classroom.'

What follows from the representation of the verbal argument structure as in (30) and the fact that *-ou* is an exponent of the eventive verbal structure in three kinds of argument-structural *-n-ou* stems is the shape of the lexical entry as in:

(32) Lexical entry for the *-ou* theme in Czech and Polish
[V_3 [V_2 [V_1]]] ⟺ *-ou*

The smallest subset of the VP structure that can be lexicalized as *-ou* is present in degree achievements, a class of *-n-ou* verbs that are, let us restate, exclusively unaccusative, as for instance in the Czech example in (33).

(33) Jan bled-n-u-l.
Jan.NOM pale-GET-OU-PART
'Jan was getting pale.'

The merger of the partially derived semelfactive stem like *bled-n* 'get pale' in (21) with the verbal feature V_1 is followed by the spell-out procedure, as shown in:

(34) Spell-out of *-ou* in an unaccusative degree achievement stem *bled-n-ou* 'get pale'

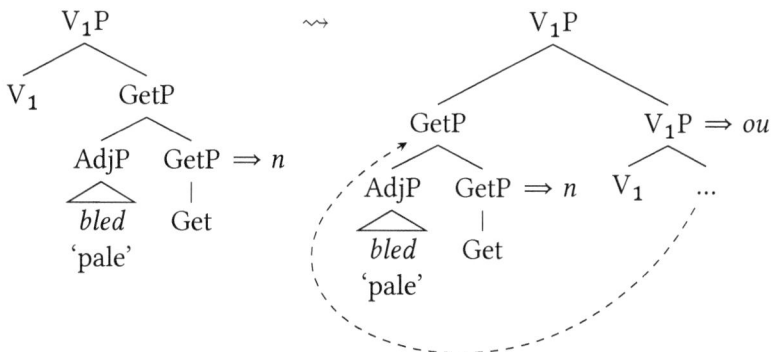

Following snowballing, *-ou* becomes spelled out as the smallest subset of (32) and ends up as the external suffix on the adjectival root *bled*.

In the case of transitive/accusative semelfactives, like the Czech/Polish *kop-n-q-ć* 'kick' in (26b), a bigger subset of the verbal structure is present, the one that includes features V_1 and V_2. Each merger of the verbal feature triggers the spell-out procedure, as outlined in (35):

55

3 Deriving the verb stem alternation

(35) Spell-out of -ou in an accusative semelfactive stem *kop-n-ou* 'give a kick'

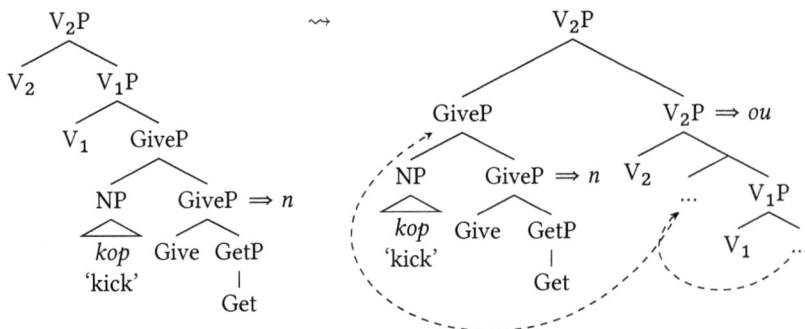

Following snowballing at the first cycle and spec-to-spec movement at the second cycle, the -*ou* theme spells out the accusative V₂P structure and comes out as the outer suffix.

In turn, the derivation of unergative semelfactives, like the Czech *syk-n-ou-t* 'hiss' or the Polish *gwizd-n-ą-ć* 'whistle' in (31a) involves the merger of the full set of V-features, resulting in the formation of the unergative superstructure, the structure that is a notch bigger than accusative semelfactive. As shown in (36) on the example of *gwizd-n-ą-ć*, the merger of each V-feature is, again, followed by spell-out.

(36) Spell-out of -ou in an unergative semelfactive stem *gwizd-n-ą* 'whistle'

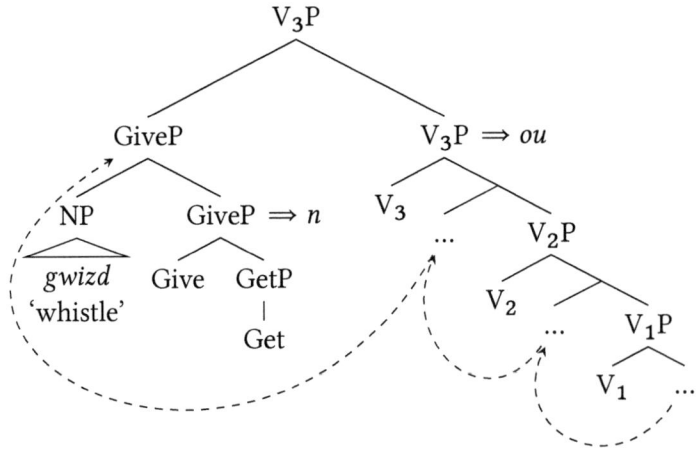

56

Following the movements of the derived -n stem, the GiveP constituent, the -ou theme spells out the unergative V₃P superstructure and, like before, comes out as the outer suffix on the nominal root.

3.4 Properties of the alternation

There are two key properties of the alternation between -n-ou and -aj stems. Namely, the alternation targets perfective stems and it preserves the argument structure of the stem.

3.4.1 Perfective stems

The semelfactive stems are inherently perfective, which means that the event they express is bounded, hence countable (Declerck 1979; Bach 1986; de Swart 1998; Willim 2006; Dickey 2016). A bounded (countable) event denoted by a semelfactive stem can be iterated, which is reflected in the alternation illustrated on the example of a few Czech and Polish verbs in the following.

(37) Examples of semelfactive-iterative alternation in Czech
    a. kop-**n-ou**-t — kop-**a**-t
        kick-GIVE-OU-INF   kick-AJ-INF
        'give a kick'   'be giving kicks, kick repeatedly'
    b. mrk-**n-ou**-t — mrk-**a**-t
        wink-GIVE-OU-INF wink-AJ-INF
        'give a wink'   'be giving winks, keep winking'
    c. kous-**n-ou**-t — kous-**a**-t
        bite-GIVE-OU-INF bite-AJ-INF
        'give a bite'   'bite repeatedly, keep biting'

(38) Examples of semelfactive-iterative alternation in Polish
    a. liz-**n-ą**-ć — liz-**a**-ć
        lick-GIVE-OU-INF lick-AJ-INF
        'give a lick'   'be giving licks, lick repeatedly'
    b. dotk-**n-ą**-ć — dotyk-**a**-ć
        touch-GIVE-OU-INF touch-AJ-INF
        'give a touch'   'touch repeatedly'
    c. bek-**n-ą**-ć — bek-**a**-ć
        burp-GIVE-OU-INF burp-AJ-INF
        'burp once'   'keep burping, burp repeatedly'

3 Deriving the verb stem alternation

The *-aj* iteratives retain the Give-readings of semelfactive *-n-ou* stems, which is expected if iteratives denote a repetition of the single stage event denoted by the corresponding semelfactive stem.[13]

Although the alternation targets a considerable subset of nominal roots that form *-n-ou* semelfactives, certain roots that form such semelfactives will not form iterative *-aj* stems. For instance, nominal roots such as the Polish *krzyk-* 'a scream' or *ryk-* 'a roar' build semelfactives *krzyk-n-ą-ć* 'give a scream', *ryk-n-ą-ć* 'give a roar' but they alternate with stative *-e* stems *krzycz-e-ć* 'to scream', *rycz-e-ć* 'to roar' rather than with iterative *-aj* stems (the unattested *krzyk-a-ć, *ryk-a-ć). This, however, is expected under a proviso that there is a syntactically sensitive typology of roots that goes beyond the basic distinction into lexical categories of N vs. Adj vs. V, a scenario we need to assume anyways in order to control for the fact that not all nominal roots form semelfactive *-n-ou* stems in the first place (let us recall here the discussion of unattested semelfactives with nominal roots such as *matk-* 'mother' or *stół-* 'table' from §3.3.1). Given the fact that *krzyk-* and *ryk-* are nouns of perception and production of sounds we correctly expect them to produce *-e* stems, which typically form this subclass of statives, rather than iteratives. Thus, in the case of such roots it is safe to state that they simply form bases for semelfactive *-n-ou* stems and *-e* stems but there is no derivational relation between semelfactives and *-e* statives.

Unlike in the case of semelfactives, bare roots of degree achievement *-n-ou* stems do not undergo the iterative alternation, as illustrated by the following examples.

(39) Czech

    a.   bled-**n-ou**-t   – *bled-**a**-t
          pale-GET-OU-INF
          'get pale'

---

[13]This comes with a caveat regarding the extensions of the iterative readings denoted by the *-aj* stems into habitual and/or frequentative readings, a class broadly labeled as activities. The morphological form of the three types of activity verbs is identical and includes the *-aj* theme to the effect that iterative, habitual, and frequentative readings can be differentiated by adverbial modifiers, in a similar way as in English, as for instance in (i) (see Carlson 2012).

(i)   a. The dog barked **for the whole night**.   (iterative)
     b. The dog barked **every time he was hungry**.   (habitual/frequentative)

Unless in the unlikely scenario that the distinction between iteratives, habituals, and frequentatives is not part of lexical aspect, this points to an analysis of *-aj* – as well as the English verbs like *bark, cough, wink* – as morphemes that are overspecified with respect to the features forming these aspectual categories, in a similar way the *-ou* theme is overspecified for argument-structural properties, the *-n* morpheme for the light Get and Give, etc.

3.4 Properties of the alternation

      b.   hluch-**n**-**ou**-t   – *hluch-**a**-t
          deaf-GET-OU-INF
          'get deaf'

      c.   mrz-**n**-**ou**-t   – *mrz-**a**-t
          freeze-GET-OU-INF
          'get frozen'

(40)   Polish

      a.   mok-**n**-**ą**-ć   – *mocz-**a**-ć
          wet-GET-OU-INF
          'get wet'

      b.   sch-**n**-**ą**-ć   – *sch-**a**-ć
          dry-GET-OU-INF
          'get dry'

      c.   chud-**n**-**ą**-ć   – *chud-**a**-ć
          slim-GET-OU-INF
          'get slim, loose weight'

This contrast follows from the fact that degree achievement stems are imperfective, which means that the event they express is unbounded, hence uncountable. An unbounded (uncountable) event denoted by such a stem cannot be iterated. However, once a degree achievement stem has a prefix which makes it perfective, such a stem can undergo the iterative alternation quite regularly, as shown in the following:

(41)   Czech

      a.   vy-bled-**n**-**ou**-t   – vy-bled-**a**-t
          PFV-pale-GET-OU-INF PFV-pale-AJ-INF
          'get pale'   'pale out repeatedly'

      b.   u-vad-**n**-**ou**-t   – u-vad-**a**-t
          PFV-wither-GET-OU-INF PFV-wither-AJ-INF
          'wither'   'wither repeatedly'

      c.   za-mrz-**n**-**ou**-t   – za-mrz-**a**-t
          PFV-freeze-GET-OU-INF PFV-freeze-AJ-INF
          'get frozen'   'freeze repeatedly'

(42)   Polish

      a.   za-mok-**n**-**ą**-ć   – za-mak-**a**-ć
          PFV-wet-GET-OU-INF PFV-wet-AJ-INF
          'get wet'   'moisten repeatedly or gradually'

3 Deriving the verb stem alternation

b. wy-sch-n-ą-ć   – wy-sych-a-ć
    PFV-dry-GET-OU-INF   PFV-dry-AJ-INF
    'get dry'   'get dry repeatedly or gradually'
c. wy-mięk-n-ą-ć   – wy-mięk-a-ć
    PFV-soft-GET-OU-INF   PFV-soft-AJ-INF
    'chicken out'   'chicken out repeatedly'

3.4.2 Argument structure preservation

The other essential property of the iterative alternation with *-n-ou* stems is the preservation of the argument structure. As shown in (43–44), accusative semelfactive *-n-ou* stems will form accusative iterative *-aj* stems.

(43) Czech
      Jan   { kopnul   / kopal }   míč.
      Jan.NOM kicked$_{semel}$ kicked$_{iter}$ ball.ACC
      'Jan kicked the ball once/repeatedly.'

(44) Polish
      Jan   { dotknął   / dotykał }   detonator.
      Jan.NOM touched$_{semel}$ touched$_{iter}$ detonator.ACC
      'Jan touched the detonator once/repeatedly.'

Unergative semelfactive *-n-ou* stems will form unergative *-aj* stems, as shown in the following:

(45) Czech
      Pes   { štěknul   / štěkal }.
      dog.NOM barked$_{semel}$ barked$_{iter}$
      'The dog barked once/repeatedly.'

(46) Polish
      Jan   { mrugnął   / mrugał }.
      Jan.NOM winked$_{semel}$ winked$_{iter}$
      'Jan winked once/repeatedly.'

The argument structure preservation holds also in the case of anticausative semelfactives, such as the Czech/Polish verb *couvnout/cofnąć* 'move back', as illustrated for Polish in the following:

(47) Motor   się   { cofnął   / cofał }.
     motorcycle.NOM REFL   moved.back$_{semel}$ moved.back$_{iter}$
     'The motorcycle moved back once/repeatedly.'

Argument structure is also preserved in iteratives formed with perfectivized stems of degree achievements prefixed with *wy-*, like for instance in the case of the Polish *wymiękać* 'chicken out repeatedly':

(48) Nasi zawodnicy   nie mogą { wy-mięknąć   / wy-miękać }.
     our players.NOM.PL   not can   chicken.out$_{deg.ach}$ chicken.out$_{iter}$
     'Our players must not chicken out this time/repeatedly.'

3.5 Representation

The properties of the alternation between perfective (bounded/countable) verbs and iteratives can be explained if we follow a strand of work on aspectual categories that argues for a compositional relation between these two types of verbs. More specifically, the properties of the alternation can be captured if iterative *-aj* stems are structurally bigger than perfective (bounded/countable) stems. This can be generally represented as in (49), where the relevant size difference is pretheoretically marked as an extra iterative-forming Asp head on top of the perfective stem:

(49)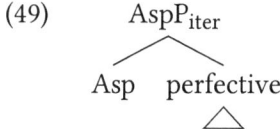

For semelfactives, this means the iterative Asp feature will apply to the *-n-ou* stem that contains the light verb Give *-n*. Since both accusative and unergative semelfactives undergo the iterative alternation, the stem that the Asp feature applies to must include, respectively, the V$_2$P subset or the V$_3$P superset of *-ou*. The addition of the iterative feature Asp to both types of semelfactives is shown on the example of an accusative *kop-n-ou-t* 'give a kick' and an unergative *gwizd-n-ą-ć* 'whistle' in the following representations, which show the stages before the spell-out of AspP as *-aj* will over-ride the *-n-ou* sequence:

3 Deriving the verb stem alternation

(50) Iterative stems based on semelfactives before the spell-out of AspP as *-aj*
    a. Czech
        Accusative *kop-n-ou-t* 'give a kick'

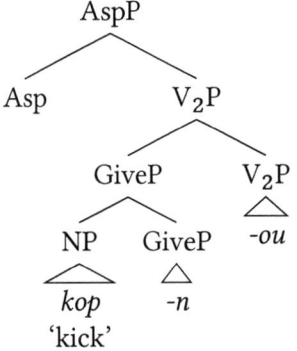

    b. Polish
        Unergative *gwizd-n-ą-ć* 'whistle'

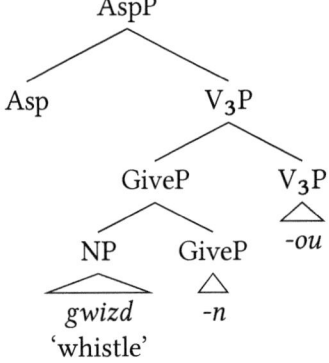

For degree achievements perfectivized with a prefix, this means the iterative Asp will apply to the *-n-ou* stem that contains the Get subset of light verb *-n*, and the V_1P subset of the *-ou*, which is present in unaccusatives. This is illustrated on the example of the Czech *za-mrz-n-ou-t* 'get frozen', which alternates with *za-mrz-a-t* 'freeze repeatedly' in (51). As for the perfectivizing prefix *za-*, which is represented below simply as the realization of the Perf(ective)P, which I will assume to merge directly with the adjectival root of a degree achievement stem (the root marked here as the AP).

3.5 Representation

(51) Czech
Iterative stem *za-mrz-a-t* 'freeze repeatedly' based on the root of a degree achievement before the spell-out of AspP as *-aj*

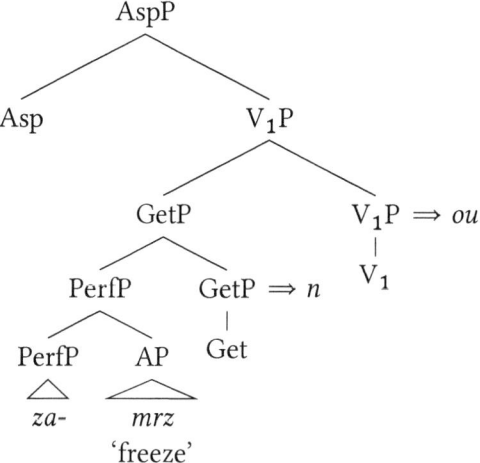

This assumption about *za-* is in agreement with observations about its low position in Polish in Svenonius (2004a) (who credits Patrycja Jabłońska with this insight), Wiland (2012), and in Slovenian in Žaucer (2005). More generally, the idea that verbal prefixes in Czech are base generated as sisters to the root is compliant with Caha & Ziková's (2016) claim that prefixed verb stems in Czech have an underlying structure as in (52), the proposal first put forth for Slavic in Svenonius (2004b).

(52) [[pref root] theme]

Apart from the formation of an iterative based on a prefixed root of a degree achievement stem, an inferential argument in favor of the size relation between iteratives and (unprefixed) semelfactives is based on the fact that we can construe an iterative reading of a semelfactive *-n-ou* verb by adding a frequency adverbial. This is illustrated for Polish by the following examples:

(53) a. Jan   kop-n-ą-ł   piłkę.   (semelfactive)
          Jan.NOM kick-GIVE-OU-PART ball.ACC
          'Jan kicked the ball once.'
      b. Jan kop-n-ą-ł   piłkę pięć razy   (iterative)
          Jan kick-GIVE-OU-PART ball   five times
          'Jan kicked the ball five times.'

3 Deriving the verb stem alternation

(54) a. Jan   kaszl-n-ą-ł.   (semelfactive)
Jan.NOM cough-GIVE-OU-PART
'Jan coughed once.'

b. Jan kaszl-n-ą-ł   pięć razy   (iterative)
Jan cough-GIVE-OU-PART five times
'Jan coughed five times.'

The opposite, that is the addition of a punctual adverbial to an iterative -*aj* verb, does not result in the semelfactive reading of the -*aj* verb, as illustrated for Polish in the following:

(55) Jan   kop-a-ł   piłkę   (o 5-tej).   (iterative)
Jan.NOM kick-AJ-PART ball.ACC at five
'Jan kicked the ball repeatedly at 5 o'clock.'

(56) Jan   kaszl-a-ł   (o 5-tej).   (iterative)
Jan.NOM cough-AJ-PART at five
'Jan coughed repeatedly at 5 o'clock.'

While there is no agreement in the literature about the identification of the semantic content of what is represented in (49) as the Asp head, the syn-sem representation of iteratives as bigger than semelfactives is in line with a strand of work on the semantics of aspectual classes that describes semelfactives as a subset structure of iterative activities. For example, in approaches that extend Vendler's (1967) description of aspectual classes, both semelfactives and activities are described as [+dynamic] situations, with activities additionally described as [+durative] (e.g. Smith 1997; Olsen 1994; 1997; Beavers 2008).

In Xiao & McEnery (2004), where the activity class is split such that iteratives constitute a separate category, iteratives that correspond to the English verbs like in:

(57) He coughed **for 5 minutes**.

are classified as derived semelfactives, as opposed to basic semelfactives like in:

(58) He coughed **once**.

In turn, in a non-Vendlerian approach such as Egg (2018), iteratives are derived either by lexical construction or aspectual coercion applied to semelfactives. Egg's (2018) analysis stands in opposition to Rothstein (2004), who proposes that iteratives are more basic than semelfactives, which effectively makes semelfactives a subclass of activity predicates, a scenario not compatible with the syn-sem description of both categories in (50). Egg shows, among others that, contrary to the predictions of Rothstein's proposal, iteratives are composed of minimal eventualities. For instance, iteratives like *tremble* clearly denote back and forth movements whereas *tremble 5 times* denotes iterations of such movements only.[14]

Assuming the structures in (50–51) represent the iterative -*aj* stems that alternate with -*n-ou* stems, let us attempt to spell out the AspP in these structures following the spell-out procedure discussed in the previous chapter.

3.6 Spelling out -*aj* stems with subextraction

We need to apply spell-out operations to the trees in (50–51) in such a way that we preserve the root in semelfactives and the prefix-root constituent in perfectivized stems of degree achievements and make sure the spell-out of the Asp head will over-ride the earlier spell-outs of -*n* and -*ou* in these structures – the procedure that will derive the reduction in the number of affixes. For the illustration of the application of the spell-our procedure recapped in §2.4 to our structures, let us first work with the semelfactive *kop-n-ou-t* in (50a).

3.6.1 Deriving the reduction

The first step of the spell-out algorithm, STAY, does not lead to the spell-out of Asp in (49) since the insertion of -*aj* in the AspP node would over-ride the entire stem including the root, counter fact. The second step, the spec-to-spec movement of GiveP shown in (59), does not lead to its spell-out either, since it results in the formation of an unattested stem **kop-n-aj*. (Let us recall from (35) that GiveP is the constituent that moves at the cycle directly preceding the merger of Asp).

(59)

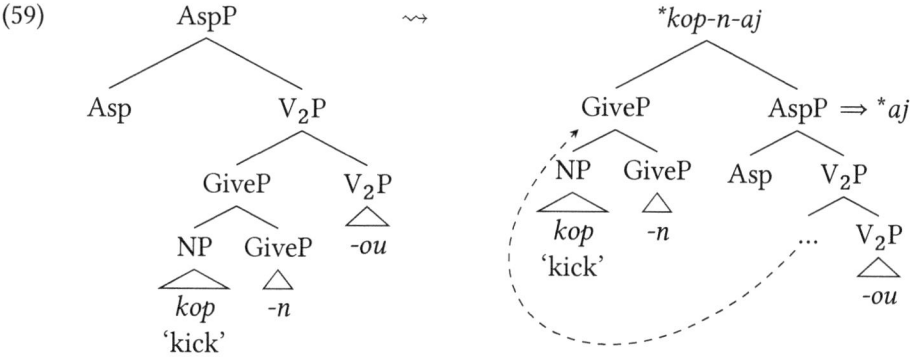

[14]See also Taraldsen Medová & Wiland (2018b: §4.1) for challenges in applying Rothstein's proposal to the morpho-semantic description of Czech and Polish semelfactives.

3 Deriving the verb stem alternation

Although the evacuation of GiveP *kop-n* in (59) allows Asp to be spelled out in such a way that the insertion of *-aj* in the sister node to the landing site of GiveP over-rides the spell-out of the VP *-ou*, *-aj* surfaces here as the second suffix on the root, counter fact. In other words, spec-to-spec movement does not derive the cutback in the number of suffixes we observe in the alternation between semelfactive *-n-ou* and iterative *-aj* stems.

In this case we need to backtrack by trying snowballing, the third step of the algorithm, as shown in:

(60)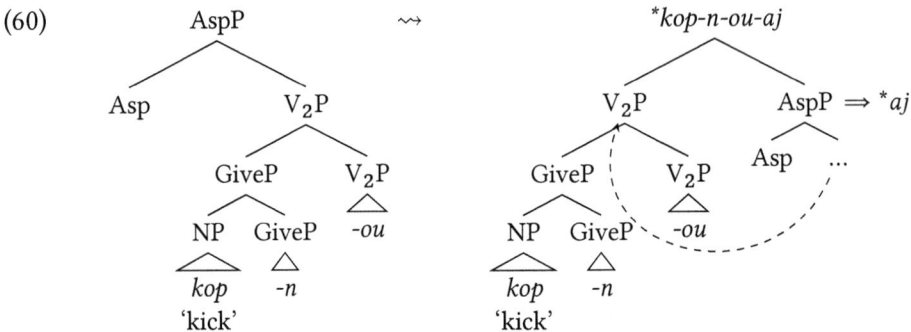

Snowballing, however, also does not derive the desired result either since now *-aj* ends up as the third suffix in the unattested stem **kop-n-ou-aj*. Let us note here that the application of the truncation rule in Slavic phonology as in (61), whereby a vowel in a cyclic morpheme (essentially, a suffix) becomes deleted before a vowel, does not help, either.[15]

(61)   Vowel truncation
       V → ∅ / _ V

This is so since the deletion of *-ou* in front of *-aj* as in (62) derives the unattested surface form **kop-n-aj*, the same result as in (59).

(62)   kop-n-ou-aj → kop-n-∅-aj

---

[15]There is a long tradition of applying the vowel deletion rule in (61), originally discovered to hold in Russian conjugation in Jakobson (1948), in the derivation of surface forms throughout Slavic, including Lightner (1972), Gussmann (1980), Rubach (1984; 1993), Halle & Nevins (2009), among others.

3.6 Spelling out -aj stems with subextraction

Snowballing exhausts the list of movement operations in the spell-out procedure discussed in Starke (2018) with the subsequent SUBDERIVE resulting in the formation of a prefix. As suggested in §2.5.3, a logical solution to the problem of spelling out Asp is to extend the list of movement operations by SUBEXTRACT and order it before SUBDERIVE. When applied to our representation in (63), the extraction of the NP *kop* from the complex specifier GiveP *kop-n* appears to derive the desired result.

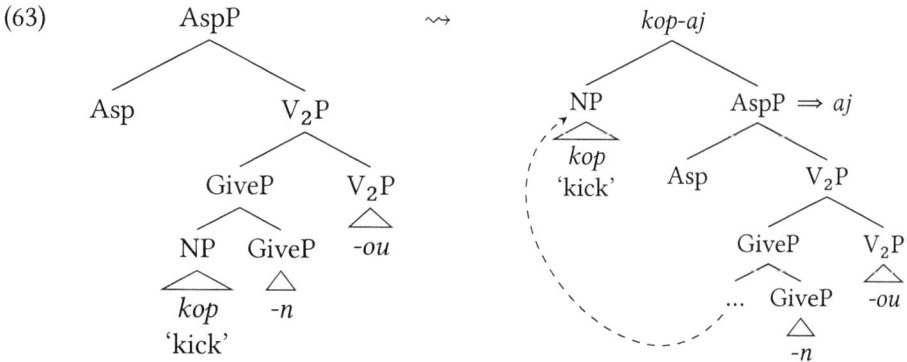

(63)

Following the extraction of the NP *kop*, the spell-out of its sister node AspP as *-aj* over-rides the earlier spell-outs of both *-n* and *-ou*, resulting in the formation of *kop-aj*, a bi-morphemic stem with a portmanteau suffix. The extraction preserves the nominal root and derives the reduction in the number of morphemes in the iterative *-aj* stem with respect to the syntactically less complex semelfactive *-n-ou* stem. Let us also point out that the lexicalization of the complex AspP as the *-aj* suffix in (63) adheres to Starke's (2018) contrast between "pre-" vs. "post-" placement in terms of a binary vs. a unary foot in their syntactic representations (cf. the discussion in §2.3.4). This is so since the subextraction that facilitates spell-out in a derivation like in (63) does not appear to create a syntactically relevant trace (i.e. an object relevant for reconstruction), which makes it identical to spell-out driven movement that involves a specifier or a complement with this respect.

The subextraction of the root node will give a similar result when it applies to the representation with the unergative semelfactives *gwizd-n-q-ć* 'whistle once' in (50b). As shown in (64), the spell-out of the remnant AspP as *-aj* produces the desired *gwizd-a-ć* 'whistle repeatedly' (modulo the infinitive suffix *-ć*).

3 Deriving the verb stem alternation

(64)
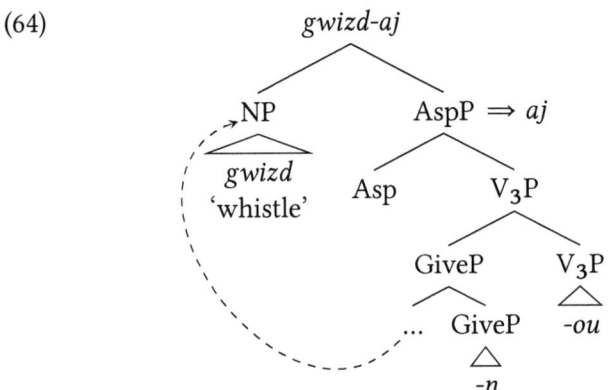

Likewise, the subextraction of the node containing the prefixed root can apply to the representation based on the degree achievement *za-mrz-n-ou-t* 'get frozen' in (51). As shown in (65), such a movement will create a remnant AspP, which can be spelled out as *-aj* in the desired *za-mrz-a-t* 'freeze repeatedly'.

(65)
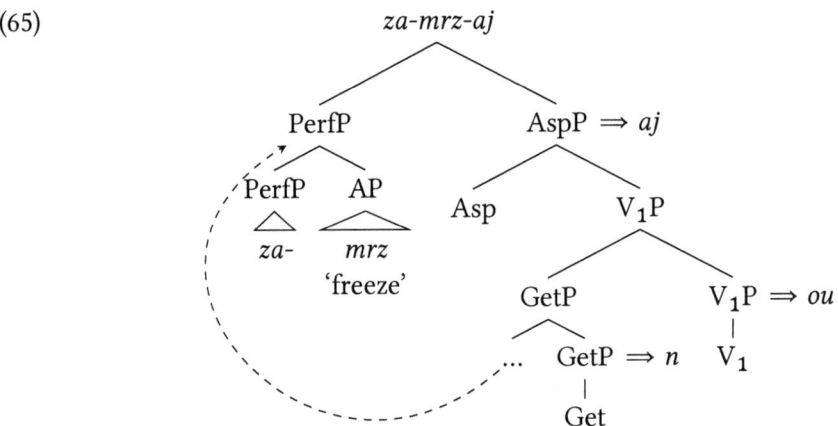

Let us observe that while we are able to obtain the reduction of a sequence of two affixes to one with SUBEXTRACT, we need to control for the fact that *-aj* spells out three different subtrees. In (63), *-aj* spells out AspP that contains GiveP and the accusative V_2P; in (64), it spells out AspP that contains GiveP and the unergative V_3P; in (51), it spells out AspP that contains GetP and the unaccusative V_1P, the smallest subset of the *-ou* theme. This raises the question: what is the shape of the lexical entry for *-aj* such that it can be inserted in these three different-looking nodes? This issue is non-trivial since the lexical insertion mechanism that is regulated by the Superset Principle requires a syntactic node to be a (sub-)constituent

3.6 Spelling out -aj stems with subextraction

of a lexically stored tree. In the case we are considering, -aj is inserted into AspP that *dominates* (sub-)constituents of two lexically stored trees: one for -n and the other for -ou. In other words, -aj is inserted into a syntactic tree that can shrink in the middle rather than on top. This issue can be resolved if the lexical entry for -aj includes pointers to the lexical items -n and -ou rather than to syntactic nodes these exponents realize.

3.6.2 Pointers

In §2.3.5 we stated that the cyclicity of spell-out enables the insertion mechanism to make reference to lexical items inserted at earlier cycles, a result achieved through a tool called a pointer. Let us consider how such a lexicalization scenario applies to the lexical entry for -aj if it includes a pointer structure as in the following.

(66) Lexical entry for the -aj theme

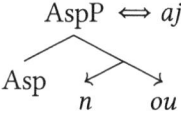

The entry for -aj defined in such a way means that it can be inserted in AspP that contains feature Asp and a pointer structure with two particular lexical items, -n and -ou, which were inserted at earlier cycles. The item -aj can, thus, spell out the following syntactic representations, which involve either the superset or the subset structures of -n and -ou:

(67) a.

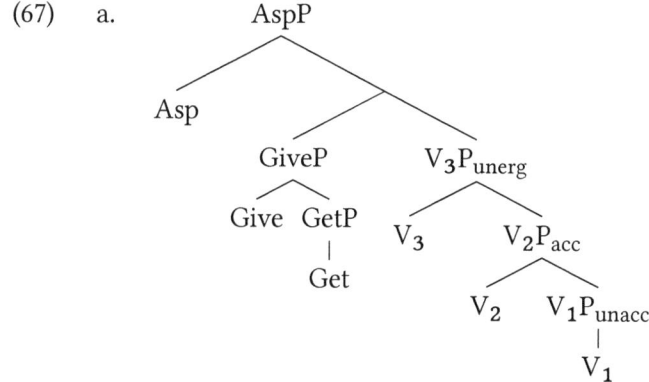

69

3 Deriving the verb stem alternation

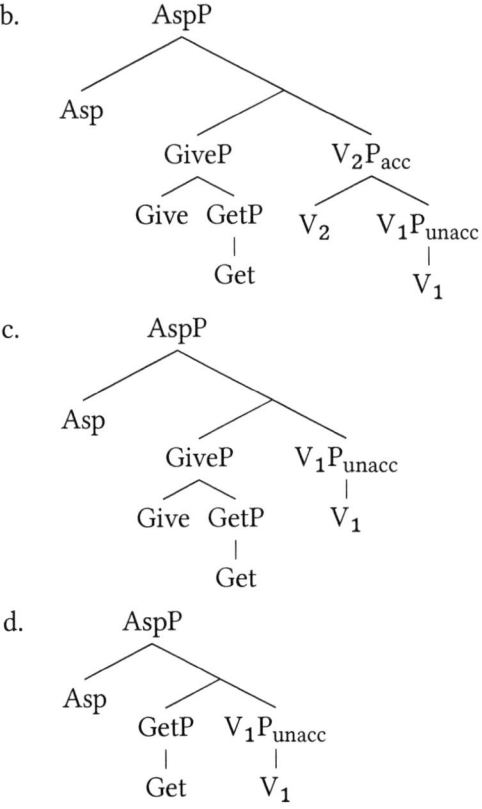

The -*aj* theme which spells out the unergative V_3P superstructure in (67a) is present in stems like *gwizdać* (Pol) 'whistle repeatedly' in (64). The -*aj* with the accusative V_2P subset structure in (67b) is present in stems like *kopat* 'kick repeatedly' (Cz, Pol) in (63). In turn, while -*aj* can also spell out the tree in (67c), that tree does not correspond to an attested syntactic representation. This is so since unaccusative -*n-ou* stems only form degree achievements, which include the light Get. Thus, the unaccusative V_1P does not merge with GiveP but with its GetP subset – the attested structure in (67d).

To sum up, the reduction in the number of morphemes can be derived with subextraction from a complex specifier followed by the spell-out of the remnant node. In the illustration of such a reduction with the iterative alternation that involves -*n-ou* stems, the desired result of the over-riding of two smaller affixes with one bigger affix can be obtained using the lexical insertion mechanism that makes reference to lexical items inserted at earlier cycles.

3.7 Subextract vs. backtracking

An alternative way of obtaining a reduction in the amount of morphemes based on backtracking has been outlined in §2.5.2 (cf. Pantcheva 2011: 160–168). According to the spell-out logic we have been working with so far, an attempt to spell-out a feature becomes undone if there is no lexical item that matches a tree structure and a different spell-out option is attempted. In a backtracking derivation, this may mean moving back several cycles. To illustrate how the backtracking derivation outlined in §2.5.2 applies to the iterative alternation that targets -n-ou stems, let us work with the example involving the Czech *kop-n-ou-t* 'give a kick' and *kop-a-t* 'kick repeatedly'.

3.7.1 Structures that shrink in the middle

The addition of the Asp head to the semelfactive stem *kop-n-ou* illustrated in (63) triggers spell-out. If movement possibilities are exhausted, the derivation backtracks to the inside of the NP root *kop* and spells out its subset structure, as shown in the following, where the structure of the NP root is represented as a sequence of N_n heads that indicate contiguous the levels of embedding.

(68)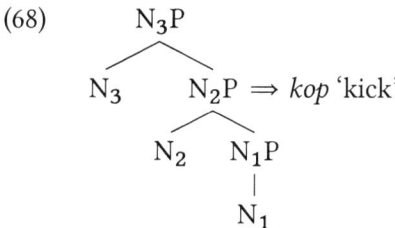

Instead of spelling out N_3 by STAY, N_3 is spelled out following the evacuation of the node spelled out at the previous cycle, as shown in (69). If the lexical entry for -*aj* has a foot in N_3, then the N_3P remnant can be now spelled out as the -*aj* suffix on the root.

(69)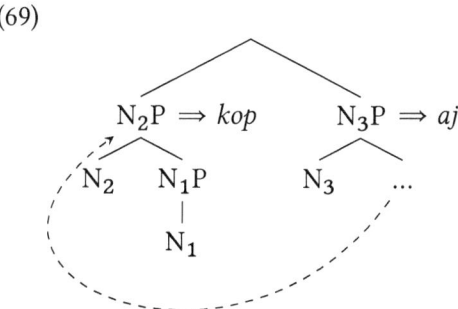

3 Deriving the verb stem alternation

Subsequent mergers of the features ranging from the up to the iterative Asp are spelled out in the same way, by successive cyclic movement of N_2P *kop*, as shown in the following.

(70)

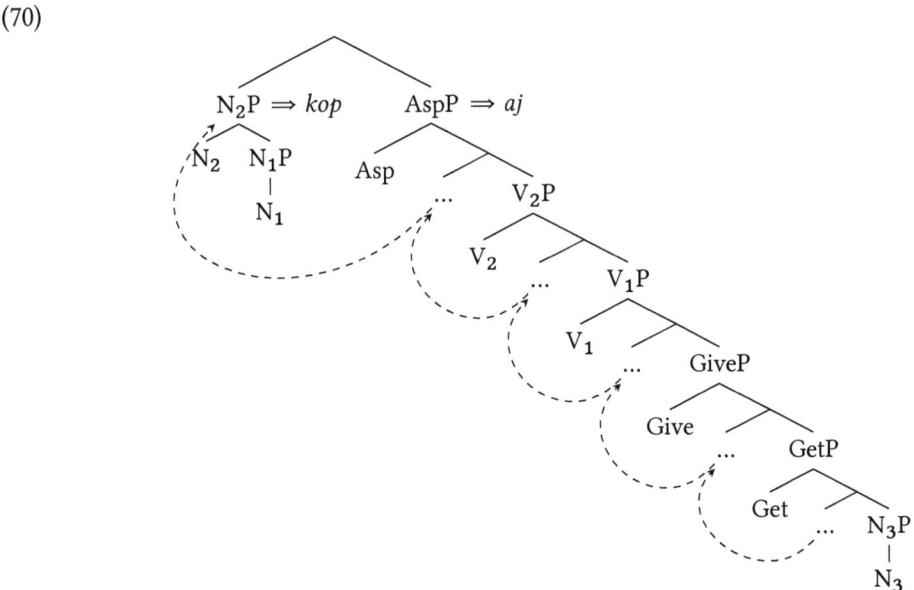

The insertion of *-aj* in AspP in (70) is possible if its lexical entry is defined as in the following:

(71) Lexical entry for the *-aj* theme (alternative to (66))
[Asp [V_2 [V_1 [Give [Get [N_3]]]]]] ⇔ *-aj*

However, while the entry defined as in (71) will be inserted in the AspP in accusative iteratives based on semelfactives like *kop-a-t*, it will not be inserted in the AspP in the other two kinds of *-aj* stems that alternate with *-n-ou* stems: those based on unergative semelfactives like *gwizd-a-ć* 'whistle repeatedly' and those based on prefixed roots of degree achievements like *za-mrz-a-t* 'freeze repeatedly'. When compared to the representation in (70), the first include an extra V_3P layer (cf. 64); the second lack two layers: GiveP and V_2P (cf. 65). The insertion of *-aj* into the AspP that dominates structures that shrink in the middle is possible in derivations involving subextract since it relies on pointers to earlier spell-outs as *-n* and *-ou*. The same solution is unavailable for the derivation involving backtracking. This is so since for *-aj* to be inserted in AspP in (70), its lexical entry must not include a pointer to *-n* and *-ou*, as these morphemes are not formed in the backtracking derivation. Assuming the way the discussion of the alternation between *-n-ou* and *-aj* stems has been set up, this constitutes an argument in favor of the analysis based on subextract over the analysis based on backtracking.

3.7.2 Shrinking at the root?

An essential theoretical contrast between subextract and backtracking is that in the backtracking derivation, the root constituent shrinks. As illustrated in §2.5.2 with an abstract sequence of features, *ROOT* in a backtracking derivation in (54) spells out a subset structure spelled out as *ROOT* in a derivation involving subextract in (55). This is also the case with the subset spell-out of the root *kop* 'kick' in the backtracking derivation discussed above. Thus, the question is whether this theoretical contrast is linked to an empirical difference. Specifically, what needs to be considered is the fact whether the form of the root stays the same in the semelfactive and in the iterative. If it always does, this fact may constitute an argument in favor of the subextraction. If the root alternates, this may be a potential argument in favor of the backtracking analysis.

Such an alternation indeed exists in a subset of Czech roots. Namely, the vowel in the root of the iterative *-aj* stem either shortens or lengthens, as shown in the following.

(72) Shortening (Czech)
    a. šláp-n-ou-t – šlap-a-t ('step on once/repeatedly')
    b. hráb-n-ou-t – hrab-a-t ('rake once/repeatedly')
    c. říz-n-ou-t – řez-a-t ('cut once/repeatedly')
    d. čís-n-ou-t – česati-t ('comb once/repeatedly')

(73) Lengthening (Czech)
    a. řek-n-ou-t – řík-a-t ('say once/repeatedly')
    b. střih-n-ou-t – stříh-a-t ('trim once/repeatedly')
    c. za-mk-n-ou-t – za-myk-a-t ('lock once/repeatedly')
    d. po-slech-n-ou-t – po-slouch-a-t ('listen once/repeatedly')

It has been suggested by a reviewer that since these vocalic changes in the roots exist alongside the majority of non-alternating roots, it is perhaps reasonable to treat them as cases of (mild) suppletion. If such an analysis is on the right track then the backtracking analysis has an advantage over subextraction, since only the first predicts that the roots in the semelfactive-iterative alternation lexicalize syntactic structures of different sizes. For example, under the backtracking derivation, the root *řík* 'say' could realize the structure as in:

(74) $N_2P \Rightarrow$ *řík*
            /\
        N_2 N_1P
               |
              N_1

while *řek* could realize a bigger structure with a pointer to *řík*, as in the following:

(75) $N_3P \Rightarrow$ *řek*
            /→
        N_3 *řík*

However, there exists a possible alternative account of the changing roots in the iterative alternation in Czech. Since we find vocalic changes in both directions (both vowel shortening and vowel lengthening takes place), this alternation strongly appears to be an instance of a templatic effect, rather than a case of (mild) root suppletion. More specifically, it has been argued in Scheer (2003; 2011) that the spell-out of the iterative stems is regulated by a prosodic template, which governs the distribution of vowel length. Assuming the structure of the Slavic verb stem that comprises the root and a separate thematic suffix, Scheer argues there exists a template that constrains the shape of iterative stems in Czech, which states the following:

(76)   Czech iteratives weigh exactly 3 morae (Scheer 2003: 112).

In order to satisfy this restriction, the suffixation of a heavy root with the heavy thematic suffix such as the iterative *-ova* will require vowel shortening to take place in the root. For example, the long vowel in *šláp-n-ou-t* 'step on' becomes short in *šlap-ov-a-t* 'step on repeatedly'. The templatic shortening is not restricted to roots that form *-n-ou* stems, as seen in *výš-i-t – vyš-ov-a-t* 'elevate'. In turn, the suffixation of a light root with a light iterative thematic suffix will require vowel lengthening to take place in the root. For example, the short vowel in *řek-n-ou-t* 'say once' becomes long in *řík-a-t* 'say repeatedly' when it merges with the short iterative suffix *-aj*. Iterative lengthening applies also to roots that do not form *-n-ou* stems, as for instance *skoč-i-t – skák-a-t* 'jump'.

The change of the vowel length that is restricted by a prosodic template accounts for the examples involving lengthening in the root in a non-arbitrary way. More generally speaking, such an account belongs to a body of work that reanalyzes instances of (mild) allomorphy that targets roots or affixes in predictable phonological terms (Steriade 2016 and Kiparsky 2018 being recent examples).

However, assuming that the *-aj* theme always weighs one mora, then the list of roots involving shortening in (72) all constitute counter-examples that must be controlled for. Scheer (2003: 115) states that both the examples with shortening in (72) as well as examples without the expected lengthening, e.g. *pad-n-ou-t – pad-a-t* 'fall down once/repeatedly', indicate that the attested cases of iterative shortening and lengthening are lexically recorded properties of templatic activity that was once active in the history of Czech but is no longer active synchronically. An argument in favor of the non-synchronic status of the iterative template is that it is no longer a productive process. The example provided in Scheer (2003) involves the lack of lengthening in *klik-n-ou-t – klik-a-t* 'click (computer)'. If the templatic restriction was active in present day Czech, we would expect a bimoraic stem in *klik-a-t* to undergo lenghtening. With *klík-a-t* rejected by native speakers of Czech, this is unconfirmed.

3.8 Remaining issues

There are two remaining issues that must be pointed out in the discussion of the alternation between perfective *-n-ou* stems and iterative *-aj* stems. The first concerns what can be called the *-n-ou* drop: the fact that certain forms of semelfactives can occur without *-n-ou* morphology but will still produce *-aj* iteratives. The other concerns the observation that there are examples of stems where the *-aj* theme seems to stack on top of the *-n* suffix.

3.8.1 -*N-ou* drop

The analysis of the alternation rests on the idea that the input to the formation of iterative *-aj* stems includes not only bare roots of semelfactives and perfectivized degree achievements but their stems, i.e. the sequences *ROOT-n-ou*. An argument in favor of such a setup has been the fact that the *-aj* stems derived from these two categories preserve their argument structure, which is associated with the *-ou* suffix, not the bare root. This fact serves as an argument in favor of either the subextraction analysis or the backtracking analysis of the alternation, since both these alternatives rely on the presence of the syntactic representation of the argument structure projected on top of the root.

3 Deriving the verb stem alternation

However, as pointed out by a reviewer, semelfactives are known to occur also without -*n-ou*, most productively with the past *l*-participle, yielding double forms, such as shown for Czech in the following:

(77) Jan { kop-n-u-l / kop-l } míč.
Jan.NOM kick-GIVE-OU-PART kick-PART ball.ACC
'Jan kicked the ball.'

The possibility to drop -*n-ou* holds also in degree achievements, as shown for Czech in the following:

(78) Jan { bled-n-u-l / bled-l }.
Jan.NOM pale-GET-OU-PART pale-PART
'Jan was getting pale.'

This raises the question about the input to the iterative alternation, namely whether forms like *kop-a-l* 'kicked repeatedly' are derived from the -*n-ou* stem or from the bare root. The second option would involve an unremarkable increase in the number of suffixes. Putting aside the argument from the conservation of the argument structure, the preservation of the idea that the alternation targets the -*n-ou* stems rather than their bare roots depends on the analysis of the -*n-ou* drop. The grammatical environment for the disappearing -*n-ou* constitutes a reason to link it with the forms of the higher *l*-participle rather than with the root, though.

While there is variation among Czech speakers, the -*n-ou* sequence tends to appear only in the masculine singular form of the past *l*-participle and it tends to drop throughout singular and plural forms of the participle. This can be illustrated with the following examples from Taraldsen Medová & Wiland (2018a):

(79) a. kop-(n-u)-l
kick-(GIVE-OU)-PART.3.MSC.SG
b. kop-($^{??}$n-u)-l-{a / i / o}
kick-($^{??}$GIVE-OU)-PART-other than MSC.SG
'gave a kick'

(80) a. bled-(n-u)-l
pale-(GIVE-OU)-PART.MSC.SG
b. bled-($^{??}$n-u)-l-{a / i / o}
pale-($^{??}$GET-OU)-PART-other than MSC.SG
'got pale'

3.8 Remaining issues

The drop is much harder to obtain in Polish than it is in Czech. By and large, it seems the easiest to obtain in 3rd person feminine and neuter singular rather than masculine, as shown in:

(81)   a.   kop-*(n-ą)-ł
            kick-*(GIVE-OU)-PART.3.MSC.SG
      b.   kop-$^{??}$(n-ę)-ł-{a / o}
            kick-$^{??}$(GIVE-OU)-PART-3.FEM.SG / 3.NEU.SG
            'gave a kick'

3.8.2 *-Aj* on top of *-n*

There are some examples in Czech where *-aj* seems to attach on top of *-n*, as in the following examples:

(82)   Czech
      a.   za-p-n-ou-t   – za-pí-n-a-t
            PREF-switch-N-OU-INF   PREF-switch-N-AJ-INF
            'switch on / repeatedly'
      b.   u-s-n-ou-t   – u-sí-n-a-t
            PREF-fall.asleep-N-OU-INF   PREF-fall.asleep-N-AJ-INF
            'fall asleep / repeatedly'

The fact that we are able to form participles with the *-n-ou* drop, *za-p-l* 'swiched on' and *u-s-l* 'he fell asleep', suggests that the roots are *p-* and *s-*, respectively. The existence of forms like in (82) thus seems to suggests that if *-aj* can attach on top of *-n* then perhaps the majority of forms where it does not should be treated as derived from bare roots.

For what it's worth, such a conclusion at the very least requires controlling for the status of the root-final *n*.

First, the status of *p-* and *s-* as roots in *zapnout* and *usnout* is challenged by the fact that, by and large, Czech roots are phonological structures bigger than a single consonant (with the theme vowel often complementing a CVC root in a CVCV stem). This can suggest that the *-n* belongs to the root in *za-pn-ou-t* and *u-sn-ou-t*, in which case the light verb structure present in semelfactives would be realized by the roots *pVn-* and *sVn-* and their prefixes, which jointly form semelfactive bases for the merger with the theme *-ou*. If so, then *-aj* does not stack on top of the light verb suffix *-n* but simply replaces the theme vowel *-ou* in *za-pín-a-t* and *u-sín-a-t*. While this calls for an explanation why *-aj* replaces

77

-ou in these examples, (82) are not genuine examples of *-aj* stacking on top of the light *-n* suffix.

Second, a related possibility to consider is a situation where *p-* is a contextual allomorph of *pVn-* before the participle as in *za-p-l* and *s-* is an allomorph of *sVn-* in *u-s-l*. A circumstantial argument that can support – or at least allow not to reject such a hypothesis right away – is the fact that in Polish, the equivalent of the Czech iterative in (82b) includes a suppletive root, as shown in the following:

(83) Polish
 za-s-n-ą-ć – za-sypi-a-ć
 PREF-sleep-N-OU-INF PREF-fall.asleep-AJ-INF
 'fall asleep / repeatedly'

The root in *za-sn-ą-ć* appears to be the same as in the noun *sen* 'a dream' or in the verb *śn-i-ć* 'to dream', where the shape of the *sVn* root is clearer than in the Czech example. The suppletive root in *za-sypi-a-ć* is shared with the verb *sp-a-ć* 'sleep'.

3.9 Concluding remarks

There is no doubt that the list of remaining issues could continue in the domain of possible and impossible alternations with the *-aj* theme. Instead of trying to bring here all possible and impossible structures of roots and stems that can be inputs to the alternations, I have concentrated on an interesting instance of a predictable alternation that involves *-n-ou* stems. On the proviso that the alternation is derivationally related, it results in the reduction in the number of affixes on the root.

Working with phrasal spell-out, I have considered two alternative possibilities for deriving this reduction, with subextraction and with backtracking, and have pointed out some of the strengths and possible challenges for both. Adopting subextraction means that the existing list of spell-out driven movements discussed in Starke (2018) must be extended to the effect that it includes all three kinds of attested phrasal movement: snowballing, spec-to-spec movement, and subextraction.

The data discussed in this chapter does not indicate how these movements should be ordered with respect to one another. One possibility is to follow the logic of trying to move first as little as possible and order subextraction before spec-to-spec movement and snowballing, an option suggested to me by Pavel

3.9 Concluding remarks

Caha (p.c.). An alternative possibility is to try to move first the node that is closest to the feature targeted by spell-out at a given cycle. In that case, the order of attempted movements will be reversed: spell-out will first try to target the complement node, then the specifier node, and then its internal node.

Both these ordering possibilities also raise the question if the so-called deep extractions (subextractions from an even more embedded node) are also attested as movements resulting in the spell-out of a newly added feature. I leave these questions open at this point. The argumentation in the subsequent chapters will not rely on subextraction. Instead, I will concentrate on how the problems with morphological containment and syncretic alignment in the domain of declarative complementizers and related categories can be resolved using phrasal spell-out and the spell-out procedure in a more general sense. By that I understand the existence of a grammar in which the merger of a feature is followed by an attempt to spell it as part of the syntactic tree either "as is", following a movement operation, or following a subderivation.

4 Resolving a morphological containment problem

4.1 Introduction

Let us move on to a different kind of problem that, I will argue, can be resolved with the application of the spell-out procedure to a singleton projection line of syntactic heads. Namely, the problem discussed in this chapter involves a situation in which the organization of a paradigm based on syncretic alignment does not seem to make the right prediction about morphological containment.

A domain where such a situation can be observed is a cross-categorial paradigm comprising the declarative complementizer (Comp for short), the demonstrative pronoun (Dem), the relativizer (Rel), and the wh-pronoun 'what' (Wh). Syncretisms between these categories have led Baunaz & Lander (2017; 2018a) to advance a thesis that they form a complexity scale as in the following:

(1) Dem > Comp > Rel > Wh

This inclusion sequence is based on the presumption that syncretism anchors structural containment since it holds only between adjacent layers of a syntactic structure, i.e. the *ABA generalization. Syncretisms between these four categories that are consistent upon the sequence in (1) are well illustrated by languages such as English, Italian, or Romanian, as shown in Table 4.1.

Table 4.1: Syncretic alignment

	DEM	COMP	REL	WH
English	that	that	that	what
Italian	quello	che	che	che
Romanian	acel	că	ce	ce

However, when we consider the set of related forms in Russian, as seen in Table 4.2, we observe that the morphological form of the demonstrative pronoun

4 Resolving a morphological containment problem

to is contained in *čto* (henceforth indicated as *č-to* where it is relevant), the form of the declarative complementizer, the relative pronoun, and the wh-pronoun.

Table 4.2: Morphological containment of Dem

	DEM	COMP	REL	WH
Russian	to	č-to	č-to	č-to
Serbo-Croatian	to	š-to, da	š-to	š-to

Such a morphological containment is opposite to what we expect if the demonstrative syntactically contains the remaining three categories.

An immediate observation that can be made about such forms as in Table 4.1, which follow the sequence in (1), and the Russian forms is that the first include demonstratives that are marked for definiteness while the second include a definiteless demonstrative. I will argue that there is a non-trivial way of accommodating demonstratives without definiteness marking, like the Russian *to*, into the same containment sequence that describes containment between the demonstrative with definiteness marking, the Comp, the Rel, and the Wh. Such a solution will allow us to explain syncretic alignment and morphological containment in the cross-categorial paradigm with these categories in a systematic way.

4.2 Syncretisms with the declarative complementizer

4.2.1 Paradigm

The sample of languages in Table 4.3 illustrates syncretic alignments consistent upon the complexity scale in (1). The set in Table 4.3 covers syncretisms with the nominal complementizer, an equivalent of the English *that*, and excludes syncretisms with verbal complementizers, the categories that are derived from forms of assertive verbs like 'say'. We find verbal complementizers for instance in Yoruba, as seen in (2).

(2) Yoruba (Lawal 1991: 75)
   a. Olú pé awon ti dé
      Olu say they have arrived
      'Olu says they have arrived.'

4.2 Syncretisms with the declarative complementizer

b. Olú gbàgbé pé Bólá ti jáde
   Olu forget COMP Bola PFV go.out
   'Olu forgot that Bola has gone out.'
c. Olú rántí pé Bólá ńsun
   Olu remember COMP Bola sleeping
   'Olu remembered that Bola was sleeping.'

Table 4.3: Syncretic alignment (continued)

	DEM	COMP	REL	WH
English:	that	that	that	what
German:	das	dass	das	was
Dutch:	dat	dat	dat	wat
Afrikaans:	dit	dat	wat	wat
Yiddish:	jenc	vos, az	vos, az	vos
Pite Saami:	dat	att	mij	mij
Finnish:	tä-	että	mi-	mi-
Modern Greek:	ekíno	pu	pu	tí
Italian:	quello	che	che	che
Romanian:	acel	că	ce	ce
French:	ce	que	que	que
Basque:	hura	-ela	-n	zer

Lawal (1991) shows that in Yoruba, *pé* is syncretic form for the verb 'say' and serves as a complementizer for clauses embedded under assertive verbs like 'say' as well as verbs of cognition like 'forget' or 'remember', as seen in (2). At the same time, Lawal (1991: 76) argues that the distribution of *pé* is that of a complementizer, as it heads preposed English-like *that*-clauses, as in (3).

(3) pé a jo lo dára
    COMP we together went good
    'that we went together was good'

Verbal complementizers are well-attested cross-lingustically (see for instance Dixon & Aikhenvald 2006) and they can co-exist with nominal complementizers within one language as for example in Hausa. Hausa has a verbal declarative complementizer *cêewaa* based on 'say', as in (4a), which is not used after the verb *cêe*, in which case the nominal complemetizer *wai* is used, as in (4b).

4 Resolving a morphological containment problem

(4) Hausa (Dimmendaal 1989: 96–97)
    a. sun tabbátaa maná [cêewaa niisan   raanaa dága nan yaa yi mîl
        3A assure us   COMP   distance sun   from here 3A do mile
        dá   yawáa]
        with many
        'They assured us that the sun is far away from here.'
    b. an cêe [wai yaa bi   wani macïijii]
        one say COMP 3A follow some snake
        'It was said that he followed some snake.'

The remainder of the discussion in this chapter focuses on the paradigm with the nominal complementizer and completely disregards verbal complementizers.

4.2.2 Analysis in Baunaz & Lander (2017; 2018a)

Baunaz & Lander propose an analysis of the syncretic alignment shown in Table 4.3 based on a complex underlying tree structure as in (6), whose left branch spells out as the prefix on a nominal base (marked here as the N triangle) and whose right branch spells out an invariant inflectional suffix (marked here as the ϕ triangle). Given the entries for the English morphemes *wh* and *th* as in (5), they come out as prefixes on the nominal stem -*a*, which is suffixed with the invariant inflectional marker -*t*.

(5) Lexical entries for the English *wh* and *th* (1st approximation)
    a. [Wh [n]] ⇔ *wh*
    b. [Dem [Comp [Rel [Wh n]]]] ⇔ *th*

Using phrasal spell-out and the Superset Principle, the phrasal nodes DemP, CompP, and RelP all spell-out as *th-* as they constitute, respectively, the superset and the subset structures of the lexical entry in (5b). The WhP node, also a subset of the entry in (5b), is spelled out as *wh* on the strength of the Elsewhere clause, since (5a) is a more specific match for the WhP node than (5b).

Two remarks are in place before we proceed. First, it is important to note that the labelling used in (6) is a simplified way to illustrate Baunaz & Lander's analysis, in the sense that a "demonstrative pronoun, a "complementizer", a "relativizer", and a "wh-pronoun" lexicalize all three branches of the tree (6) in their analysis, irrespective of morphological complexity of these categories. This is a natural consequence of phrasal spell-out. For instance, in Baunaz & Lander's architecture, the Italian *che* is analyzed as a bi-morphemic *ch-e*, where the *ch-*

4.2 Syncretisms with the declarative complementizer

morpheme spells out both the left branch and the nominal stem of the representation in (6) as a portmanteau while -*e* spells out the right branch, the invariant ϕ suffix, as in (7).[1]

(6)   Lexicalization of the English *that* and *what* in Baunaz & Lander (2017)[2]

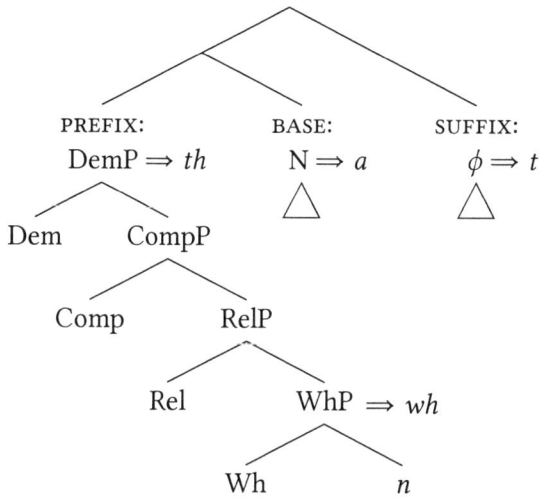

(7)   a.   Italian complementizer *che*

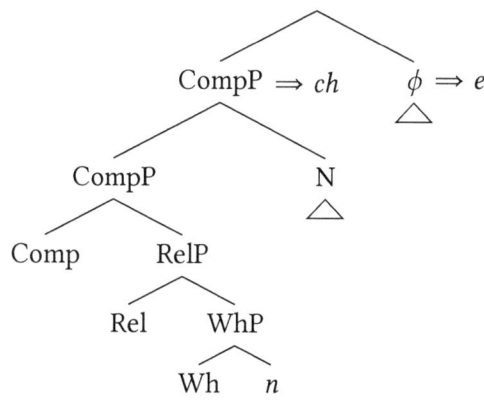

---
[1] The drawback of the analysis where *ch-* is a portmanteau realization of two independent branches of an underlying representation is that the constituent that corresponds to the the morphological stem (the middle branch) cannot be overtly identified, since its decomposition is not possible.

[2] For the sake of concreteness, let us note that the nominal element at the bottom of the left branch of this tree, the stem for the merger of the Wh feature labelled here as *n*, is described as a classifier-like lexical noun in Baunaz & Lander (2018a) and as non-lexical indeterminate noun in Baunaz & Lander (2018b). This issue is, however, orthogonal to what follows.

4 Resolving a morphological containment problem

b. Italian relativizer *che*

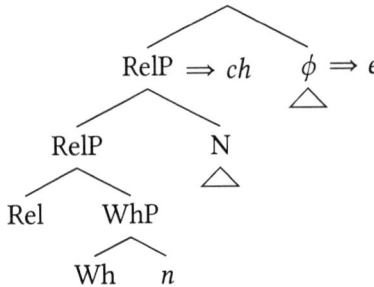

c. Italian wh-pronoun *che*

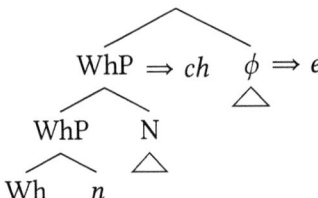

The terminal nodes labelled as Dem, Comp, Rel, and Wh should be understood here as subcomponents of the demonstrative, the complementizer, etc., rather than features that solitarily encode the properties of the categories they head. For example, the spatial deictic contrast in English demonstratives *th-is/th-at* is morphologically realized by *-is/-at*, not by the definite prefix *th-*. For this reason, Baunaz & Lander (2018a) describe the DemP in (6) as an instantiation of the definite article, a subcomponent of the demonstrative rather than the source of spatial deixis, an issue that will be taken up in a greater detail in what follows.

The other thing to bear in mind is that the four categories – Dem, Comp, Rel, and Wh – should not be necessarily treated as inherently simplex beyond the containment relation that holds between them. For example, it is clear that the RelP-layer of structure that corresponds to the relativizer (as a grammatical category) must be inherently complex enough to cover two types of relativizers found for instance in Polish: the invariant *co*, which is syncretic with the wh-pronoun 'what', and the case-inflected inflected *który*, which morphologically includes the person wh-pronoun *kto* 'who', but which, just like the invariant relativizer *co*, is compatible with +/−person] and +/−animate head nouns, as in (8).

4.2 Syncretisms with the declarative complementizer

(8) Polish
   a. pociąg { co / który } przyjechał za późno
      train.NOM REL$_{inv}$ REL.MSC.NOM arrived.3SG.MSC too late
      'the train that arrived too late'
   b. dziewczynę { co / którą } widzieliśmy w kinie
      girl.ACC REL$_{inv}$ REL.FEM.ACC saw.1PL in cinema
      'the girl that we saw in the cinema'

While both *co* and *który* can appear in subject and object relative clauses in Polish, as in (9), there are certain differences between relative clauses with both types of relativizers.

(9) Polish
   a. zegar { co / który } wybił dwunastą
      clock REL$_{inv}$ REL.MSC.NOM struck.3SG.MSC twelve
      'the clock which struck twelve o'clock'
   b. dziewczyna { co / która } widziała nas w kinie
      girl REL$_{inv}$ REL.FEM.NOM saw.3SG.FEM us in cinema
      'the girl that saw us in the cinema'

For instance, as noted in Mykowiecka (2001), the resumptive pronoun (the neuter accusative *je* 'it' in 10) must be adjacent to *co* but it does not appear in *który*-relatives, as in (11):

(10) wino, co (je) Adam (*je) przyniósł
    wine REL$_{inv}$ it Adam it brought
    'the wine that Adam brought'

(11) wino, które (*je) Adam (*je) przyniósł
    wine REL.NEU.ACC it Adam it brought
    'the wine that Adam brought'

As observed in Szczegielniak (2005), when the resumptive pronoun is embedded, it can appear in both types of relatives, as seen the following:

(12) wino, { co / które } wszyscy wiedzą, że (je) Adam
    wine REL$_{inv}$ REL.NEU.ACC everybody know.3PL COMP it Adam
    przyniósł
    brought
    'the wine that everybody knows that Adam brought'

4 Resolving a morphological containment problem

The degree of the inherent complexity of the categories Dem, Comp, Rel, and Wh is largely irrelevant to the containment relation which holds between them, though. That is, we find some cross-linguistic evidence beyond syncretism for the claim that such a relation holds between these categories. For instance, in Hungarian, the uninflected stem of the wh-pronoun *mi-* 'what' is morphologically contained within the stem of the relativizer *a-mi-*, as seen in Table 4.4.

Table 4.4: Hungarian paradigm

DEM	COMP	REL	WH
az-	hogy	a-mi-	mi-

The following examples illustrate the use of *mi-* as a wh-pronoun and *a-mi-* as a relativizer (both suffixed with the accusative *-t*):

(13) Hungarian (Kenesei et al. 1998: 11)
 Mi-t talált mindenki?
 what-ACC found.3SG everyone
 'What did everyone find?'

(14) Hungrian (Rounds 2001: 136)
 Elolvostam a könvet ami-t küldét nekem.
 sent.1SG the book.-ACC REL-ACC sent.2SG me
 'I read the book that you sent me.'

The morphological containment of Wh in Rel is an instance of a more general pattern in Hungarian, where relativizers are formed by adding the prefix *a-* to wh-pronouns other than 'what', as for instance *a-ki* 'REL-who', *a-melyik* 'REL-which', or *a-mennyi* 'REL-how.many' (cf. Kenesei et al. 1998: 40). This yields a structure of *a-mi-* as in the following:

(15) [$_{\text{RelP}}$ a [$_{\text{WhP}}$ mi]]

However, while the containment of Wh inside Rel in Hungarian is in agreement with the hierarchy in (1), defined on the basis of cross-linguistically attested syncretisms, the morphological containment of a demonstrative pronoun inside the remaining three categories that we find in Russian and Serbo-Croatian is not.

4.3 An ordering paradox with the demonstrative

Assuming the way the facts are described and set up in Baunaz & Lander (2017; 2018a), the Dem=Comp syncretism found in certain languages, in particular in the West Germanic subgroup (English, Dutch, and German) as shown in Table 4.3, points to the hierarchy "Dem > Comp > Rel > Wh". Some other languages, however, indicate that the order between these categories is different. In particular, a challenge to "Dem > Comp > Rel > Wh" comes from morphological containment of Dem in the structure of the other three categories, which we find in Slavic languages like Russian or Serbo-Croatian, as shown in Table 4.2 (repeated below):

Table 4.5: Morphological containment of Dem

	DEM	COMP	REL	WH
Russian	to	č-to	č-to	č-to
Serbo-Croatian	to	š-to, da	š-to	š-to

The Russian paradigm has the neuter singular demonstrative pronoun *to* included in the structure of all three remaining categories. The Serbo-Croatian shows a slightly different paradigm in that *što* serves as a complementizer with only a subset of verbs selecting for declarative clauses. For instance, as shown in the following, the complementizer *što* heads clauses embedded under the verb *smetati* 'bother, annoy' while the complementizer that heads declarative clauses introduced by the verb *misliti* 'think' is *da*.

(16)   Serbo-Croatian (Mihalicek 2012: 114)
    a.   Ani   smeta   { što / *da }   Marko   stalno spava.
        Ana.DAT bother.3SG COMP COMP Marko.NOM always sleep.3SG
        'It bothers Ana that Marko is always sleeping.'
    b.   Ana   misli   { *što / da }   Marka   spava.
        Ana.NOM think.3SG COMP COMP Marko.NOM sleep.3SG
        'Ana thinks that Marko is sleeping.'

Descriptively speaking, the morphological containment of Dem within Comp, Rel, and Wh is paradoxical – or counter-intuitive at best – if the demonstrative pronoun is the structurally biggest category in the paradigm.

This problem is recognized in Baunaz & Lander (2018a), who propose to solve it by eliminating demonstratives without definiteness marking (Dem$_{indef}$ for short) from the sequence so that it applies only to languages with morphologically marked definiteness on demonstratives (Dem$_{def}$ for short). The updated complexity scale looks now as in:

(17)   Dem$_{def}$ > Comp > Rel > Wh

More precisely, Baunaz & Lander (2018a) argue that only Dem$_{def}$ projects as the top layer of the left branch of the tree in (6) and in languages like Russian and Serbo-Croatian Dem$_{indef}$ is restricted to the nominal stem, i.e. the middle branch of the tree in (6) marked as "N".

However, such a solution creates a paradox: on the one hand the hierarchy in (17) applies to the categories that are supposed to always spell-out all three branches of the tree in (6) (either synthetically as in English or as a portmanteau in Italian), on the other hand it is defined only on the basis of the left branch of that tree, excluding the middle and the right branch.

In order to keep the demonstrative pronouns that are not marked for definiteness in the picture (i.e. in Slavic languages like Russian, Polish, or Czech that lack definiteness morphology), unless indicated otherwise, I will use the "Dem" label more broadly so that it describes both kinds of demonstrative pronouns. Whenever it will be needed to differentiate between demonstratives with and without definiteness morphology, I will refer to them specifically as Dem$_{def}$ and Dem$_{indef}$, respectively.

Since the Russian *čto* covers three cells of the paradigm in Table 4.2 and, unlike the Serbo-Croatian *što*, is the only possible form of the declarative complementizer, I will be focusing mostly on the Russian paradigm. To the extent that I can tell, the result for the Russian *čto*, however, carries over to the Serbo-Croatian paradigm with the syncretic Wh/Rel/Comp *što*, too.

4.4 Low indefinite demonstratives

It appears that what constitutes an obstacle in resolving the ordering paradoxes for the sequence in (17) is that it describes the categories realized by the three branches of the tree in (6) while the sequence applies only to the properties ofABC the left branch. Let us, thus, consider what happens if we relax Baunaz & Lander's constraint that a demonstrative, a complementizer, a relativizer and a wh-pronoun are always realizations of the three branches of the tree in (6).

4.4.1 Severing spatial deixis from definiteness

I have argued elsewhere (Wiland 2018a) that the base for the formation of the pronoun 'what' in Slavic is the indefinite demonstrative, which constitutes the bottom of a monotonically growing singleton projection line, as in:

4.4 Low indefinite demonstratives

(18)　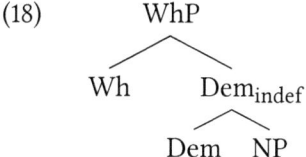

More precisely, I have argued there that the base for the formation of the Polish *co* 'what' and Russian *čto* 'what' is the medial demonstrative *to*. The evidence comes from the decomposition of spatial deixis into three categories: the proximal (close to speaker), the medial (close to hearer), and the distal (far from speaker and hearer) advanced in Lander & Haegeman (2016), who argue that such a three-way contrast reflects a universal syntactic structure, as in (19) (where $Deix_n$ stands for an abstract spatial deictic feature).

(19)　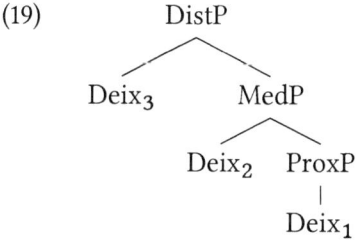

In a phrasal spell-out approach made a case for in the present work, deictic morphology is the realization of the subset(s) or the superset of that representation. For example, the proximal-medial-distal contrast in Japanese is realized sui generically by three distinct morphemes.

(20)　Japanese (Hoji et al. 2003: 97)
　　　ko-　/ so-　/ a-
　　　PROX　MED　DIST

This reveals that Japanese has the lexical entries for *ko*, *so* and *a* as specified in:

(21)　Lexical entries for the Japanese *ko*, *so*, and *a*
　　a.　$[_{ProxP}\ Deix_1\ ] \Leftrightarrow ko$
　　b.　$[_{MedP}\ Deix_2\ [_{ProxP}\ Deix_1\ ]] \Leftrightarrow so$
　　c.　$[_{DistP}\ Deix_3\ [_{MedP}\ Deix_2\ [_{ProxP}\ Deix_1\ ]]] \Leftrightarrow a$

which results in each layer of the tree in (19) being lexicalized unequivocally, as indicated in the following:

4 Resolving a morphological containment problem

(22) Spell-out of the tree in (19) in Japanese

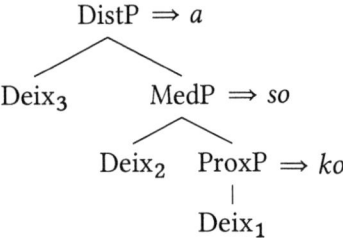

Languages differ with respect to the number of exponents which realize the representation in (19). For instance, the proximal-medial-distal contrast is realized in French by a singleton lexical item *ce* (and its allomorphs), as in:[3]

(23) French

ce journal
PROX/MED/DIST newspaper.MSC
'this/that newspaper'

Such a one-to-many relation indicates that the French *ce* is specified for a superset of features which describe the proximal–medial–distal contrast, as indicated in (24).

(24) Lexical entry for the French *ce*

[$_{DistP}$ Deix$_3$ [$_{MedP}$ Deix$_2$ [$_{ProxP}$ Deix$_1$]]] ⇔ *ce*

In fact, if we follow Baunaz & Lander's bi-morphemic analysis of the Italian *che* as in (7) for a little longer and extend it to the French *ce*, it is only the *c*- morpheme that appears to realize the spatial deictic contrast while the *-e* is an invariant "ϕ-agreement" suffix. Hence, on the strength of the Superset Principle, the French

---

[3] The French syncretic Prox=Med=Dist demonstrative *ce* modifies masculine nous that begin with a consonant, the other two allomorphs are *cet*, which modifies masculine nouns that begin with a vowel, as in (i) and *cette*, which modifies feminine nouns, as in (ii):

(i) cet oncle
PROX/MED/DIST uncle.MSC
'this/that uncle'

(ii) cette taverne
PROX/MED/DIST tavern.FEM
'this/that tavern'

4.4 Low indefinite demonstratives

lexical item *c-* spells out either the superset or any subset of that tree, as in (25), resulting in its different readings depending on its size, as indicated in (25).

(25) a. French distal *ce*

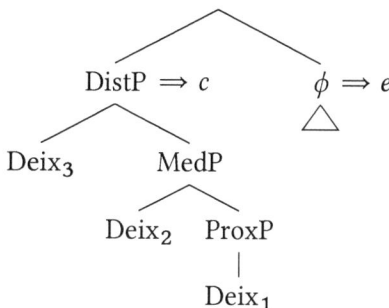

b. French medial *ce*

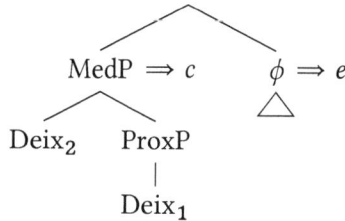

c. French proximal *ce*

$$\text{ProxP} \Rightarrow c \quad \phi \Rightarrow e$$
$$|$$
$$\text{Deix}_1$$

Just like the English *this* and *that*, Polish and Russian have two distinct pronouns that realize the three-way deictic contrast. The Polish *to* describes closeness to speaker and hearer, while *tamto* univocally describes remoteness from both speaker and hearer, as seen in (26).

(26) Polish

    to   / tamto auto
    PROX/MED   DIST   car.NEU.NOM

Unlike in Polish, the Russian *eto* univocally describes closeness to the speaker while the Russian *to* describes closeness to the hearer and remoteness from both speaker and hearer, as for instance in (27):

4 Resolving a morphological containment problem

(27) Russian
èto / to okno
PROX MED/DIST window.NEU.NOM

This clearly shows that the only subset of the tree in (19) which is realized by both Polish and Russian *to* is the medial subtree, as in (28), the observation that will become important in what follows.

(28) Simplified representation of the medial demonstrative pronoun *to* in Polish and Russian

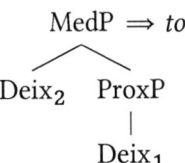

Before the representation of *to* in (28) is refined into a separate stem *t-* and an inflection suffix *-o*, a short excursus about the structure of the Polish distal demonstrative *tamto* is called for here. Namely, it morphologically contains the proximal/medial *to* along the distal locative *tam* 'there'. I have argued in Wiland (2018a) that *tam-to* is in fact an instance of a reinforcer-demonstrative construction, a pattern more widely attested in Romance and Germanic (see e.g. Bernstein 1997), as for instance in Afrikaans, where the locative reinforcer is prefixed onto the demonstrative in the pre-nomininal position, as seen in the following.

(29) Afrikaans (Roehrs 2010: 226–227)
hier-die mooi meisie
here.this pretty girl
'this pretty girl'

The argument for the reinforcer-demonstrative analysis of the Polish *tam-to* is based on the observation that there is a contrast between the distribution of the Polish proximal locative *tu* 'here' and distal locative *tam* 'there' with demonstrative pronouns. While *tu* 'here' can be optionally placed after the proximal/medial demonstrative pronoun *to* as in (30) (just like *here* in a substandard English *this here big house*), *tam* 'there' cannot function as free form reinforcer placed in the distal demonstrative *tam-to*, which contains it, as seen in (31):

(30) to { tu / tam } dziecko
PROX/MED here there child.NEU.NOM
'this here child'

4.4 Low indefinite demonstratives

(31) tamto (*tam) dziecko
      DIST   there child.NEU.NOM
      intended 'that there child'

At the same time, *tu-to 'here-PROX/MED' is ill-formed in Polish, a scenario which indicates that only the distal demonstrative *tam-to* but not the proximal/medial demonstrative *to* includes a locative reinforcer in its structure. Thus, the structure of the distal *tam-to* appears to be derived along the lines of Leu's (2007) analysis of Germanic demonstratives, whereby the locative *tam* raises from its canonical pre-nominal position to the pre-demonstrative position yielding the reinforcer-demonstrative item, as indicated in the following:

(32) a. to   tam dziecko
          PROX/MED there child.NEU.NOM
          intended 'that there child'
      b. tam-to t dziecko
          ↑_____|

Before we turn the observation that *to* spells out the medial layer in both Polish and Russian into a solution to the problem of morphological containment of the demonstrative *to* inside the Russian *č-to*, let us first refine the representation of the demonstrative pronoun in (28).

It is clear that spatial deixis is not inherently pronominal, a point also made explicit in Lander & Haegeman (2016). For instance, the Japanese spatial deictic markers *ko-*, *so-*, and *a-* can merge with pronominal, determiner, and adverbial stems, as seen in Table 4.6, forming demonstrative pronouns, demonstrative determiners, and demonstrative adverbs.[4]

Table 4.6: Categories of demonstratives in Japanese (Kuno 1973)

	pronoun	determiner	adverb
proximal	ko-re	ko-no	ko-ko
medial	so-re	so-no	so-ko
distal	a-re	a-no	a-soko

---

[4]The stem *-re*, as in *so-re* in Table 4.6, means 'thing' and the stem *-ko*, as in *so-ko*, means 'place'. Japanese demonstratives can also merge directly with other nominal stems, as e.g. *ko-tira* 'PROX-way', *so-tira* 'MED-way', *a-tira* 'DIST-way', or *ko-itu* 'PROX-guy', *so-itu* 'MED-guy', *a-itu* 'DIST-guy' (Hoji et al. 2003: 97).

4 Resolving a morphological containment problem

In turn, what indicates that spatial deixis in the Polish and Russian demonstrative pronoun *to* merges with a nominal stem is the fact that it is inflected for case, which shows up in the obligatory case concord between the demonstrative pronoun and the head noun. This is illustrated in (33) on the example of the Polish singular accusative suffix of the feminine declension and instrumental suffix of the masculine declension.

(33)   a.   przez t-ę   lamp-ę
             by   PROX/MED-ACC.FEM.SG lamp-ACC.FEM.SG
             'by this/that lamp'
     b.   t-ym   klucz-em
             PROX/MED-INST.MSC.SG key-INST.MSC.SG
             'with this/that key'

The -*o* suffix in the bi-morphemic *t-o* is a syncretic marker for neuter nominative and accusative, as indicated in the singular declension paradigms in Table 4.7.

Table 4.7: Declension of *to* in Polish (left) and Russian (right)

	MSC	FEM	NEU		MSC	FEM	NEU
NOM	t-en	t-a	t-o	NOM	t-ot	t-a	t-o
ACC	t-ego	t-ę	t-o	ACC	t-ogo	t-u	t-o
GEN	t-ego	t-ej	t-ego	GEN	t-ogo	t-oj	t-ogo
DAT	t-emu	t-ej	t-emu	DAT	t-omu	t-oj	t-omu
LOC	t-ym	t-ej	t-ym	LOC	t-om	t-oj	t-om
INST	t-ym	t-ą	t-ym	INST	t-im	t-oj	t-im

At this point, let us return for a moment to the inventory of Russian demonstratives shown in (27), involving the proximal *èto* and the medial/distal *to*. Given that the Russian *èto* is realizing a subset structure of *to* and the description of the -*o* as a suffix, the morphological structure of the Russian proximal pronoun appears to be *èt-o*. The alternative with a tri-morphemic *è-t-o* would require a substantially different analysis of the Russian demonstratives (plus perhaps controlling for the fact that *è-* does not appear in a related context elsewhere). I will therefore cautiously assume that the Russian *èt-* is a singleton morpheme.

The presence of the case suffix in the structure of *t-o* indicates that the *t-* is not a "pure" marker of spatial deixis like the Japanese *ko-*, *so-*, and *a-* are, but that it realizes both spatial deixis and a stem which is inflected for case. The two kinds of stems that form case inflected categories in Polish and Russian are

4.4 Low indefinite demonstratives

nouns and adjectives (these two classes obviously include not only lexical nouns and adjectives but also the categories that are based on nominal and adjectival roots, such as case inflected numerals and quantifiers). Along personal pronouns, case inflected *to* can serve as a pro-form for noun phrases rather than adjective phrases, as illustrated by the following example from Polish:[5]

(34) Opowiedział ze szczegółami o **twoim problemie**, mimo
 told.3SG with details about your problem.LOC.SG despite
 że miał zakaz nawet o { **nim / tym** } wspominać.
 COMP had.3SG ban even about it DEM-LOC.SG mention.INF
 'He told about your problem with details, even though he had a ban on even mentioning { it / that }.'

For this reason, it is more more plausible to go along with the idea that, apart from spatial deixis, *to* contains a nominal rather than adjectival ingredient (though nothing in what follows is going to rely on that particular choice).[6]

---

[5]The presence of a locative *tym* in (34) is not accidental as it gives us a clearer example of a nominal pro-form than a neuter singular *to* does. The latter form can both serve as a sentential pro-form, as for instance in the Polish

(i) ... ale **to** nie może być prawda
 but it not can be truth
 '... but it cannot be true'

and it is also syncretic with (what can be pre-theoretically described as) an invariant particle present in a range of sentences including foci, topics, and clefts, as partially illustrated in:

(ii) Polish *to* in sentences with a focused object (Wiland 2016: 147)
 To Marię okradli jej sąsiedzi
 PRT Mary.ACC.FOC robbed her neighbors.NOM
 'Mary's neighbors robbed her.'

(iii) Polish *to* in cleft sentences (Tajsner 2008: 354)
 Marka **to** Ania spoktała w kinie
 Marek.ACC.TOP PRT Ania.NOM met in cinema
 'It was Marek that Ania met in the cinema.'

For analyses of clauses with the sentential *to* in Polish see for instance Tajsner (2008; 2015; 2018) and Mokrosz (2014); for a related discussion of the sentential *to* in Czech see Šimík (2009).

[6]In other words, what needs to be accommodated in the representation of the demonstrative pronoun is the source of case, which deictic features $Deix_n$ in (28) are not. In Polish and Russian this source of case can be attributed to the presence of either a nominal or an adjectival stem, which is reflected by what is often described as nominal or adjectival case declensions (cf. Nagórko 1998: 130–131, 146).

4 Resolving a morphological containment problem

This nominal ingredient is responsible for the projection of a separate case fseq on its top (marked below as K_1, a stand-in for neuter nominative singular), in agreement with Caha's (2009) case representation discussed in §2.3.3. All these layers are merged in the one and only projection line, as in the structure with a bare Dem_{indef} in (35a) and WhP in (35b), a refined version of (18):

(35)

To wrap it up, under the decomposition analysis of the demonstrative into three deictic features detailed in Lander & Haegeman (2016), the Polish and Russian *to* in (35a) realizes the following sequence:

(36)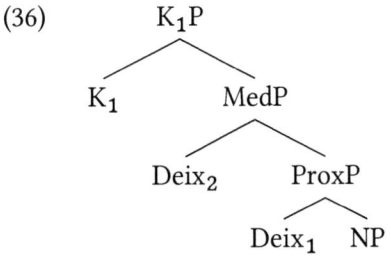

Note, however, that while decomposing the Dem_{indef} layer into separate features that describe the spatial deictic contrast enables us to better identify the Polish/Russian *t-* as an exponent of the medial, our main point merely relies on the fact that the *t-* is an exponent of a certain demonstrative pronoun without a definiteness marker. For this reason, I will continue to represent such demonstratives in this chapter and onwards simply as "Dem_{indef} headed by Dem" since the argument is not based on the degree of its internal decomposition.

4.4.2 Lexicalization in Polish and in Russian

Let us consider how the structures in (35) are lexicalized in Polish, a language with bi-morphemic forms for all four categories, as shown in Table 4.8. These forms reveal that Polish has the following list of the lexical entries:

4.4 Low indefinite demonstratives

(37) Lexical entries in Polish
  a. [Dem NP] ⇔ t
  b. [Rel [Wh [Dem NP]]] ⇔ c
  c. [Comp [Rel [Wh [Dem NP]]]] ⇔ ż
  d. [K_1] ⇔ o

Table 4.8: Polish paradigm

DEM	COMP	REL	WH
t-o	ż-e	c-o	c-o

In Polish, the spell-out of the "Wh > Dem$_{indef}$" subsequence involves a simple over-riding: the merger of the Wh feature on top of Dem$_{indef}$ is spelled out by STAY, the first step of the algorithm. Given the lexical entries in (37a) and (37b), the spell-out of the WhP-layer over-rides the earlier spell-out of Dem$_{indef}$, as in:

(38)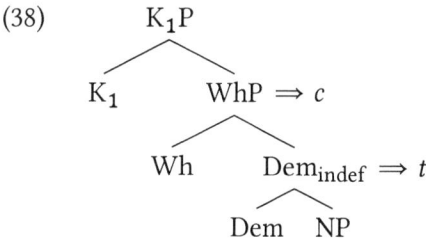

In turn, the spell-out of K_1 requires the evacuation movement of its complement, as in (39), in a typical way in which nominative is lexicalized in Slavic, as illustrated on the example of *win-o* 'wine-NOM' in (24) in §2.3.4.[7]

(39)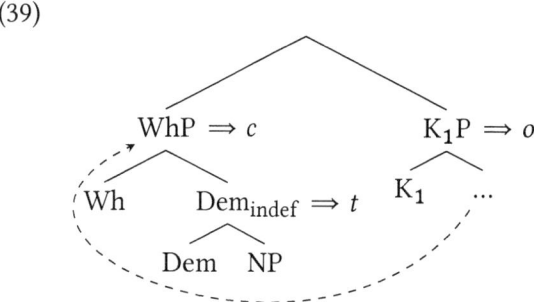

---

[7]The case suffix on the complementizer *ż-e* does not require a separate lexical entry other than the one for *-o* in (37d). As Baunaz & Lander (2018a) point out, the suffix *-o* /o/ shifts into *-e* /e/ after a soft consonant *ż-* /ʒ/.

99

4 Resolving a morphological containment problem

There is no need to postulate a second branch (e.g. the N triangle in 6) if Dem_{indef} is already part of Wh > Dem_{indef}. With the lexical entries in (37), the lexicalization of Rel and Comp layers takes place, again, by spelling out the one and only projection line:

(40) Lexicalization of the sequence in Polish

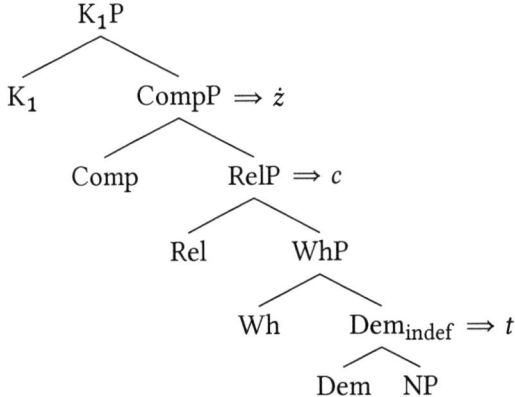

Note that the hypothesis that there is a single underlying projection line for the sequence "Comp > Rel > Wh > Dem_{indef}" does not exclude the possibility that it may have to be reshaped in order to facilitate spell-out. This is a natural consequence of the spell-out procedure but it does not equal the idea that a reshaped tree is base generated as anything more complex than a singleton sequence of heads.

As detailed in Chapter 2, the essence of Starke's (2018) contribution is that the subderivation of the left branch takes place as a last resort operation which facilitates spell-out only after STAY and MOVE (cyclic and snowballing movements) do not lead to lexical insertion. This is precisely the source of the difference between the pattern we see in Polish and Russian (and Serbo-Croatian), as argued for in Wiland (2018a). That is, while the shape of the lexical entries in Polish allow the fseq in (40) to be spelled-out by STAY (ignoring case), the shape of the lexical entry for the Russian č- as in (41) requires the formation of the left branch.

(41) Lexical entry in Russian
 [Comp [Rel [Wh Dem]]] ⇔ č

If the lexical entries for the demonstrative t- and the neuter case suffix -o are identical in Polish and Russian, then the lexicalization of Wh, Rel, and Comp will require the formation of the left branch in Russian, given the entry for č- in

4.4 Low indefinite demonstratives

(41). In contrast to Polish, only the bottom Dem$_{indef}$ of the fseq in (40) can be spelled out by STAY (as *t-*) and none of the available movement operations of the updated spell-out algorithm (cyclic, snowballing, extraction) are able to reshape the tree in (40) in such a way that it matches (the subset or the superset of) the entry for *č-* in (41), either. As discussed in §2.3.4, the final available option is to launch a subderivation by providing the feature from the mainline, e.g. the Dem feature of Dem$_{indef}$, as the basis for the merger of the Wh feature. Such a merger will result with a binary foot, as in (42), and will require a separate lexical entry to be spelled out.

(42)   WhP
        / \
       Wh Dem

Upon the merger of this subderivation with Dem$_{indef}$, the resulting structure comes out as a bi-morphemic *č-t-* (ignoring, again, the neuter case suffix *-o*):

(43)

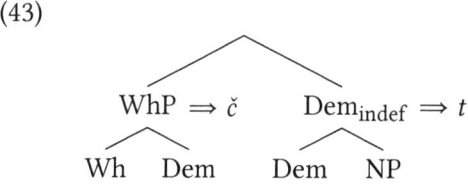

Subsequent mergers of features forming RelP and CompP will extend (what comes out as) the left branch, yielding (44).

(44)   Lexicalization of the sequence in Russian

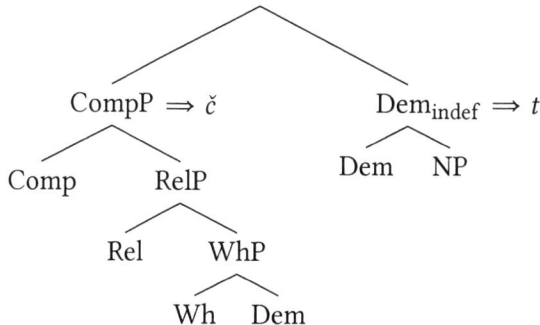

If this analysis is on the right track, then the contrast in the shapes of the lexical items in Polish and Russian directly implies that the Polish pattern is more basic, in the sense that the lexicalization of the same fseq is achieved by STAY, while

4 Resolving a morphological containment problem

its lexicalization in Russian requires SUBDERIVE, the last resort. We can, thus, conclude that the underlying fseq comprises the indefinite demonstrative at its bottom, as in (45).

(45)   Comp > Rel > Wh > Dem$_{indef}$

The geometry of the tree in (44) resembles the structure for the Russian *č-t-* as in *čto* in Baunaz & Lander (2018a), where it is based on a complex underlying tree in (6). Note, however, that there are two essential differences between these two representations. The first one is that in Baunaz & Lander's analysis the Russian *t-* is an invariant nominal core, a kind of base component, while the *t-* in (44) is the medial demonstrative pronoun (modulo the case suffix). The second difference concerns the nature of both representations. In Baunaz and Lander's analysis, the bi-morphemic *č-t-* realizes the nominal base and the prefix branch of complex representation in (6). In the alternative in (44), the bi-moprhemic *č-t-* is created solely as a result of the spell-out algorithm, hence, there is technically no base component or a pre-defined prefix branch; instead, the underlying representation is a simple projection line just like it is in Polish (or any other language, for that matter).

At this point let us note that while the *t-* stem of the inflected demonstrative *t-o* is retained in the Russian Comp and nominative and accusative forms of the Wh and the Rel *čto*, it disappears in non-nominative forms of the Wh and the Rel, as shown in Table 4.9.

Table 4.9: Declension of the Russian *čto*

NOM	č-t-o
ACC	č-t-o / č-evo (informal)
GEN	č-evo
DAT	č-emu
LOC	č-om
INST	č-em

The disappearing *t-* stem is found in Slavic beyond Russian and Polish, too, and targets also forms of person wh-pronoun 'who'. For example, as noted in Wiland (2018a), if we follow the logic of decomposing *čto* into *c-t-o* and analyze *kto* 'who-NOM' as *k-t-o*, the same form in Russian and Polish, *t-* disappears in all other cases, as shown in Table 4.10.

4.5 High definite demonstratives

Table 4.10: Declension of the Russian and Polish *kto* 'who'

	Russian	Polish
NOM	k-t-o	k-t-o
ACC	k-ovo	k-ogo
GEN	k-ovo	k-ogo
DAT	k-omu	k-omu
LOC	k-om	k-im
INST	k-em	k-im

If we consider the case hierarchy in (21) in §2.3.3, the *t-* stem in wh-pronouns disappears in cases that are all bigger than nominative in the complexity scale. This suggests that the disappearing *t-* is a result of spell-out of cases bigger than nominative (perhaps involving backtracking). In the remainder of the chapter, I will restrict the discussion to the nominative form of *čto* only, as it is the only attested form of the declarative complementizer, and will not offer an analysis of the disappearing *t-* in forms other than the nominative.

The sequence in (45) is enough to cover languages like Polish or Russian, but it needs to be updated with definite demonstratives in order to describe languages like English. This issue essentially reduces to the question about the place of definiteness morphology among the other categories in (45).

4.5 High definite demonstratives

There are at least two scenarios to consider. The first one is a variant of (45) in which definiteness (indicated below as Def) is projected as a separate category at the bottom of the sequence, as in:

(46)   Comp > Rel > Wh > Dem$_{def}$ > Def

Initially, this looks like an attractive option since not only does it suggest that definiteness applies directly to the nominal root, as in (47), but it also reflects the fact that definite markers can be contained in the structure of a demonstrative pronoun (e.g. English *th-at* or Italian *quel-lo*).

(47)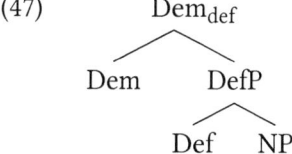

4 Resolving a morphological containment problem

The idea that definiteness applies to the nominal root also parallels with the situation observed with lexical nouns, as e.g. *the car*, where the definite article can appear without demonstrative morphology.

However, extending such a structure into WhP, RelP, and CompP leads to the *ABA violation: if the English definiteness marker *th-* and the medial/distal demonstrative marker *-at* spell out such a structure, the demonstrative *-at* will come out as the suffix, following the evacuation movement of DefP, as indicated in the following:

(48)
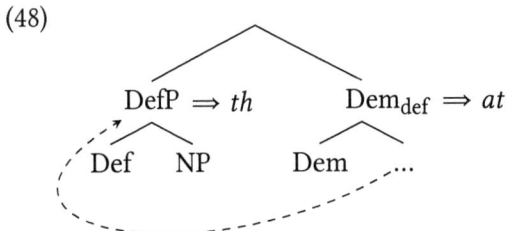

The structure obtained by the Def-movement in (48) appears to give a desired result. However, if the remainder of the sequence is "Comp > Rel > Wh", then the addition of these layers will result in the *ABA pattern by sandwiching the *wh-* for Wh between a lower *th-* for Def and a higher *th-* for Rel and Comp (i.e. the *ABA-violating "$th_{Comp} > th_{Rel} > wh_{Wh} > at_{Dem} > th_{Def}$").

In the alternative scenario, definiteness applies to the entire fseq with the nominal root at its bottom, as indicated in the following:

(49)   The updated singleton fseq

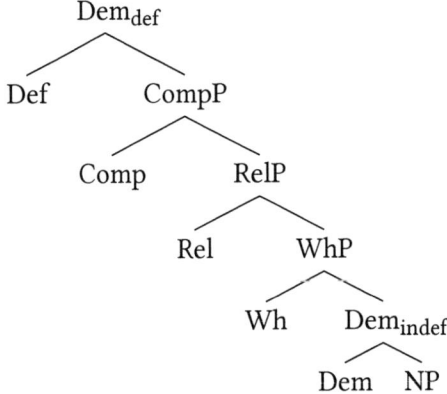

4.5 High definite demonstratives

This sequence differs from the one that applies to both Polish and Russian (cf. 40) only by the top layer and captures the fact that the deictic demonstrative is a stem for the formation of all higher categories.[8]

Given the shape of the English lexical items as in (50), the spell-out of the updated fseq in English requires the formation of the complex left branch, as shown in (51).

(50) Lexical entries in English (2nd approximation, replaces 5)
    a.   [Def [Comp [Rel [Wh Dem]]]] ⇔ *th*
    b.   [Wh Dem] ⇔ *wh*
    c.   [Dem NP] ⇔ *at*

(51) Lexicalization of the English *wh-at* and *th-at*

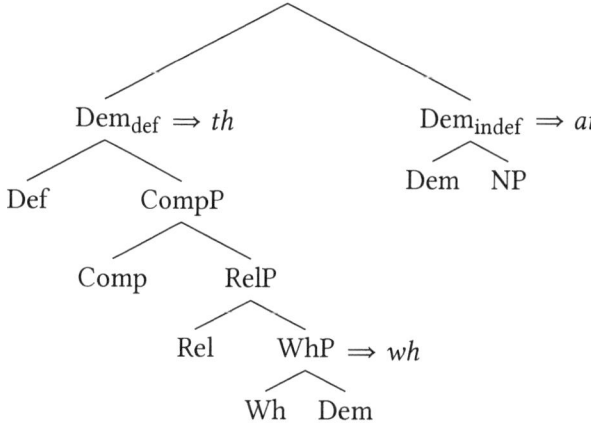

---

[8]This option, shown in (i) below without the intermediate Wh, Rel, Comp layers, is in essence compliant with Leu (2015: §2).

(i)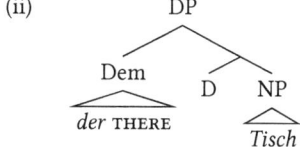

Leu's work makes a case for the architecture of the Germanic definite demonstrative which contains the definite article and a proper deictic element — an abstract HERE/THERE in Leu's (2015: 15) analysis of German *der Tisch* 'the table', as shown in:

(ii)
            DP
          /   \
     Dem
    /   \   D   NP
  der THERE   *Tisch*

Thus, with the addition of Def, the lexicalization of the updated fseq in (49) in English mimics what we see in Russian in (44), modulo the Def added on top.

To sum up, defining the sequence as in (49) leads to the reordering in the paradigms of languages without definiteness marking, which should be represented as in Table 6.3.

Table 4.11: English via-à-vis Russian

	DEM$_{def}$	COMP	REL	WH	DEM$_{indef}$
English	th-at	th-at	th-at	wh-at	-at
Russian		č-to	č-to	č-to	to

The *-at* morpheme in *th-at* /ðæt/ and in *wh-at* /wɑt/ has different exponents, even across the varieties of English involving also /wɔt/ but not */wæt/. This contrasts with what we observe in Russian, where *to* is syncretic in all four forms. This fact does not seem to result in an ABA pattern in Table 6.3 but — on the proviso that the contrast in the phonological shape of the stem *-at* in *th-at* and in *wh-at* as /æt/ vs. /ɑt/ or /ɔt/ is not an instance of a purely phonologically conditioned allomorphy — it may suggest that the syntactic size of stem in Wh, Rel, Comp, and Dem$_{indef}$ is not constant throughout the English paradigm. That is, the English /ɑt/ and /æt/ may reflect the subset-superset relation that is realized by different exponents, a plausible scenario given that the Dem$_{indef}$ stem is internally complex. I will return to the issue of the variable size of the bottom constituent in the next chapter on the example of the Latvian *kas*, a syncretic form for pronominal 'what' and 'who'.[9]

4.6 Summary

Cross-categorical syncretisms with the declarative complementizer discussed in Baunaz & Lander (2017; 2018a; 2018b) indicate that the wh-pronoun, the rela-

---

[9]The complexity of Dem$_{indef}$ concerns both the spatial deictic contrast as in Lander & Haegeman's (2016) decomposition in (19) but also its (pro)nominal component, marked in (49) and elsewhere in this chapter as the NP constituent at the bottom of the fseq in (49). In Wiland (2018a) I have explored a possibility where the Russian and Polish NP *t-* of the bi-morphemic *t-o* spells out subsets of a nominal sequence specified for Thing and Person (in the sense of Cysouw 2004; 2005), a scenario more transparently visible in the English forms *wh-at* and *wh-o* rather than in the Russian *č-to* 'what' and *k-to* 'who' with a syncretic stem *to*. I will discuss the distinction between pronominal Person and Thing in wh-queries in Latvian in the next chapter.

tivizer, the complementizer, and the definite demonstrative pronoun form an fseq. Thus, morphological containment of indefinite demonstrative pronouns in the structure of the wh-pronoun, the relativizer, and the complementizer in languages like Russian poses a problem for such an fseq in that it does not apply uniformly to languages with and without definiteness marking.

This problem can be resolved by inserting indefinite demonstratives at the bottom of this fseq to the effect that the definite demonstrative is a category which syntactically ranges from the indefinite demonstrative, through Wh, Rel, Comp, and is closed up by a high Def. This result is possible to achieve if the underlying representation of these categories is simplified to a single projection line and its partition into multiple morphemes is solely a result of the spell-out procedure, not the geometry of a tree in an underlying representation.

5 Beyond Slavic: Sorting out a Latvian paradigm

5.1 Introduction

We expect the proposed hierarchy in (1) (repeated from the previous chapter) to hold outside Slavic, too, irrespective of whether indefinite demonstratives are morphologically contained in the bigger categories of this sequence, like it is in the case of Russian *čto*, or not.

(1) Dem_{def} > Comp > Rel > Wh > $\text{Dem}_{\text{indef}}$

In Chapter 2 we discussed the reason why morphological containment is a possible but not a necessary effect of the presence of a particular category in an fseq. Namely, morphological containment is either a result of spell-out driven movement or the formation of the left branch (the "pre-" distribution in morphosyntax). Both these operations that are both ranked after STAY in the spell-out procedure.[1] This means that the layers of the sequence of heads lexicalized by STAY will not visibly (i.e. morphologically) contain the smaller categories of the same sequence of projections in syntax.

Incorporating $\text{Dem}_{\text{indef}}$ into the bottom of the fseq that covers syncretisms with the declarative complementizer makes a correct prediction about a curious paradigm found in Latvian (Baltic). In Latvian, the nominative case marker *-s* is part of the morphological structure of Dem, Wh, and Rel, but it is absent from the morphological structure of Comp. This is shown in Table 5.1. While Latvian does not have definite articles, it marks definiteness on adjectives to the effect that the contrast between definite and indefinite noun phrases is fully meaningful, as shown in (2) (see for instance Budina Lazdina 1966; Nau 1998; Praulinš 2012, among others).

---

[1] The term "spell-out driven movement" is understood here as a cover term for all three kinds of movement subsumed in the MOVE leg of the spell-out scheme: spec-to-spec movement, snowballing, and subextraction.

5 Beyond Slavic: Sorting out a Latvian paradigm

Table 5.1: Latvian paradigm

DEM	COMP	REL	WH
ta-s	ka	ka-s	ka-s

(2) Latvian (Lyons 1999: 84)
    a. liel-s kok-s
       big-NOM tree-NOM
       'a big tree'
    b. liel-ai-s kok-s
       big-DEF-NOM tree-NOM
       'the big tree'

Despite this fact, the arrangement of the Latvian paradigm in the way shown in Table 5.1 creates a problem since the case suffix -s is present in three non-adjacent cells. While this is not an instance of the *ABA violation since the -s represents the same (non-syncretic) nominative marker in all the cells, it is unexpected for the case marker to be absent on a category (Comp) that is sandwiched in the paradigm by the categories this case marker is a part of (Dem and Rel).

Let us discuss how the sequence in (1) and the representation of polymorphemic categories as singleton projection lines in syntax help us describe the Latvian paradigm in a more insightful way.

5.2 Latvian demonstratives

While Latvian does not have articles, it morphologically distinguishes between definite and indefinite adjectives, often described as long and short forms. Just like Latvian nouns, they are inflected for case (see for instance Mathiassen 1997: 57–58). The definite marker can be identified as suffix -ai or -aj, which is placed between the adjectival root and the case suffixes, as illustrated in Table 5.2 on the example of the masculine declension of the adjective *labs* 'good' (examples from Eckert et al. 1994: 293–294).

Latvian morphologically distinguishes between two forms of the demonstrative: the proximal *šis* and the medial/distal *tas* (e.g. Budina Lazdina 1966; Lyons 1999: 111). The definite function of the long form of the adjective is further manifested by the fact that an occurrence of the medial/distal demonstrative *tas* together with an adjective, requires the adjective to come in the definite form. This is illustrated in (3).

5.2 Latvian demonstratives

Table 5.2: Declension of the Latvian *labs* 'good'

	SINGULAR		PLURAL	
	INDEF.	DEF.	INDEF.	DEF.
NOM	lab-s	lab-ai-s	lab-i	lab-ie
ACC	lab-u	lab-o	lab-us	lab-os
GEN	lab-a	lab-ā	lab-u	lab-o
DAT	lab-am	lab-aj-am	lab-iem	lab-aj-iem
LOC	lab-ā	lab-aj-ā	lab-os	lab-aj-os

(3) Latvian (Fennell & Gelsen 1980: 318)

    a. Kur ir tas vec-ai-s kok-s?
        where is DEM old-DEF-NOM tree-NOM
        'Where is that old tree?'

    b. Ko tu lasi tajās jaun-aj-ās grāmat-ās?
        what you read those new-DEF-LOC book-LOC
        'What are you reading in those new books?'

In a similar way to what we have observed on the examples of Polish and Russian, Latvian demonstrative pronouns *tas* and *šis* can be decomposed into spatial deictic stems and case suffixes: *ta-s* and *ši-s* in the nominative. This is so since they are inflected just like possessive pronouns, as shown in Table 5.3.[2] The demonstratives share the same declension class with *kas*, a syncretic form for Wh/Rel. *Kas*, however, appears only in the singular and the locative adverb *kur* 'where' is used in the locative, as shown in Table 5.4.

Let us consider the Latvian declarative complementizer *ka*.

(4) Latvian declarative complementizer *ka* (Holvoet 2016: 229)

    Es zinu ka tu atbrauksi paciemoties
    I know.1SG COMP you come.FUT.2SG visit.INF
    'I know you will come on a visit.'

Unlike the demonstratives *tas*, *šis* and the syncretic Wh/Rel *kas*, the complementizer *ka* is uninflected for case. This situation contrasts with complementizers

---

[2] Let us take note of the fact that Tables 5.2 and 5.3 list only a subset of exponents while Latvian distinguishes three masculine and three feminine declensions. The list provided here, however, is sufficient to identify case marking on the demonstratives.

5 Beyond Slavic: Sorting out a Latvian paradigm

Table 5.3: Masculine declension of the Latvian demonstratives: distal/medial *tas* and proximal *šis*

	SG	PL	SG	PL
NOM	ta-s	t-ie	ši-s	ši-e
ACC	t-o	t-os	š-o	š-os
GEN	t-ā	t-o	š-ā, š-ī	š-o
DAT	t-am	t-iem	š-im	š-iem
LOC	ta-jā	ta-is	ša-jā	ša-jos

Table 5.4: Singular declension of the Latvian syncretic Wh/Rel *kas*

NOM	ka-s
ACC	k-o
GEN	k-ā
DAT	k-am
LOC	k-ur 'where'

such as the Russian *čto* or the Serbo-Croatian *što*, which include a neuter nominative case suffix *-o*, and also the Polish complementizer *że*.[3] The fact that the Latvian declarative complementizer *ka* lacks the invariant case suffix leads to an interesting observation: while the Latvian noun phrase such as e.g. 'that old tree' in (3a) includes a definite marker in its structure, this marker must be distinct from the Def category of the "Dem_{def} > Comp > Rel > Wh > $\text{Dem}_{\text{indef}}$" sequence. This follows from the fact that equating the adjectival definite marker with the Def category in our sequence results in the arrangement of the paradigm as in Table 5.1. In Table 5.1, on the one hand Comp is a category intermediate in terms of complexity and on the other hand it is the only category which does not comprise the case marker.

This puzzle becomes less absorbing if the Latvian demonstrative, which itself does not comprise the definite marker, instead corresponds to the $\text{Dem}_{\text{indef}}$ at the bottom of our fseq, yielding the order as in Table 5.5. When compared to the arrangement in Table 5.1, the one in Table 5.5 keeps the syncretic span of the

---

[3] Assuming with Baunaz & Lander (2018a) that *że* should be analyzed as a bi-morphemic *ż-e*, where the usual neuter nominative case suffix *-o* surfaces as /e/ after a soft consonant *ż-* /ʒ/ (see Footnote 7 in Chapter 4).

stems of Comp=Rel=Wh and groups the case-inflected categories into a different span including Rel, Wh, and Dem.

Table 5.5: Reordered paradigm in Latvian

COMP	REL	WH	DEM
ka	ka-s	ka-s	ta-s

While the arrangement of the paradigm as in Table 5.5 by itself does not provide an answer to the question why the Latvian declarative complementizer *ka* does not take any (invariant) case suffix the way other languages we have so far looked at do, it at least allows us to identify the pattern in the noise.

What has helped us resolve the morphological containment problem of indefinite demonstratives in Slavic is the idea that an underlying syntactic representation of morphologically complex categories in the sequence "Dem$_{def}$ > Comp > Rel > Wh > Dem$_{indef}$" has a shape of singleton projection line. Such a simplex sequence becomes partitioned into geometrically more complex trees only as a result of spell-out driven operations. Let us now move on to consider how this sequence is lexicalized and extended by the case feature(s) in Latvian, bearing in mind that – just like in Russian and Polish but unlike in Germanic – it reaches only up to the CompP layer in Latvian and does not include the top Def layer.

5.3 Refining the pronominal base

The comparison of *tas* and *kas* with other interrogative pronouns suggests that the stems for the merger of the case suffix are morphologically complex, too. Namely, while *kas* is a syncretic form for 'what' and 'who', the forms of other interrogative pronouns in Latvian comprise the initial *k-* and a different ending, as listed in Table 5.6.

Table 5.6: Latvian interrogative pronouns

kas	'what', 'who'
kur	'where'
kā	'how'
kāpēc	'why'

5 Beyond Slavic: Sorting out a Latvian paradigm

If *k-* is a wh-prefix added to different stems in the formation of interrogative pronouns, then the Latvian pattern adheres to what we find throughout Indo-European, including the English pattern involving *wh-at, wh-o, wh-ich, wh-en, wh-ere*.[4]

This leads us to a tri-morphemic analysis of the Latvian *t-a-s* and *k-a-s* in a similar way to the Russian *č-t-o* 'what', with – in the case of *k-a-s* – more than one syncretic morpheme in its structure. Apart from the syncretic prefix *k-* covering Wh, Rel, and Comp, also the nominal stem *-a*, which is the base for the merger of *t-* and *k-* in *t-a-s/k-a-s*, must be syntactically complex since *kas* is syncretic for 'what' and 'who'. In this respect the Latvian *kas* stands out from a well-attested pattern where the stems for the wh-prefix in morphological forms of kind and person queries are non-syncretic (including the English *wh-at, wh-o* or the Italian *ch-e* 'what', *ch-i* 'who').

We can fairly straightforwardly account for the complexity of the Latvian stem *-a* by identifying it as an internally complex NP, the (pro)nominal base component in our fseq. The fseq, repeated in (5) for convenience, projects only up to the Comp layer in Latvian and it excludes Def, the top-most ingredient whose presence results in the formation of definite demonstratives, which Latvian lacks.

(5)

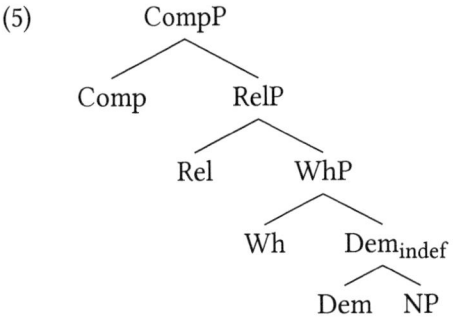

---

[4]To a large extent, this pattern is also present in Slavic but it can be sometimes blurred by phonological factors. In Polish for instance, the personal interrogative pronoun *kto* 'who' includes the wh-prefix *k-*, which is present in *k-iedy* 'when' and *k-ędy* 'through where' but, as stated in Wiland (2018a), it is also present in forms such as *g-dzie* 'where' or *g-dy* 'when', where /g/ is a voiced allomorph of /k/ appearing before a voiced /d/ in the onset of the stem. Also, the form of the Polish *do-k-ąd* 'where to', as in (i), includes the interrogative prefix *k-*, which is merged directly with the locative stem, and the external prefix denoting path *do-* 'to'.

(i) Polish
Dokąd idziecie?
where.to go.2PL
'Where are you going to?'

5.3 Refining the pronominal base

The complexity of Dem_indef can in principle apply not only to the Dem component but also to its (pro)nominal NP component. That is, the decomposition of the Dem in (5) into independent features that encode spatial deictic contrast, discussed in (19) in Chapter 4, renders the representation of the Dem_indef as in (6), with deictic features projected on top of the (pro)nominal NP base.

(6)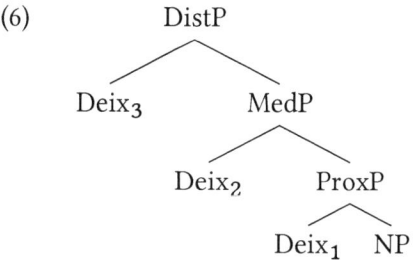

There exists independent evidence that what we have so far been referring to as the (pro)nominal NP base in the structure of Dem_indef has its own complex structure, too. Namely, the decomposition of the NP base into a sequence of nominal features N_n as in (7) captures the different sizes of stems present in wh-pronouns denoting Thing ('what'), Person ('who'), and Place ('where').

(7) Refined NP base

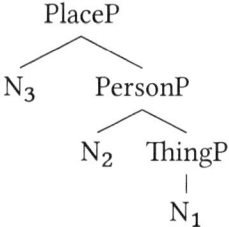

An argument in favor of a partial hierarchy in (7) can be found in Baunaz & Lander (2018c), who organize the list of closed class light nouns. The full list includes interrogative words denoting the concepts listed in (8), which are organized into a sequence based on their syncretisms and morphological containment.[5]

(8) a. Thing ('what')
    b. Person ('who')
    c. Place ('where')

---

[5] See Cysouw (2004; 2005) for the topology of wh-pronouns including Thing, Person, and Person wh-queries. See also Vangsnes (2013), who on the basis of syncretic alignment argues that the Person wh-pronuns are syntactically more complex than Thing wh-pronouns in Germanic.

5 Beyond Slavic: Sorting out a Latvian paradigm

    d.   Manner ('how')
    e.   Amount ('how much/many')
    f.   Time ('when')

Let us briefly go through the evidence provided in Baunaz & Lander (2018c) in support of syntactic inclusion of Thing inside Person and Person inside Place before we move on to represent the Latvian *kas* as a form which comprises subsets of (7) in its syntactic structure.

The argument in favor of the inclusion of Thing inside Person wh-queries comes from morphological containment found in Amuecha (Arawakan) and in Muna (Austronesian), as shown in:

(9)   Amuecha (Wise 1986: 573 as cited in Cysouw 2004)
        es   THING
        es-eša   PERSON

(10)   Muna (Van den Berg 1989: §8.6.2 as cited in Baunaz & Lander 2018c)
        hae   THING
        la-hae   PERSON

In turn, the argument in favor of the inclusion of Person inside Place inside wh-queries comes from morphological containment found for instance in Sanumá (Yanomaman) and Pipil (Uto-Aztecan):

(11)   Sanumá (Borgman 1990: 67, 70)
        witi   PERSON
        witi ha   PLACE

(12)   Pipil (Campbell 1985: 114)
        ka: PERSON
        ka:n   PLACE

Apart from morphological containment, an argument for the 'Place > Person > Thing' sequence comes from syncretic alignment. Baunaz & Lander (2018c) note that there are cross-linguistically attested syncretisms between the Person query and the Place query, as for instance in Awa Pit (Barbacoan).

(13)   Awa Pit (Curnow 2006: 225)
        shi   THING
        mɨn   PERSON
        mɨn=   PLACE

5.3 Refining the pronominal base

At the same time syncretism involving the Thing query and the Place query to the exclusion of the Person query has not been attested.[6] Given the *ABA generalization, the structure of Person comes out as intermediate in terms of syntactic complexity between Place and Thing.

To summarize, while syncretism indicates that the three forms constitute a paradigm with the Person-cell intermediate in terms of complexity, as in Table 5.7 morphological containment facts indicate that Place is more complex than both Person and Thing, as indicated in the fseq in (7).

Table 5.7: Syncretic alignment of wh-pronouns

	PLACE	PERSON	THING
English	where	who	what
Latvian	kur	kas	kas
Awa Pit	min=	min	shi
unattested			

The essential difference between the Latvian *kas* and forms for 'what' and 'who' in languages like Amuecha or Muna is two-fold: the *k-* marker in *kas* is a prefix and the *-a* is a syncretic stem. Given the refined nominal base in (7), we are able to describe the lexical entry for the Latvian pronominal stem *-a* as comprising the two bottom layers of (7), as specified in (14), to the exclusion of a separate *k-* prefix, as specified in:

(14) Lexical entry for the Latvian pronominal stem *-a*

  [$_{PersonP}$ N$_2$ [$_{ThingP}$ N$_1$]] $\Leftrightarrow$ a

Such an entry not only allows us to straightforwardly derive *k-a-s*, the syncretic form for 'what', 'who', and Rel, but also to explain the contrast in the morpho-

---

[6]The Person=Place syncretism can also be found in Modern Greek if we qualify the dative *pú* 'to whom' as a Person wh-query in sentences as (ib):

(i) Modern Greek *pú* 'where'/'to whom' (Roussou 2016: ex. 12)
  a. Pú   pas?
    where go.2SG
    'Where are you going?'
  b. Pú   to edhoses?
    where it gave.2SG
    'Who did you give it to?'

logical structure between the medial/distal demonstrative pronoun *t-a-s* and the proximal demonstrative pronoun *si-s*, which has a mono-morphemic stem.

Let us discuss the structure and spell-out of the proximal *ši-s* first, since the medial/distal *t-a-s* and the Wh/Rel *k-a-s* include bigger structures that build up on the structure of *šis*.

5.4 Proximal *šis* and medial *tas*

Assuming the decomposition of demonstratives in Lander & Haegeman (2016) in (6) and the refinement of the pronominal stem in (7), the syntactic representation of proximal demonstrative pronouns minimally includes the pronominal Thing-forming feature N_1 and the Prox-forming feature $Deix_1$, as in (15). On the strength of the Superset Principle, the Thing layer of such a representation is realized as *-a* as the subset spell-out of the lexical entry in (14).

(15) ProxP
      / \
    $Deix_1$ ThingP $\Rightarrow$ a
              |
              N_1

In order to lexicalize the Prox layer of this structure there needs to exist another lexical entry in the Latvian lexicon: the one which includes the $Deix_1$ feature. While the lexical entry for *-a* in (14) lacks $Deix_1$, the lexical entry for the proximal stem *ši-* defined as in (16) includes it.

(16) Lexical entry for the Latvian (uninflected) proximal demonstrative pronoun *ši-*

  [$_{ProxP}$ $Deix_1$ [$_{ThingP}$ N_1]] $\Leftrightarrow$ *ši*

The insertion of *ši-* in the ProxP node in the syntactic representation results in the over-riding of *-a*, as shown in (17).

(17) Spell-out of the Latvian proximal demonstrative stem *ši-*
        ProxP $\Rightarrow$ *ši*
        / \
      $Deix_1$ ThingP $\Rightarrow$ a
                |
                N_1

In this way, *ši-* comes out as a portmanteau stem that realizes the pronominal base and the proximal deictic feature.

5.4 Proximal šis and medial tas

The pronominal base, however, is visibly retained in other forms in Latvian. Whereas the proximal feature is realized in the stem of *ši-s*, the medial feature is realized in the prefix *t-* in the demonstrative *t-a-s*, not in the stem *-a*. The lexicalization of the medial feature as part of the stem would result in an ABA pattern, as it requires the realization of MedP and ThingP as syncretic *-a* to the exclusion of ProxP, which is intermediate in terms of complexity, as *ši-*, as outlined in (18).

(18)   Unattested spell-out (*ABA violation)

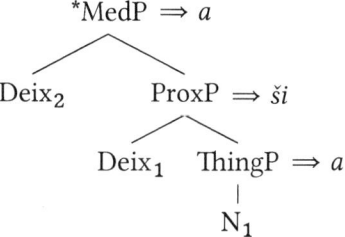

The preservation of the *-a* stem in *t-a-s* indicates that there is no lexical item in the Latvian lexicon which realizes both the pronominal base ThingP and the Med-forming feature $Deix_2$. In turn, the lack of morphological containment of *ši-* in the structure of *t-a-s* indicates that the *t-a-* sequence is not derived by MOVE but by a last resort SUBDERIVE, which results in the merger of an XP with the mainline derivation, the procedure resulting in the formation of the complex left branch discussed in §2.3.4.

The decomposition of indefinite demonstratives into independent $Deix_n$ features projected on top of a pronominal structure in (6) comes out as a necessary result in identifying the base feature for spawning the subderivation. We are only able to capture the distinction between the proximal stem *ši-* and the medial *t-a-* if it is precisely the proximal feature $Deix_1$ of the split category Dem_{indef} which is provided as the base feature for the formation of the left branch. Its merger with the next feature in line, the Med-forming feature $Deix_2$, as shown in (19), forms an XP constituent that is subsequently merged with the pronominal ThingP of the mainline derivation.

(19)   Spell-out of the Latvian medial demonstrative stem *t-a-*

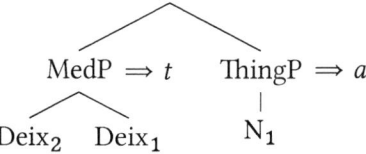

5 Beyond Slavic: Sorting out a Latvian paradigm

The left branch of such a tree can be spelled out as *t-* if its lexical specification includes a constituent specified as in (20), where Deix_2 and Deix_1 are sisters.[7]

(20) Lexical entry for the Latvian medial prefix *t-*

$[_{\text{MedP}} \ \text{Deix}_2 \ \text{Deix}_1 \ ] \Longleftrightarrow t$

The decomposition of demonstratives in the way seen in (6) is here necessary since the Prox-forming feature Deix_1 spells out together with ThingP as a single portmanteau morpheme *si-* only when there is no higher Med-forming Deix_2 added to the derivation. The addition of Deix_2 requires backtracking and the formation of the left branch, which becomes merged with the pronominal stem *-a*, the subset of the proximal *si-*.

Importantly, for the present derivation of *t-a-* to work, the subderivation of the complex left branch in (19) must be able to enforce backtracking. As pointed out by a reviewer, this is different than in Starke (2018), where SUBDERIVE does not involve backtracking. When we compare *ši-* in (17) with *t-a-* in (19), for the present analysis to work, the derivation must backtrack down to ThingP and start the subderivation of the left branch from that level. If the subderivation started from ProxP, i.e. the stage in (17), we would expect an unattested form like *t-ši-s* to be generated.

The suffixal case marking on *ši-s* and *t-a-s* follows straightforwardly if the case fseq projects on top of the categories forming the "Dem_{def} > Comp > Rel > Wh > $\text{Dem}_{\text{indef}}$" sequence rather than directly on the pronominal base, the subset of $\text{Dem}_{\text{indef}}$. Thus, assuming (21) to be a stand-in entry for the Latvian nominative singular marker *-s*,

(21) $[_{K_1 P} \ K_1 \ ] \Longleftrightarrow s$

the merger of the nominative feature K_1 on top of the proximal *si-* and the medial *t-a-* becomes spelled out in both instances following complement movement, as illustrated in (22–23).[8]

---

[7] In line with Starke's (2018) insight that prefixes but not suffixes have a binary foot in their syntactic representations, a consequence of SUBDERIVE.

[8] The *-s* marker is the nominative exponent of the 1st declension class in the Latvian conjugation system, which includes demonstrative pronouns (see Mathiassen 1997 and Nau 2011).

5.4 Proximal *šis* and medial *tas*

(22) Spell-out of the Latvian *ši-s*

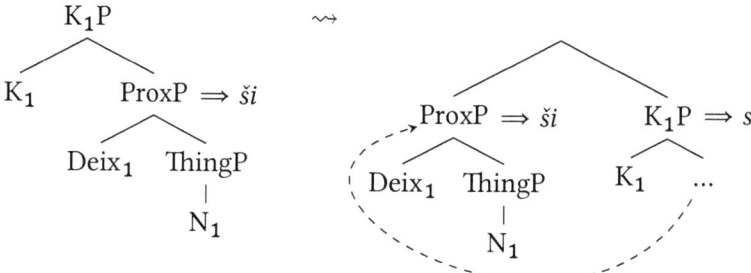

(23) Spell-out of the Latvian *t-a-s*

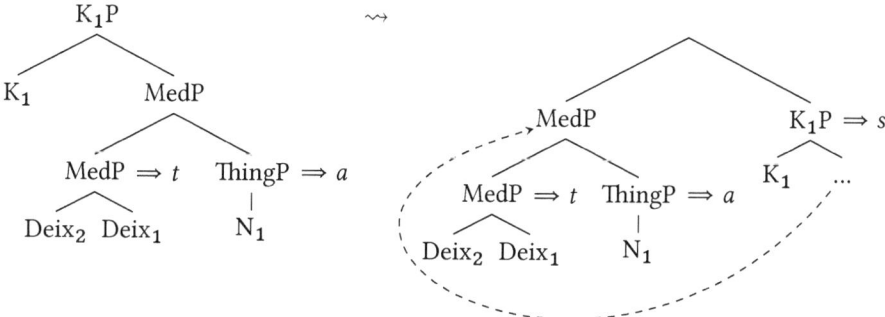

Let us observe that if case fseq projects on top of the "Dem$_{def}$ > Comp > Rel > Wh > Dem$_{indef}$" sequence, case suffixation in *ši-s* and in the complex *t-a-s* is possible only if the left branch constituent *t-* in the second is a complex head. By "complex head" I understand the node that provides its label for the merger with its sister. For *t-a-s*, MedP *t-* must be a head (rather than a non-projecting specifier) on the ThingP stem *-a*. This result is in agreement with Starke's (2004) reanalysis of specifiers as complex heads. If, against this idea, the prefix *t-* in *t-a-s* is a non-projecting specifier and what projects is the pronominal ThingP *-a*, the case fseq will have to apply to the latter. Such an alternative is illustrated in (24).

(24) Unattested sequence K$_1$P > ThingP > MedP derived by non-projecting left branches

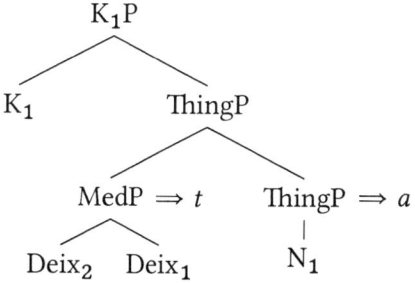

121

5 Beyond Slavic: Sorting out a Latvian paradigm

The scenario with non-projecting left branches in (24) would create a contradictory situation: we would have one sequence "K_1P > ProxP > ThingP" for the proximal *šis* and another sequence "K_1P > ThingP > MedP" for the medial *tas*. With ThingP listed as smaller than ProxP in the first and as bigger than MedP in the second, we would incorrectly expect to have a sequence "ProxP > ThingP > MedP", suggesting that proximal demonstratives structurally contain medial demonstratives. The evidence for (6) discussed in Lander & Haegeman (2016) shows the opposite to be true. We avoid this contradiction if we follow (23), where left branches formed by SUBDERIVE are complex heads.[9]

5.5 Deriving the three readings of *kas*

Kas is a declinable syncretic form for wh-pronouns denoting Thing ('what') and Person ('who') as well as the relative pronoun, as shown below for nominative *kas*, accusative *ko*, and genitive *kā*.[10]

(25)   Latvian *kas* as pronominal 'what' (Praulinš 2012)

    a.   Kas   vainas?
           what.NOM fault.ACC
           'What's the matter?'

    b.   Ko   jūs   darāt?
           what.ACC you.2PL do.2PL.PRES
           'What are you doing?'

---

[9]If we return to the discussion of spell-out driven extraction in the domain of Czech and Polish semelfactive *-n-ou* stems in Chapter 3, we can observe the difference between the projecting vs. non-projecting status of specifier-like XPs. In semelfactives like the Czech *kop-n-ou-t* 'give a kick', following the roll-up derivation, the constituent *kop-n-* ends up as non-projecting specifier of the verbalizing theme vowel *-ou*. Thus, distinction between projecting and non-projecting specifier-like XPs appears to be running along the following description: internally merged XPs form non-projecting specifiers whereas externally merged XPs are complex heads. See also Caha et al. (2019b), who reach the same conclusion about projecting vs. non-projecting specifiers in the domain of Czech comparative morphology.

[10]Both Wh and Rel *kas* are inflected for all the cases in the Latvian paradigm, as shown in Table 5.4 above, but the use of the genitive form of Rel is rare. However, it is nevertheless possible in contexts such as in the following:

(i)   Latvian (Nicole Nau, p.c.)
       suns,   no kā   man   bail
       dog.NOM of REL.GEN me.DAT afraid.1SG.PRES
       'the dog of which I am afraid'

5.5 Deriving the three readings of kas

(26) Latvian *kas* as pronominal 'who'
    a. Kas   nozaga manu maku?
       who.NOM stole my wallet.ACC
       'Who stole my wallet?'
    b. Kā   cepure ir   tā?
       who.GEN hat.NOM be.3SG.PRES that.GEN
       'Whose hat is that?'

(27) Latvian *kas* Rel (Tatjana Navicka, p.c.; Nau 2009)
    a. cilvēks kas   tur   sēž
       man.NOM REL.NOM there sit.3SG.PRES
       'the man who is sitting there'
    b. Vai ir   kāds liels sapnis, ko   gribētos īstenot?
       PRT be.3SG.PRES any great dream REL.ACC want.2PL realize.INF
       'Do you have any great dream you want to realize?'

If both Wh and Rel are based on the indefinite medial demonstrative, we can straightforwardly derive the Wh=Rel syncretism of *kas* by extending the structure of *t-a-* in (19) by adding the higher features Wh and Rel as shown in (29) below. More specifically, features Wh and Rel must belong to the lexical entry for *k-* (as in 28), which is bigger than the entry for *t-* (in (20) above).

(28) Lexical entry for the Latvian prefix *k-* (1st approximation)
    [Rel [Wh [$_{MedP}$ Deix$_2$ Deix$_1$]]] ⇔ *k*

This can be inferred from the fact that, given the 'Rel > Wh > Dem$_{indef}$' sequence, *k-* over-rides *t-* to the exclusion of the stem *-a*.

(29) Spell-out of the Latvian Wh/Rel *k-a-*

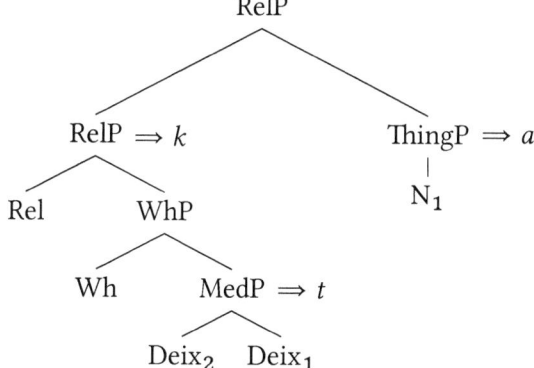

5 Beyond Slavic: Sorting out a Latvian paradigm

With the lexical entry in (28), the Rel=Wh syncretism of *kas* results from the subset spell-out of *k-* as Rel or its Wh subset (while the stem *-a* is invariant in both categories).

The subsequent merger and spell-out of the case fseq on top of *k-a-* takes place exactly as in *tas* in (23), as shown below with the suffix *-s* spelling out the nominative feature K_1 following complement movement.

(30)   Spell-out of the Latvian Wh/Rel *k-a-s*

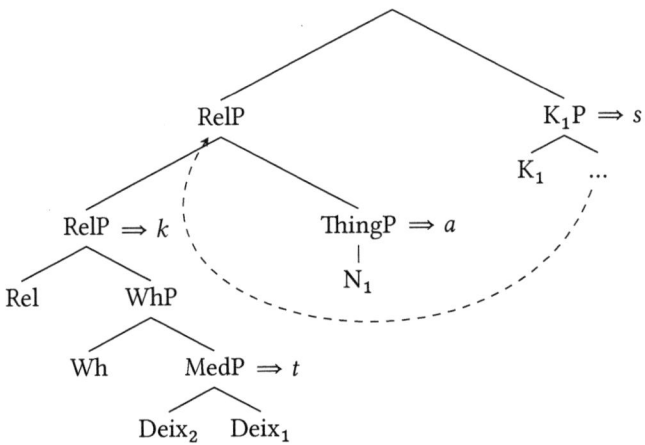

This leaves us with the pronominal 'who' reading of *kas* to explain. That is, we now need to structurally differentiate not between the categories from the "Comp > Rel > Wh > Dem$_{indef}$" sequence but between two wh-pronouns: *kas* 'what' and *kas* 'who'. Descriptively speaking, we need to represent the structural difference between the two vertical cells in the following two-dimensional paradigm (Table 5.8).

Table 5.8: Two-dimensional paradigm in Latvian

COMP	REL	WH	DEM$_{indef}$
ka	kas	kas $_{what}$ kas $_{who}$	tas

With the refined pronominal stem in (7), we can represent the difference between both wh-pronouns as the size difference of the *-a* stem, as in (31) (modulo case).

(31) Spell-out of the Latvian *k-a-* 'who'

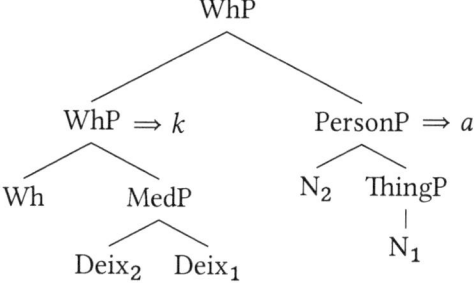

The difference between the stem in the pronominal *kas* 'what' and *kas* 'who' reduces to the presence of the Person-forming feature N_2 in the latter. Given the lexical entry in (14), the stem comes out in both wh-pronouns as *-a*.

If we extend this logic to the English *who*, we can analyze it as a bi-morphemic *wh-o* with *-o* lexicalizing the PersonP superstructure and *-at* lexicalizing its ThingP subset. One difference between the Latvian *-a* stem in *kas* 'what' and the English *-at* stem in *wh-at* is that the latter also contains the deictic medial (and perhaps also distal) features, as specified in (50c) in Chapter 4.

5.6 Place *-ur* as a pronominal superstructure in *kur*

Let us move on to *kur* 'where', which unlike other case forms of *kas* does not comprise the *-a* stem, as shown in Table 5.9 (both the demonstrative *tas* and *kas* belong to the 1st declension class).

Table 5.9: Singular declension of *tas* and *kas*

	tas	kas
NOM	tas	kas
ACC	to	ko
GEN	tā	kā
DAT	tam	kam
LOC	tajā / tai / tanī	

Whereas in the accusative *ko* we can explain the deletion of the exponent of the *-a* stem in front of the vocalic case suffix by vowel truncation, *kur* simply does not have a locative case suffix and hence there is no ground to describe it as a locative form of *kas*.

5 Beyond Slavic: Sorting out a Latvian paradigm

That *kur* is a locative pronoun 'where' rather than the prefix-stem complex *k-a-* with an added locative case suffix is inferred from the fact that *kur* is preserved in a caseless form *kaut kur* 'somewhere'. Moreover, the forms of *kur* 'where' and the locative demonstrative *tur* 'there' indicate that *k-* and *t-* are distinct morphemes, which both can merge with the locative stem, the bound morpheme *-ur* (see e.g. Praulinš 2012).

The latter fact points toward the analysis of *kur* as comprising the *k-* prefix and the stem *-ur* denoting Place, the superset of the (pro)nominal features in (7). The lexical entry is defined as follows:

(32) Lexical entry for the Latvian stem *-ur*

$$[_{\text{PlaceP}} \, N_3 \, [_{\text{PersonP}} \, N_2 \, [_{\text{ThingP}} \, N_1 \,]]] \Leftrightarrow ur$$

The description of *-ur* as Place in both *t-ur* 'there' and *k-ur* 'where' is in agreement with Katz & Postal's (1964) description of the English *here*, *there*, and *where* as involving an underlying PP structure as in:

(33) *here* = at this place
      there = at that place
      where = at what place

Likewise, it is in agreement with Kayne's (2007) description of *there* and *where* as containing a silent noun Place, as in (34).[11]

(34) *there* = [at [that [Place]]]
      where = [at [what [Place]]]

In what is essentially a refinement of the descriptions above, Vanden Wyngaerd (2018a) proposes that the English *there* be described as in (35), which explains the distribution of *there* with manner of motion and directed motion verbs.

(35) [Dir [Loc [Dem [Place]]]]

Such a refinement stems from a body of work on spatial expressions which shows that directions are more complex than locations (see Koopman 2000; Kracht 2002;

---

[11] By and large, Kayne's (2007) abstract Place corresponds to a silent noun proposed in Katz & Postal (1964) to be present in *where*, which they analyze to be a pro-form of *at which place*. There is a short history of applying Kayne's (2007) analysis to the description of locative expressions as involving a pronominal Place in other languages (see Pantcheva 2008 for Persian, Leu 2015 for Germanic, Caha & Pantcheva 2016 for Shona, Botwinik-Rotem & Terzi 2008 for Hebrew and Greek, Wiland 2018a for Russian and Polish).

Zwarts 2005; Cinque 2010; den Dikken 2010; Svenonius 2010; Pantcheva 2011). In such an analysis, the syn-sem structure of a VP with a directional preposition (e.g. *to that place*) contains the structure of the locative preposition (e.g. *in that place*), as outlined in the following:

(36)   [V [Dir [Loc [Dem Place]]]]

More specifically, Vanden Wyngaerd argues that manner of motion verbs like *walk, dance, run* will merge with *there* which is ambiguous between direction and location, as in (37).[12]

(37)   She danced *there* (= to that place/in that place).

In turn, directed motion verbs like *go* or *come* will merge with only a locative *there*, as in:

(38)   She went *there* (− *to that place/in that place).

In Vanden Wyngaerd's (2018a) analysis, this contrast reflects the fact that manner of motion verbs are process verbs, a class of verbs which do not include the Dir layer in their own lexical entries. This means that in a VP headed by a manner of motion verb, the Dir layer is part of a different lexical item than the verb. Consequently, such verbs can select either a directional PP (when the Dir layer is selected) as indicated in (39) or its locative subset (when the Dir layer is absent) as indicated in (40).

(39)   [V$_{process}$ [Dir [Loc [Dem Place]]]]
               dance   to   that place
                           there

---

[12] The descriptions in (35–36) include Dem, which Vanden Wyngaerd (2018a) does not list as a separate category in the structure of *there*. Dem, however, must remain a category distinct from both Dir/Loc and Place to allow for the deictic contrast between the English proximal *here* and the medial/distal *there*. Moreover, the fact that the PP *in that place* as in (ia) below can be described as either *in there* in (ib) or *there* in (ic) but not as a periphrastic **that there* points to an analysis of *there* as realizing demonstrative *that* as its ingredient.

(i)   a.   She danced *in that place*.
        b.   She danced *in there*.
        c.   She danced *there*.
        d.   *She danced (*in*) *that there*.

5 Beyond Slavic: Sorting out a Latvian paradigm

(40) [V$_{process}$ [Loc [Dem Place]]]]
      ⏟   ⏟   ⏟
      dance   in   that place
                ⏟_____⏟
                   there

Thus, the directional 'to that place' reading of *there* in (37) follows from the lexicalization of the directional superstructure, whereas the 'in that place' reading of *there* follows from the lexicalization of its syncretic locative subset. In contrast, the Dir layer is always lexicalized as part of a directed motion verb leaving only the Loc layer to be lexicalized by the PP. Hence, the *there* in (38) spells out only the locative subset of the directional superstructure, as indicated in (41).

(41) [V$_{process}$ [Dir [Loc [Dem Place]]]]
      ⏟   ⏟   ⏟   ⏟
      go   in   that place
                 ⏟_____⏟
                    there

We can add to these observations the fact that the locative but not the directional *there* can be preceded by *in* with both manner of motion and directed motion verbs, as in (42).

(42) a. She danced *in there* (= *to that place/in that place).
      b. She went *in there* (= *to that place/in that place).

This indicates that in such cases *there* corresponds only to *that place*, the complement of the locative PP, which is predicted by the analysis of the locative preposition *in* as a subset of the directional *to*.[13] Using the notational convention in Vanden Wyngaerd (2018a), the above can be summarized as in Table 5.10.

Note that since the English *there* can appear as a complement to prepositions *to* and *in*, we must be able to define the minimal syntactic structure *there* can lex-

---

[13] As pointed out by a reviewer, *here/there* in expressions such as *dance in here/there* is analysed in Svenonius (2010) as a PP modifier that is crossed by a PP with a silent pronominal Ground, as shown in the the following:

(i)   [$_{PP}$ [$_{PlaceP}$ *in pro*][$_{PP}$ { here/there } t$_{PlaceP}$]]
              ↑_____|

This contrasts with the representation of *there* here as a complement to the preposition. While it is certainly interesting to see to what extent the analysis of the Latvian demonstratives can be informed by Svenonius's analysis, I will continue to work with a simpler representation. As long as *there* is not a sister to the prepositional Dir or Loc, however, expressions such as *in there* can in principle still be analyzed as structures involving a silent pronominal Ground, as in: [in *pro* there].

5.6 Place -ur as a pronominal superstructure in kur

Table 5.10: Readings of *there*

PROCESS	DIR	LOC	THAT	PLACE
dance	to			there
dance			there	
dance	×	in		there
dance	×		there	
go		in		there
go			there	

icalize without relying on Dir and Loc layers. If this logic is carried over to the Latvian *tur* we can describe it as comprising the medial prefix *t-* and the pronominal base Place *-ur* as the minimal subset of features it lexicalizes, as shown in (43) below.[14]

(43) Minimal spell-outs of the Latvian *tur* 'there' and *kur* 'where'

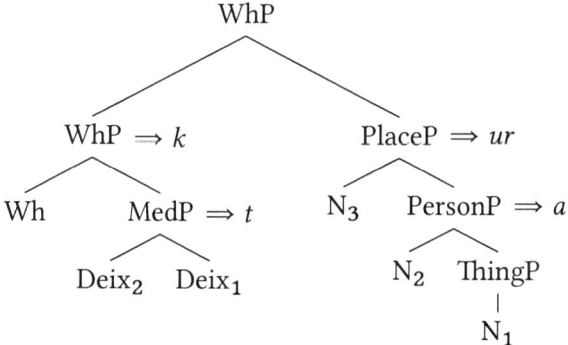

In such a representation, the difference between the stems *tas*, *kas*$_{\text{what}}$ and the locative *tur*, *kur* is in the size of the (pro)nominal base, Thing vs. Place, in line with the containment hierarchy in (7), rather than in the locative case suffix. In turn, the contrast between the forms for the locative 'there' and 'where', which is realized by a prefix, is by no means specific to Latvian or English as essentially

---

[14]"Minimal" in the sense that if we take any feature out of the equation from what spells out as *tur* in (43), we are going to end up with other forms. The pronominal base that is a notch smaller than Place in (43) gives us the stem *t-a-* of the medial demonstrative *tas* in (23). In turn, stripping the pair of deictic features in (43) down to the sole Deix$_1$ allows us to construe nothing more than the stem *ši-* of the proximal demonstrative *šis* in (22).

5 Beyond Slavic: Sorting out a Latvian paradigm

the same pattern holds for example in Czech, where these forms are, respectively, *t-am* and *k-am*.[15]

To wrap up the discussion of the locative *kur*, this form is best described as belonging to the vertical (inter-categorial) set of the Wh forms in the two-dimensional paradigm in Table 5.11 rather than to the case declension paradigm of *kas*$_{what}$ given in Table 5.9.

Table 5.11: Locative *kur* in a two-dimensional paradigm

COMP	REL	WH	DEM$_{indef}$
ka	kas	kas $_{what}$	tas
		kas $_{who}$	
		kur$_{where}$	

Before we move on to the Latvian caseless complementizer *ka*, let us juxtapose English *there*, *where* against Latvian *tur*, *kur*.

An essential difference between these categories is that the English *there* includes the *th*-prefix, which is syncretic not only with the Rel and Comp but also with the Def-marker, which Latvian lacks. In the previous chapter, we reduced the differences between syncretic alignment of Wh, Rel, and Comp with definite and indefinite and demonstratives to the "Dem$_{def}$ > Comp > Rel > Wh > Dem$_{indef}$" containment sequence, which is closed by Def, the top-most category in the fseq. This allowed us to describe the structure realized by the English *wh-* as a subset of the structure realized by *th-* (see (51) in §4.5). This result is seamlessly retained for *th-ere* and *wh-ere* if the entries for *th-* and *wh-* are refined by a decomposed spatial deixis and the entry for *-ere* is defined as Place, as specified in (44).

(44) Lexical entries in English (3rd and final approximations for *th* and *wh*, which supersede the ones in (50) in §4.5)
    a. [Def [Comp [Rel [Wh [Deix$_2$ Deix$_1$]]]]] ⇔ *th*
    b. [Wh [Deix$_2$ Deix$_1$]] ⇔ *wh*
    c. [$_{PlaceP}$ N$_3$ [$_{PersonP}$ N$_2$ [$_{ThingP}$ N$_1$]]] ⇔ *ere*

---

[15] See also Greenberg (2000) and the references cited there for a lists of Indo-European forms comprising the *-r* stem, a likely source of present day Latvian locative stem *-ur*, in adverbs and certain verbal compounds. In particular, Greenberg (2000: 147) also cites Pokorny (1959: 1087), who reconstructs forms parallel to the Indo-European locative *-r* based on the demonstrative *t-* as **tor* or **tēr* as 'there' including the Latvian *tur*.

These items realize a syntactic representation in which the spell-out of (at least) the Med-forming feature Deix_2 is unachievable by STAY or MOVE and its lexicalization takes place in the left branch, as shown in (45).

(45)　Minimal spell-outs of *there* and *where*

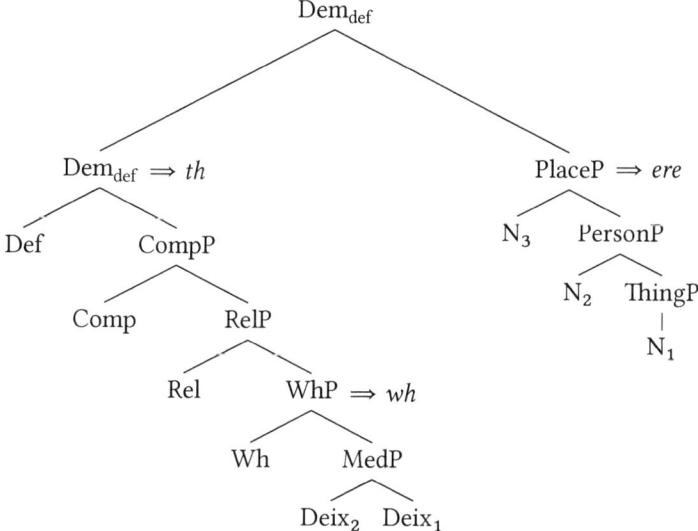

As indicated in (45), subsequent mergers of Wh, Rel, Comp, and Def on top of WhP will extend the subderivation (the left branch) in a familiar way.[16]

With the lexical entries covering *tas*, *kas*, and *kur*, we are in a position to discuss the Latvian complementizer *ka*.

5.7 Caseless complementizer *ka*

On the one hand, we have seen in §5.5 that suffixal case marking on demonstratives *šis* and *tas* as well as *kas* 'what'/'who'/Rel follows straightforwardly if case is projected on top of the categories of the "Dem_{def} > Comp > Rel > Wh > $\text{Dem}_{\text{indef}}$" sequence rather than directly on top of the categories of the (pro)nominal base PersonP > ThingP. On the other hand, setting up the paradigm like in

---

[16] Let us note that the spell-out of Place as *-ere* in (45) does not appear to trivially over-ride the lexical entry for *-at*. This follows from the fact that only the second includes the overt marking of the deictic contrast, as in *th-is* vs. *th-at*, which indicates that the lexical entry for *-at* includes $\text{Dem}_{\text{indef}}$ rather than a bare pronominal base Thing, as specified in (50c) in §4.5. We do not find overt evidence for the deictic contrast between *th-ere* vs. *h-ere* to be lexicalized in *-ere*, unless the proximal *here* /hir/ is analyzed as an allomorph of a bound morpheme *-ere* /er/.

5 Beyond Slavic: Sorting out a Latvian paradigm

Table 5.5 allows us to assemble the categories with the case suffix into an adjacent span of cells. This leads to the observation that the projection of the case is delimited by the Rel layer.

There is independent evidence that the case fseq is ordered on top of the Rel > Wh > Dem$_{indef}$ sequence in Lavian as part of a more general pattern. If we recall the representation of the Polish bi-morphemic Dem$_{indef}$ *t-o*, Rel=Wh *c-o*, and Comp *ż-e* in (39–40) in Chapter 4, whose prefixless structure indicates that the "Comp > Rel > ..." sequence is all lexicalized by the most basic spell-out option STAY, we observe that case is projected on top of all its categories. This is the only possible location of the case markers to come out as suffixes. We can, thus, conclude that case is projected on top of the categories that comprise the "Comp > Rel > ..." sequence irrespective of the geometry of the tree, whose segregation into multiple subtrees is solely a matter of the spell-out mechanism.

An exception to the first part of this statement is the Latvian Comp *ka* once we break it down into a complex *k-a*. Such an analysis comes naturally as it keeps the lexical entry for the stem *-a* in (14) intact and it only requires us to update the entry for *k-* with the Comp feature on top, as in the following.

(46) Lexical entry for the Latvian prefix *k-* (2nd and final approximation, replaces 28)

[Comp [Rel [Wh [$_{MedP}$ Deix$_2$ Deix$_1$]]]] ⇔ *k*

With a complex *k-a*, we arrive at a picture where the subset structures of the cross-categorial sequence comprising Dem$_{indef}$ (*tas* in 23), Wh and Rel (*kas* in 30) are all extended by the case features while the Comp superset structure in (47) is not.

(47) Latvian complementizer *ka*

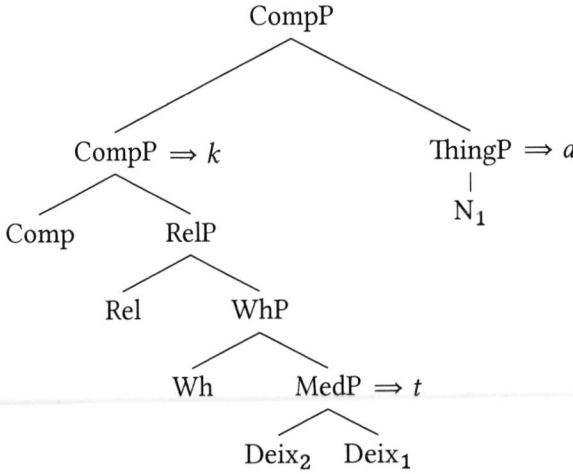

Technically speaking, the Latvian RelP delimits the projection of the case fseq but this result leads to a new more arduous question: why?

A possible answer can be informed by the contrasts with the Polish invariant Rel *co* and the Russian invariant Rel/Comp *čto*, whose suffix *-o* is the exponent of the neuter nominative (see Table 4.7 in Chapter 4). If the status of the Slavic neuter *-o* suffix teaches us about default case morphology (in the sense that it need not show concord), then the lack of neuter gender in Latvian results in a caseless invariant *ka*. In this way Comp *ka* contrasts with Dem *tas* and Wh/Rel *kas* with respect to case concord with masculine and feminine nouns, as shown for instance in (2) or (26b).

5.8 Multi-dimensional morphological paradigms as homeomorphic singleton projection lines in syntax

One final remark about the ordering of the case fseq with respect to the categories of the "Dem_{def} > Comp > Rel > Wh > Dem_{indef}" sequence is in place at this point.

On the one hand we have seen an argument from syncretic alignment and morphological containment for a strict ordering between the categories as seen in the tree in (49) in Chapter 4. On the other hand, in principle every category in this sequence can project case on its top: Dem_{def} in German; Dem_{indef}, Wh, Rel, and Comp in Polish and Russian. Though, the invariant categories like the Polish Rel *co* only project a default neuter nominative. In Latvian, Dem_{Indef}, Wh, and Rel all project the case fseq on their top except for the Comp. In this respect, the combination of case marking and the categories of the "Comp > Rel > ... " sequence results in the formation of two-dimensional paradigms, as shown on the example of Polish and Latvian declensions in Table 5.12 and in Table 5.13. This begs the following question: how are the horizontal Dem, Wh, Rel, and Comp features ordered with respect to case-forming vertical K_n features so that their mergers create two-dimensional paradigms?

In the approach to a syntactic representation of multi-morphemic forms advanced here both horizontal and vertical cells must result form a monotonically growing singleton projection line in syntax. This result can be achieved if the features forming the same fseq are ordered both with respect to each other, as in (48), and with respect to the features in the other fseq, as in (49).

(48)   a.   ... > K_3P > K_2P > K_1P (case fseq)
         b.   Comp > Rel > Wh > Dem_{indef} (complementizer fseq)

(49)   ... > K_3P > K_2P > K_1P > Comp > Rel > Wh > Dem_{indef}

5 Beyond Slavic: Sorting out a Latvian paradigm

Table 5.12: Neuter case declension of the categories syncretic with the declarative complementizer in Polish

	COMP	REL	WH	DEM$_{indef}$
STEM	ż-	c-	c-	t-
NOM	ż-e	c-o	c-o	t-o
ACC			c-o	t-o
GEN			cz-ego	t-ego
DAT			cz-emu	t-emu
LOC			cz-ym	t-ym
INST			cz-ym	t-ym

Table 5.13: Masculine case declension of the categories syncretic with the declarative complementizer in Latvian

	COMP	REL	WH	DEM$_{indef}$
STEM	ka	ka-	ka-	ta-
NOM		ka-s	ka-s	ta-s
ACC		k-o	k-o	t-o
GEN		k-ā	k-ā	t-ā
DAT		k-am	k-am	t-am
LOC				ta-jā

The familiar sequences in (48a) and (48b) form the vertical and the horizontal paradigm; their combination in (49) incorporates both paradigms into one complex morphological system.

All we need to do to derive case-marked forms of Dem, Wh, Rel, and Comp (if applicable) is to accommodate the basic premise that the fseqs in (48a) and (48b) can appear as subsets.[17] For instance, the Dem$_{indef}$ subset of (48b) can be directly extended by K_1, K_2, etc. when features forming Wh, Rel, Comp are not selected as in the formation of case-inflected demonstratives. However, when these features are selected, they must be strictly ordered with respect to the other features within the same fseq (on top of Dem$_{indef}$) and with respect to the case fseq (below K_1).

---

[17] Different classes of ordered features (fseqs) that form a singleton projection line are informally referred to as "fseq zones" in Taraldsen Medová & Wiland (2018a,b).

Let us point out that the fact that *co* in Table 5.12 forms a syncretic triplet targeting adjacent horizontal and vertical cells is expected in two-dimensional paradigms (see Taraldsen 2012 and Caha & Pantcheva 2012). The paradigms covered in Taraldsen (2012) and Caha & Pantcheva (2012) include morphologically simplex forms while the ones discussed here include multi-morphemic forms. More specifically, Taraldsen (2012) discusses abstract exponents organized into feature sets and Caha & Pantcheva (2012) discuss syncretisms between monomorphemic dative, allative, and locative markers. However, if the hypothesis advanced here that paradigms can be described as a singleton fseq is on the right track, then there is no reason to differentiate between two-dimensional paradigms on the basis of the number of morphemes they involve since multimorphemic forms are solely a result of the segregation of a single projection line in the syntactic representation into multiple subtrees at spell-out. While such a system allows for the accommodation of case features with different stems, we are not able to rule out (partial or complete) caselessness of certain forms in the paradigm (e.g. the Polish invariant Rel *co*), an explanation for which must come from elsewhere, as suggested for the Latvian caseless *ka* above.

The representation of two-dimensional paradigms as a sequence of syntactic heads, a de facto one-dimensional space, leads to the conjecture that any *n*-dimensional paradigm can be represented as a homeomorphic fseq. This conjecture can be illustrated for a three-dimensional paradigm that includes the three Latvian wh-pronouns, the syncretic *kas* 'what'/'who' and *kur* 'where', that form a backward coordinate (the aisle) in the paradigm in (50).

(50)

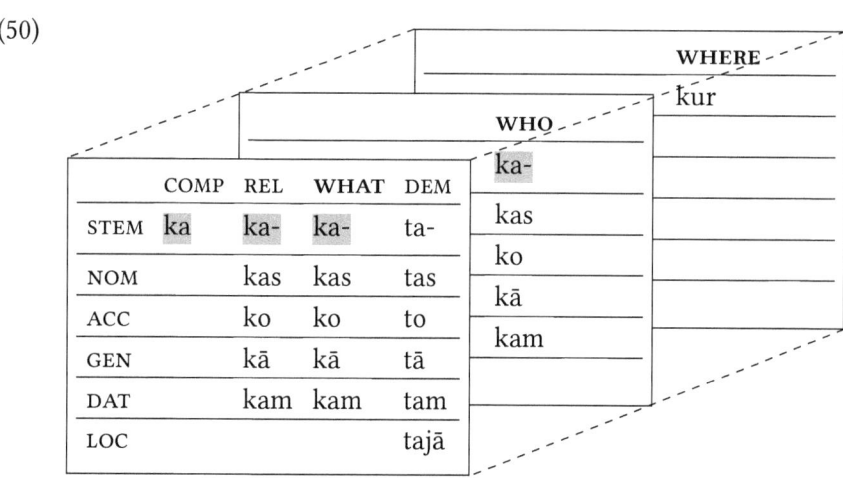

Only one of these wh-pronouns, *kas* 'what', is a cell in the cross-categorial paradigm (the horizontal coordinate) and both 'what' and 'who' are inflected for case (the vertical coordinate). The values of the vertical coordinate in (50) are described by the case fseq in (48a), the values of the horizontal coordinate by (48b), and the values of the backward aisle by a decomposition of the (pro)nominal base in (7), the subset of the wh-pronouns, repeated below.

(51)   Place > Person > Thing

The ordering of the refined (pro)nominal base with respect to the other fseqs gives us the updated singleton sequence, as in the following:

(52)   ... > K_3P > K_2P > K_1P > Comp > Rel > Wh > Dem_{indef} > Place > Person > Thing

If the *ABA generalization follows from the Superset Principle that applies to an ordered fseq, then we correctly expect syncretism to be restricted to adjacent cells in n-dimensional paradigms, a result described independently for two-dimensional paradigms earlier in Caha & Pantcheva (2012) and Vanden Wyngaerd (2018b). In (50) we observe the syncretic span restricted to adjacent cells of the horizontal and the backward coordinates that includes the 'what'-cell at their juncture.

With the decomposition of Dem_{indef} into "Dist > Med > Prox", we are able to further refine the singleton sequence of projections as in:

(53)   ... > K_3P > K_2P > K_1P > Comp > Rel > Wh > Dist > Med > Prox > Place > Person > Thing

With this refinement in place, the distinction between the Latvian proximal *šis* and the medial/distal *tas* belongs to the third coordinate in the paradigm (the forward aisle), as in (54).

The representation of the Prox *šis* as a cell forming the third coordinate reflects the fact that both Prox *šis* and Med/Dist *tas* are case inflected but only the latter is a cell in the cross-categorical paradigm with Comp, Rel, and Wh. Such an ordering also captures the observation we can make on the basis of the data discussed so far, namely that proximal demonstratives by and large do not belong to the "Dem_{def} > Comp > Rel > Wh > Dem_{indef}" sequence, the statement which appears to hold both for languages with "high" Dem_{def} (e.g. English *that - what* or Spanish *aquél - qué*) and the "low" Dem_{indef} (e.g. Russian *to - čto* or Polish *to - co*). Though, more typological work is required before this can be turned into a generalization.

(54)

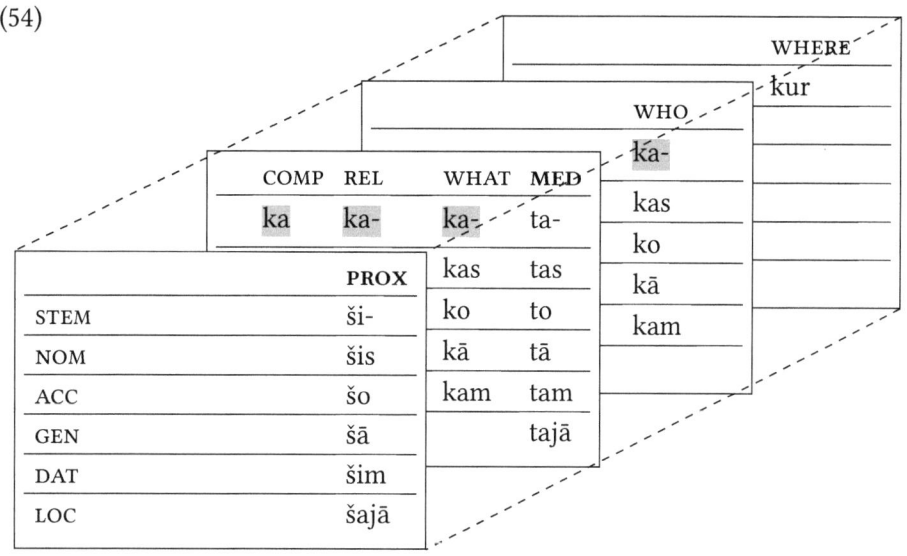

5.9 Summary

The inclusion of the indefinite demonstrative pronoun as the bottom category in an fseq which covers syncretisms with the declarative complementizer allowed us to explain morphological containment and syncretic alignment in such a paradigm in Slavic. The same holds true for Latvian, too, which enabled us to describe the paradigm with the Comp *ka*, the only suffixless item in the fseq in (55), as a caseless category in a sequence where case marking is delimited by Rel.

(55)   Comp > Rel > Wh > Dem$_{indef}$

Such a result follows naturally from the representation of these morphologically complex categories as a singleton sequence of syntactic projections, whose segregation into more complex subtrees is exclusively an effect of the spell-out procedure, not of the complexity of an underlying syntactic representation. One consequence of that approach is a possibility to describe multi-dimensional paradigms as a single homeomorphic sequence of syntactic projections, a conjecture shown to hold for a three-dimensional paradigm in Latvian.

6 An apparent *ABA violation in Basaá

6.1 Introduction: an ABA paradigm

The inclusion of Dem$_{indef}$ as the bottom of the hierarchy in (1) proposed in Chapter 4 constitutes an essential ingredient of sorting out what appears to be an ABA pattern of syncretism in Basaá (Bantu, A.43).

(1)   Dem$_{def}$ > Comp > Rel > Wh > Dem$_{indef}$ (reiterated)

Namely, as shown in Table 6.1, the Basaá paradigm shows a Dem=Rel syncretism to the exclusion of Comp.

Table 6.1: Basaá

DEM	COMP	REL	WH
nú	∅, lé	nú, lé	kíí

The arrangement of the cells in the Basaá paradigm in the same way as in the Germanic languages, as for instance in English, Dutch, German or Swiss German in Table 6.2 (partially repeated from §4.2.1), results in the violation of the *ABA generalization.

Table 6.2: Germanic

	DEM	COMP	REL	WH
English	that	that	that	what
Dutch	dat	dat	dat	wat
German	das	dass	das	was
Swiss German	das	dass	∅	was

6 An apparent *ABA violation in Basaá

The description of the Swiss German relative pronoun as the phonologically null marker in Table 6.2 requires qualification, which shows a direction toward working out a solution for the refractory Basaá paradigm in Table 6.1.

6.1.1 Excursus on the Rel-cell in Swiss German

In Swiss German, an invariant particle *wo* introduces both locative relatives, as in (2a), and headed relative clauses, as in (2b). It is syncretic with the locative 'where'.

(2) Swiss German (van Riemsdijk 2003: ex. 42a,b)
    a.   s   huss wo de Hans wont
        the house wo the Hans lives
        'the house where Hans lives'
    b.   s   fäscht wo i ghöört han das de Hans anegaat
        the party wo I heard have that the Hans to.goes
        'the party that I have heard Hans is going to'

However, van Riemsdijk (1989, 2003) shows that *wo* is not a genuine relativizer despite the fact that headed relatives in Swiss German are never preceded by a distinct relative pronoun. We can see this, among others, when we compare Swiss German with certain other Upper German dialects where *wo* either can or must be preceded by a relative *d*-pronoun (see also Salzmann 2006 and Brandner & Bräuning 2013). This is shown in the following examples contrasting Bavarian with Swiss German (more precisely, the Züritüütsch dialect):

(3) Bavarian (Bayer 1984: 216)
    I   schenk 's dem   Kind (des) wo mid da Katz spuid.
    I   give it the.DAT child REL wo with the cat plays
    'I give it to the child that plays with the cat.'

(4) Swiss German - Züritüütsch (van Riemsdijk 2003: 4)
    I   schänk 's em   chind (*das) wo mit de chatz spilt.
    I   give it the.DAT child REL wo with the cat plays
    'I give it to the child that is playing with the cat.'

The *d*-pronoun strongly appears to qualify as a genuine relativizer (in the sense that it belongs to the cross-categorial paradigm with the declarative Comp).

The contrast illustrated above, however, begs a question why *wo*-relatives come with a relative pronoun in dialects like Bavarian but not in Swiss German.

There is more than one possibility, including an analysis advanced in Penner & Bader (1995) where it is argued on the basis of the Bernese dialect of Swiss German that the relative pronoun is a silent *pro*. Also, an interesting insight about *wo*-relatives in the Züritüütsch dialect is offered in van Riemsdijk (2003), who argues that they are similar to the so-called aboutness 'such that' relatives, which are found in Japanese (Kuno 1973: 257) and also in English (Grosu 2002: 157), as in *A mathematical system such that two and two are four is Peano arithmetic*. If on the right track, this account further speaks against classifying *wo* as a relative pronoun.

While working out the right analysis of the *wo*-relatives is a task of its own, what is important for the purposes of the data classification is that *wo* is not a relative pronoun on par with *das* and must therefore be kept separate from the paradigm in Table 6.2 in a similar way verbal complementizers are kept separate form the paradigm with the nominal complementizer (as for instance in Yoruba or Hausa as seen in (2–4) in §4.2.1).

The point of this observation is that while describing the Swiss German relative pronoun either as ∅ or *wo* does not have consequences for syncretic alignment as neither form shows syncretism with the remaining three categories in Table 6.2, the examination of the syntax behind the Dem-cell in Basaá is going to inform us about the solution to the *ABA problem.

6.1.2 Back to the Basaá paradigm

Perhaps an immediate attempt to resolve the *ABA violation in Table 6.1 is to assume that since the complementizer that appears to disrupt the syncretic span between Dem and Rel is phonologically null, then the Comp layer is not projected in Basaá at all. Such an explanation is challenged by the fact that a dialect of Basaá does have an overt form of the declarative complementizer *lέ*, as shown in:

(5)   Basaá (Bassong 2010: ex. 30a in §3)

     mɛ ŋ́-kâl   lέ   Tonye a ŋ́-kŋ́   yààní
     I   PRES-say COMP Tomye SM PRES-go tomorrow
     'I say that Tonye will go tomorrow.'

This variant of the complementizer is syncretic with the relativizer, as in shown in the following:

(6)   Basaá (Bassong 2010: ex. 22b in §4)

     ɓaúdú   ɓá gwě malĕt lέ a ŋ́-kâl   ɓɔ́   mam
     students SM have teacher REL SM PRES-tell them things
     'The students have a teacher that tells them stories.'

6 An apparent *ABA violation in Basaá

According to Bassong, the relativizer *lé* is indeclinable and its distribution in relative clauses is more restricted than in the case of *nú*. An intuitive option would be, thus, to further assume that Comp is a layer of structure that can be skipped – but only on top of the paradigm with the Rel *nú* and not on top of the paradigm with the Rel *lé*. The liaison of these two assumptions, however, is unnecessary if the Basaá demonstratives are indefinite since, as argued earlier, only definite demonstratives of the type found in Germanic languages are the categories that are structurally bigger than declarative complementizers and relativizers.

In what follows, I consider a wholesale different approach to resolving the *ABA problem in Basaá, the one which relies on inspecting the syntax of the categories behind the Dem and Rel cells in the offending paradigm in Table 6.1.

6.2 Basaá demonstratives

The first step toward resolving this problem involves contrasting the demonstrative *nú* with the Germanic demonstratives and classifying it as the smallest rather than the biggest category in the "Dem_{def} > Comp > Rel > Wh > Dem_{indef}" sequence. The classification of the demonstrative *nú* as indefinite, however, requires qualification since Basaá does have morphological marking of specificity.

Let us consider the following. Basaá demonstratives show noun class concord with the noun they apply to. The demonstratives are morphologically distinguished between the proximal (close to speaker), the medial (close to hearer), and the distal (far from speaker and hearer), as shown on the example of class 1 *nú* and class 5 *lí* below (examples 7–9) are from Makasso 2010).[1]

(7) a. { líní / lí / líí } liwándá
      5.PROX 5.MED 5.DIST 5.friend
      'this/that friend'
   b. { núnú / nú / núú } mut
      1.PROX 1.MED 1.DIST 1.person
      'this/that person'

In Basaá, the demonstratives can appear before or after the nouns they modify. Pre-nominal demonstratives receive a focus interprctation, while a noun that is post-modified by a demonstrative is unmarked with respect to information structure (non-focus) and it is obligatorily prefixed with the augment *í-*, which marks definiteness/specificity (Jenks et al. 2017), as shown in the following:

---

[1] See Hyman (2003) for an exhaustive list of demonstratives of all nominal classes in Basaá.

(8) a. í-mut₁   nú
       AUG-1.person 1.that.DEM
       'that person'
    b. nú   mut
       1.that.DEM 1.person
       'THAT person'

This description holds for all classes of demonstratives and for all values of the proximal-medial-distal contrast:

(9) a. { líní   / lí   / líí }   liwándá
       5.PROX 5.MED 5.DIST 5.friend
       'this/that friend'
    b. lí↓-wándá   { líní   / lí   / líí }
       AUG.-5.friend 5.PROX 5.MED 5.DIST
       'this/that friend'

Since these demonstratives do not have definiteness morphology, we can classify them as indefinite on par with Russian, Polish, Czech, and Latvian demonstratives. What sets the Basaá demonstratives apart from the latter is that, descriptively speaking, the first participate in contextual licensing of an augment prefix on the noun they modify, but other than that there is no trace of the Def ingredient in their structure that qualifies them as the biggest category in the sequence in (1).

However, the fact that we are able to accommodate indefinite demonstratives as the smallest category in this sequence, which results in the reordering of the cells as in Table 6.3, does not resolve the *ABA problem but merely pushes it to a different place of the paradigm where the non-syncretic Wh is now sandwiched between the syncretic forms for Rel and Dem$_{indef}$.

Table 6.3: Reordered paradigm in Basaá

DEM$_{def}$	COMP	REL	WH	DEM$_{indef}$
	∅, lέ	nú, lέ	kíí	nú

6.3 Non-wh-relatives in Basaá

The key to resolving this problem is the observation that a similar distribution between the augment *í*-prefix on the head noun and a demonstrative pronoun we see in (8–9) holds in headed relative clauses, too, with the one essential difference: the augment *í*-prefix is optional in relative clauses.

In both subject and object relative clauses in Basaá, the medial demonstrative pronoun is the one which shows syncretism with the relative pronoun. This is shown below on the example of class 1 medial *nú*.

(10) Makasso (2010: 153–4)
    a. mɛ ŋ́ gwɛ́s mût$_i$ (nú) [_$_i$ a yé mbóm]
        I PRES like 1.person 1.REL 1.SBJ COP 9.big
        'I like a person that is big/important.'
    b. mɛ ń yéŋ mááŋgɛ́$_i$ (nú) [mɛ ń yí _$_i$]
        1SG PRES seek 1.child 1.REL 1SG PR know
        'I'm looking at the child that I know.'

As pointed out in Makasso (2010), while the augment *í*- is obligatory on nouns post-modified by demonstratives, it is optional on nouns that are heads of relative clauses, as shown in (11), in which case the noun phrase is interpreted as indefinite.

(11) a. (í)-mut$_i$ nú [_$_i$ a bí ↓jɛ́ bíjɛ́k]
       AUG-1.person 1.REL 1.SBJ PST eat 8.food
       'that person that ate the food'
    b. nú (*í)-mut$_i$ [_$_i$ a bí ↓jɛ́ bíjɛ́k]
       1.that AUG-1.person 1.SBJ PST eat 8.food
       'THAT person that ate the food'

A two-step analysis of relativization in Basaá which covers these facts is put forward in Jenks et al. (2017), whose central ingredient of the solution the *ABA problem involves the derivation of the pre-nominal placement of the demonstrative in the noun phrase from its post-nominal placement, as outlined in (12).

(12) [$_{DP}$ nú$_{Dem}$ (*í-) [$_{NP}$ mut] t]

Such a derivation captures the complementary distribution between the augment marker *í*- and the pre-nominal demonstrative in terms of blocking. Specifically, in

Jenks et al.'s (2017) account this instantiates a "generalized Doubly-filled Comp Filter" (DFCF), whereby either a head or its specifier can be lexically realized. For (12) it means that *í-* in the D-head position cannot be lexicalized when the demonstrative moves to its specifier from a post-nominal position. The analysis advanced here does not depend on the explanation based on a generalized DFCF, instead, it is enough for us to observe that the fronting of Dem blocks the merger of the augment marker.

The other ingredient of Jenks et al.'s (2017) account involves the derivation of relative clauses in Basaá via head raising in the way advanced in Kayne (1994). Let us note that such an approach to the relative clause formation is in agreement with what has been argued for other Bantu languages (see e.g. Ngonyani 2001 and Carstens 2005).

In Kayne's (1994) analysis, the head nouns are merged as specifiers of the relative clause, which can be selected by the D-head. This gives us the following result for the derivation of headed relative clauses (labelled as RelP in the derivations below) with the pre-nominal demonstrative in Basaá.

(13) Derivation of a relative clause with a post-nominal demonstrative following Jenks et al. (2017: 34)

    a. í-mut$_i$ nú [_$_i$ a bí ↓jɛ́ bíjɛ́k]
        AUG-1.person 1.REL   1.SBJ PST eat 8.food
        'that person that ate the food'

    b.

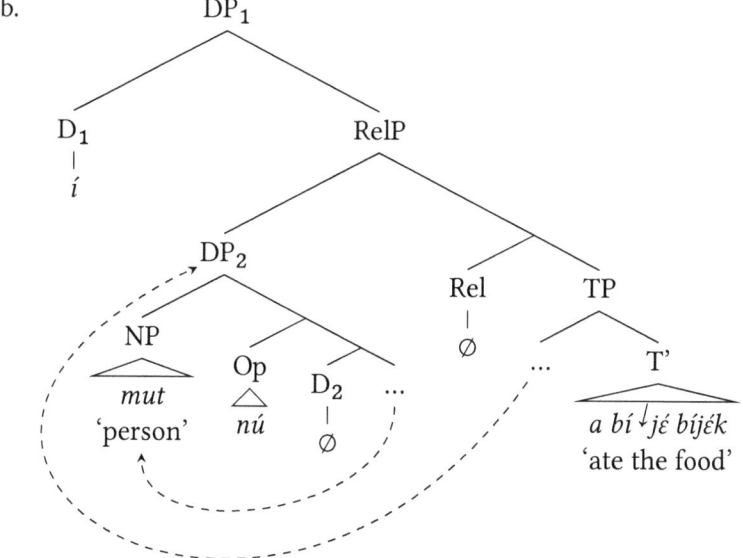

In the first step of this derivation, the noun phrase *mut* 'person' is fronted to a position before the demonstrative *nú* in its own DP$_2$ (described as the "Op(erator)" position in Jenks et al. 2017).[2] In the second step, the entire DP$_2$ is fronted to the specifier of RelP. The augment marker *í-* spells out the top selecting head D$_1$ and comes out as the prefix on the head noun *mut*.

In Jenks et al.'s (2017) account, the post-nominal "operator" position of the demonstrative does not receive a focus reading when the DP$_2$ is in the specifier of the relative clause. In contrast, in the derivation of relative clauses with a pre-nominal *nú*, the *nú* is a genuine demonstrative rather than the "operator". In this case, the entire relative DP$_2$ is raised out of RelP to a higher position where the demonstrative *nú* receives a focus reading, as outlined in (14).

(14) Derivation of a relative clause with a pre-nominal demonstrative following Jenks et al. (2017: 35)

a. nú   mut$_i$ [_$_i$ a   bí ↓jɛ́ bíjɛ́k]
    1.that 1.person 1.SBJ PST eat 8.food
    'THAT person that ate the food'

b.

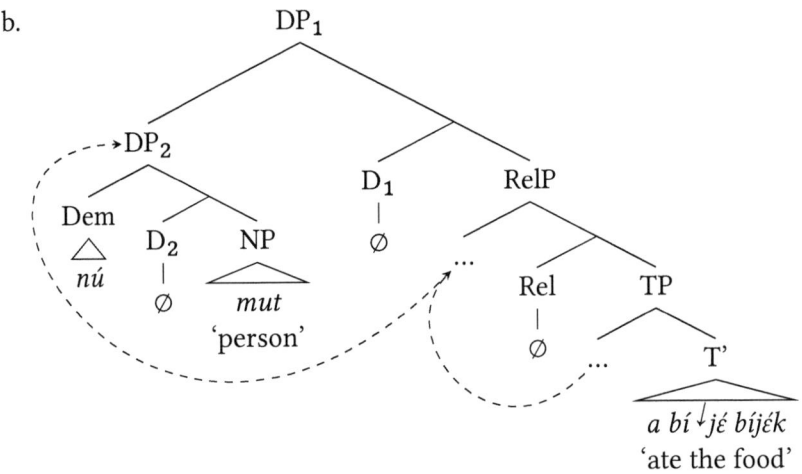

A particularly telling argument in support of such an analysis is that it accounts for the complementary distribution between demonstratives and what (appears

---

[2]Jenks et al. (2017) follow Kayne (1994) in labelling the relative clauses simply as CP. RelP is used instead in the diagrams below in order to disambiguate the head of the relative clause, Rel, with the head of the clause headed by a complementizer, Comp, as these are structurally distinct categories in the strand of research we explore in the present work. This is a technical remark with no consequences for the constituent structure of relative clauses or for the essence of Jenks et al.'s (2017) analysis.

to be) a separate relativizer in all types relative clauses involving a gap. The relative clauses involving a gap are subject and object relatives with pre- and postnominal demonstratives. These are shown in the following:

(15) í-maaŋgɛ́ᵢ nú (*nú) [mɛ ń yí _ᵢ]
AUG-1.child 1.DEM 1.REL 1SG PRES know
'this/that child that I know'

(16) lí lí-wándáᵢ (*lí↓) [_ᵢ lí bí ↓jɛ́ bíjɛ́k]
5.DEM 5-friend 5.REL 5.SBJ PST eat food
'THAT friend that ate the food'

Such a complementary distribution of the medial demonstrative pronoun and the relativizer in relative clauses involving a gap shows that the relation between these two categories in Basaá is robust and hence the problematic Dem=Rel syncretism to the exclusion of Wh cannot be attributed to an accidental homophony.

If we follow Jenks et al.'s (2017) analysis of the formation of non-wh-relatives in Basaá, we can directly resolve the *ABA problem present in Table 6.3. The juxtaposition of the syntax of non-wh-relatives in Basaá with the syntax of non-wh-relatives in languages like English reveals that the second involves a genuine relativizer, which does not form a constituent with the head noun, as outlined by the following example:

(17) a. the person that found our cat
b.

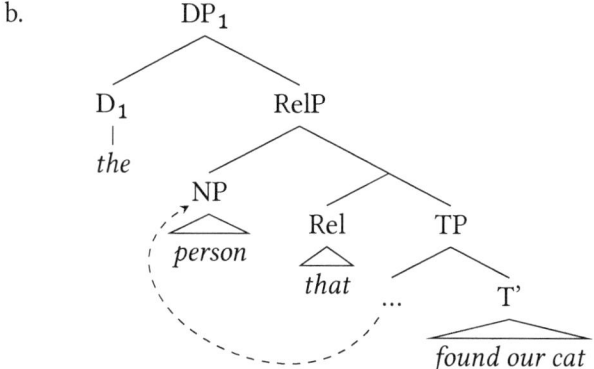

This contrasts with the Basaá *nú*, which comes out as a genuine demonstrative pronoun, which forms a constituent with the head noun. In turn, the relativizer, understood as the head of the relative clause, is null. This result requires the problematic paradigm in Basaá to be rewritten as in Table 6.4, which removes the

6 An apparent *ABA violation in Basaá

*ABA violation with the demonstrative and keeps the syncretic span Comp=Rel in the parallel paradigm with *lέ*.

Table 6.4: Final version of the Basaá paradigm

DEM$_{def}$	COMP	REL	WH	DEM$_{indef}$
Ø, lέ	Ø, lέ		kíí	nú

The reanalysis of the paradigm with a zero relativizer allows us to correctly predict that it will be able to cooccur with elements other than the demonstrative – class 1 *nú* or any other – in the D head of the relative clause. For instance, treating the English *that* as a relativizer, the head of the relative clause does not need a demonstrative, as in:

(18) John saw { three men/somebody } that Mary had fired.

Indeed, as already indicated in the example of a relative clause with a postnominal demonstrative in (13a), the null relativizer can cooccur with the D head of the relative clause that is lexicalized as the *í-* prefix. More generally, as already seen in (10), *nú* can be generally dropped in both subject and object relative clauses. This optionality holds also with other nominal classes as shown in the following example from Jenks et al. (2017: 18):

(19) hínuní$_i$ (hí) [liwándá lí   bí ↓téhĕ $_{\_i}$]
      AUG.19.bird DEM 5.friend 5.SBJ PST see
      'the bird that the friend saw'

6.4 Resumptive relative clauses

A final comment about the Basaá relative clauses involving resumption is in order. Resumptive relative clauses provide a circumstantial argument that supports both the idea that relativizers in Basaá are genuine demonstratives as well as the conjecture made earlier on the basis of Slavic, Germanic, and Latvian that it is specifically the medial demonstratives that serve as the base category in the sequence in (1).[3]

---

[3]The argument is circumstantial in the sense that it depends on a particular analysis of the formation of relative clauses that involve resumption (see for instance Bianchi 2004; 2011 or Salzmann 2017: chapters 2–3).

Namely, the complementarity between the demonstrative pronoun and (what appears to be a distinct) relativizer is more limited with relative clauses that involve resumption. In this environment, it is only the medial demonstrative that cannot co-occur with the relativizer, while the non-syncretic proximal and distal demonstratives can co-occur with the relativizer, as shown in the example of object of comparison relative clauses in (20).

(20) Resumptive (object of comparison) relative clause (Jenks et al. 2017: 27)
    a. í-maaŋgɛ́ᵢ { núnú / *nú / núú } (nú) [ŋgwɔ́ i ye ikɛ́ɲí
        AUG-1.child 1.PROX 1.MED 1.DIST 1.REL 9.dog 9.SBJ be 9.big
        ilɛ́l ŋyɛ́ᵢ]
        exceed 1.PRON
    b. { núnú / *nú / núú } maaŋgɛ́ᵢ (nú) [ŋgwɔ́ i ye ikɛ́ɲí
        1.PROX 1.MED 1.DIST 1.child 1.REL 9.dog 9.SBJ be 9.big
        ilɛ́l ŋyɛ́ᵢ]
        exceed 1.PRON
        'this/that child that the dog is bigger than'

This restriction is hard to account for if the relativizer is not a genuine demonstrative pronoun in the Basaá relative clauses given that it must show class concord with the head noun, unlike the genuine relativizer *lɛ́*, as shown in (6).

6.5 Summary

The resolution of what comes out as an apparent ABA pattern in the Basaá paradigm is possible if we inspect the syntax behind the offending Rel-cell, in a similar way the description of *wo*-relatives in Swiss German indicates that *wo* is not on a par with relative pronouns like the German *das* or the English *that*. Specifically, if we follow the analysis of non-wh-relative clauses in Basaá in Jenks et al. (2017), the offending relative pronoun turns out to be a genuine DP-internal demonstrative that is placed after the head noun. We end up with a picture where overt realization of the cross-categorial paradigm is restricted in Basaá to its two adjacent cells, in agreement with the *ABA generalization and the proposal to insert indefinite demonstratives as the bottom category of the "Dem_{def} > Comp > Rel > Wh > Dem_{indef}" sequence.

7 Overview

7.1 Summary

In the broad sense, I have investigated the nature of the relation between the lexical (linear) and the syntactic (hierarchical) structure in an approach to grammatical representations that keeps up with ongoing work on structuralization of the semantics of lexical items. The results discussed here contribute to the picture that has been getting clearer and clearer for over ten years now which shows that the three descriptive domains – morphology, lexical semantics, and syntax – form a single module of grammar as they operate on the same class of features, like [person], [place], [proximal], [definite], etc.

Such a scenario has two immediate consequences for our understanding of the interface between syntax and the lexicon. One is that morphological structures come out as linear realizations of syn-sem representations which are seamless with respect to the grammatical features. In other words, a morpheme does not have any more or any fewer features than a syntactic tree it lexicalizes. The other one is that a lexicon of a language stores syntactic subtrees paired with their exponents (a view that implies that there is no such thing as a pre-syntactic lexical storage). Following the research program outlined in Starke (2009; 2014a), both these consequences have been discussed for a few empirical domains in recent years and, in the broad sense, this contribution merely adds up to the growing body of work produced in a similar vein.

In the narrow sense, I have investigated a spell-out procedure whereby an ordered set of grammatical operations facilitates the lexicalization of syntactic structures in a way that allows us to predict exactly (i) how many morphemes a given sequence of syntactic heads is going to be realized by and (ii) what positions these morphemes are going to take ("pre-" vs. "post-" placement). Specifically, I have examined an alternation in the domain of Slavic verbs which exhibits a reduction in the number of affixes on the root and considered prospects to derive this reduction by adding subextraction to the existing list of spell-out driven movements, an option that I compared to deriving the reduction with backtracking.

7 *Overview*

Next, I have argued that we can resolve a morphological containment problem found in certain Slavic paradigms that cover syncretisms with declarative complementizers by, on the one hand, extending the sequence of syntactic heads and, on the other, by simplifying its underlying geometry to a singleton projection line. In other words, in order to be able to derive the attested patterns of morphological containment and syncretisms that conform to the *ABA generalization, polymorphemic structures must be represented as singleton syntactic projection lines whose partition into more geometrically complex trees is exclusively a result of the application of the spell-out algorithm. This rules out any syntactic representation of morphological forms as underlying geometrically complex tree structures beyond the single projection line.

Such a description of polymorphemic forms effectively allows us to represent two- and three-dimensional morphological paradigms as a de facto one-dimensional space, a sequence of syntactic projections. This reduction makes correct predictions about syncretic alignment of morphemes forming subclasses of pronominal categories in Latvian.

7.2 Loose ends

Despite these results, there are at least two significant gaps in the analyses considered here that remain to be closed in future work.

The first one concerns spell-out driven subextraction. The inclusion of subextraction in the list of spell-out driven movements can in principle reduce the amount of affixes observed in an alternation. However, it remains to be figured out if the so-called deep extractions are also permissible operations in the spell-out procedure. Likewise, the material discussed here does not reveal how subextraction should be ordered with respect to successive-cyclic movement and complement movement in the algorithm. That is, it remains unclear if attempting spell-out by moving the smallest possible piece of structure is ordered before or after attempting spell-out by moving the node that has been formed at the previous cycle. The first option suggests that subextraction is the first option in the algorithm, the second one suggests the opposite.

The other missing piece concerns the representation of multi-dimensional morphological paradigms as singleton projection lines in syntax. In an approach that adopts the Superset Principle defined as in (8) in Chapter 2, Caha & Pantcheva (2012) explored the representation of two-dimensional paradigms based on monomorphemic forms as singleton sequences of heads. In this work, this hypothesis has been illustrated to hold also for polymorphemic forms that form two- and three-dimensional paradigms in Latvian. However, its extension to any n-dimensional paradigms remains only a conjecture at this point.

References

Abels, Klaus. 2007. Towards a restrictive theory of (remnant) movement. *Linguistic Variation Yearbook* 7. 53–120. DOI:10.1075/livy.7.04abe

Acedo Matellán, Víctor. 2010. *Argument structure and the syntax-morphology interface. A case study in Latin and other languages.* University of Barcelona dissertation. http://ling.auf.net/lingbuzz/001242.

Acquaviva, Paolo, Alessandro Lenci, Carita Paradis & Ida Raffaelli. to appear. Models of lexical meaning. In Vito Pirrelli, Ingo Plag & Wolfgang U. Dressler (eds.), *Word knowledge and word usage: A cross-disciplinary guide to the mental lexicon.* Berlin/New York: Mouton de Gruyter.

Bach, Emmon. 1986. The algebra of events. *Linguistics and Philosophy* 9. 5–16. DOI:10.1007/BF00627432

Bacz, Barbara. 2012. Reflections on semelfactivity in Polish. *Studies in Polish Linguistics* 7(1). 107–128. http://www.ejournals.eu/SPL/2012/SPL-vol-7-2012/art/1163/.

Baerman, Matthew, Dunstan Brown & Greville Corbett. 2005. *The syntax-morphology interface: A study of syncretism.* Cambridge, UK: Cambridge University Press.

Bassong, Paul. 2010. *The structure of the left periphery in Basaá.* University of Yaounde I MA thesis. http://ling.auf.net/lingbuzz/001692.

Baunaz, Lena & Eric Lander. 2017. Syncretisms with the nominal complementizer. *Studia Linguistica* 72(3). 537–570. DOI:10.1111/stul.12076

Baunaz, Lena & Eric Lander. 2018a. Cross-categorial syncretism and the Slavic containment puzzle. In Brian Joseph & Iliyana Krapova (eds.), *Balkan Syntax and (Universal) principles of Grammar*, 218–246. Berlin: Mouton de Gruyter.

Baunaz, Lena & Eric Lander. 2018b. Deconstructing categories syncretic with the nominal complementizer. *Glossa: a journal of general linguistics* 3 (1). 31. DOI:10.5334/gjgl.349

Baunaz, Lena & Eric Lander. 2018c. The internal structure of ontological categories. In Pavel Caha, Karen De Clercq & Guido Vanden Wyngaerd (eds.), *The unpublished manuscript. A collection of LingBuzz papers to celebrate Michal Starke's 50th birthday*, 1–18. http://ling.auf.net/lingbuzz/003993.

References

Bayer, Josef. 1984. Comp in Bavarian syntax. *The Linguistic Review* 3(3). 209–274. DOI:10.1515/tlir.1984.3.3.209

Beavers, John. 2008. Scalar complexity and the structure of events. In Johannes Dölling, Tatjana Heyde-Zybatow & Martin Schäfer (eds.), *Event structures in linguistic form and interpretation*, 245–265. Berlin: Mouton de Gruyter.

Bernstein, Judy. 1997. Demonstratives and reinforcers. *Lingua* 102(2–3). 87–113. DOI:10.1016/S0024-3841(96)00046-0

Bianchi, Valentina. 2004. Resumptive relatives and LF chains. In Luigi Rizzi (ed.), *The structure of CP and IP*, 76–114. New York: Oxford University Press.

Bianchi, Valentina. 2011. Some notes on the 'specificity effects' of optional resumptive pronouns. In Alain Rouveret (ed.), *Resumptive pronouns at the interfaces*, 319–342. Amsterdam: John Benjamins.

Blevins, James. 2008. Declension classes in Estonian. *Linguistica Uralica* 44(4). 241–267. DOI:10.3176/lu.2008.4.01

Bobaljik, Jonathan. 2007. On comparative suppletion. http://ling.auf.net/lingbuzz/000443.

Bobaljik, Jonathan. 2012. *Universals in comparative morphology*. Cambridge, MA: MIT Press.

Bobaljik, Jonathan. 2017. Distributed Morphology. In Mark Aronoff (ed.), *Oxford research encyclopedia of linguistics*. Oxford University Press.

Boeckx, Cedric. 2008. *Bare syntax*. Oxford: Oxford University Press.

Boeckx, Cedric & Kleanthes Grohmann. 2007. Putting phases in perspective. *Syntax* 10(2). 204–222. DOI:10.1111/j.1467-9612.2007.00098.x

Booij, Gert. 2002. Constructional idioms, morphology, and the Dutch lexicon. *Journal of Germanic Linguistics* 14(4). 301–329. DOI:10.1017/S1470542702000168

Borer, Hagit. 2003. Exo-skeletal and endo-skeletal explanations: Syntactic projections and the lexicon. In John Moore & Maria Polinsky (eds.), *The nature of explanation in linguistic theory*, 31–67. Stanford, CA: CSLI Publications.

Borer, Hagit. 2005. *The normal course of events. Structuring sense vol. II*. Oxford: Oxford University Press.

Borgman, Donald. 1990. Sanuma. In Desmond C. Derbyshire & Geoffrey K. Pullum (eds.), *Handbook of Amazonian languages*, vol. 2, 15–248. Berlin: Mouton de Gruyter.

Botwinik-Rotem, Irena & Arhonto Terzi. 2008. Greek and Hebrew locative prepositional phrases: A unified case-driven account. *Lingua* 118(3). 399–424. DOI:10.1016/j.lingua.2007.08.001

Brandner, Ellen & Iris Bräuning. 2013. Relative *wo* in Alemannic: Only a complementizer? *Linguistische Berichte* 234. 131–169.

Browning, M.A. 1991. Bounding conditions on representations. *Linguistic Inquiry* 22(3). 541–562.

Budina Lazdina, Tereza. 1966. *Teach yourself Latvian*. London: The English Universities Press.

Burzio, Luigi. 2007. Phonologically conditioned syncretism. In Fabio Montermini, Gilles Boyé & Nabil Hathout (eds.), *Selected papers of the 5th décembrettes: morphology in Toulouse*, 1–19. Sommerville, MA: Cascadilla.

Caha, Pavel. 2009. *The nanosyntax of case*. CASTL/University of Tromsø dissertation.

Caha, Pavel. 2011a. Case in adpositional phrases. Manuscript, http://ling.auf.net/lingbuzz/001325.

Caha, Pavel. 2011b. The parameters of case marking and spell out driven movement. *Linguistic Variation Yearbook* 10. 32–77.   DOI:10.1075/livy.10.02cah

Caha, Pavel. 2013. Explaining the structure of case paradigms by the mechanisms of Nanosyntax. The classical Armenian nominal declension. *Natural Language & Linguistic Theory* 31(4). 1015–1066.   DOI:10.1007/s11049-013-9206-8

Caha, Pavel. 2018. Notes on insertion in Distributed Morphology and Nanosyntax. In Lena Baunaz, Karen De Clercq, Liliane Haegeman & Eric Lander (eds.), *Exploring Nanosyntax*, 57–87. New York: Oxford University Press.

Caha, Pavel, Karen De Clercq & Guido Vanden Wyngaerd. 2019a. On the difference between a √ and a root. Manuscript, https://ling.auf.net/lingbuzz/004391.

Caha, Pavel, Karen De Clercq & Guido Vanden Wyngaerd. 2019b. The fine structure of the comparative. *Studia Linguistica*.   DOI:10.1111/stul.12107

Caha, Pavel & Marina Pantcheva. 2012. Datives cross-linguistically. Slides for the presentation at CASTL/University of Tromsø, October 23.

Caha, Pavel & Marina Pantcheva. 2016. Locatives in Shona and Luganda. Manuscript, http://ling.auf.net/lingbuzz/002220.

Caha, Pavel & Marketa Ziková. 2016. Vocalic alternations in Czech prefixes: Evidence for prefix movement. *Acta Linguistica Hungarica* 63(3). 331–377. DOI:10.1556/064.2016.63.3.3

Campbell, Lyle. 1985. *The Pipil language of El Salvador*. Berlin/New York: Mouton de Gruyter.

Cardinaletti, Anna & Michal Starke. 1999. The typology of structural deficiency: A case study of the three classes of pronouns. In Henk van Riemsdijk (ed.), *Clitics in the language of Europe*, 145–253. Berlin: Mouton de Gruyter. DOI:10.1515/9783110804010.145

Carlson, Greg. 2012. Generic and habitual aspect. In Robert Binnick (ed.), *The Oxford handbook of tense and aspect*, 828–851. Oxford: Oxford University Press.

References

Carstens, Vicki. 2005. Agree and EPP in Bantu. *Natural Language & Linguistic Theory* 23(2). 219–279. DOI:10.1007/s11049-004-0996-6

Cetnarowska, Bożena. 2002a. Adjectival past-participle formation as an unaccusativity diagnostic in English and in Polish. In Sabrina Bendjaballah, Wolfgang U. Dressler, Oskar E. Pfeiffer & Maria D. Voeikova (eds.), *Morphology 2000: Selected papers from the 9th Morphology Meeting, Vienna, 24–28 February 2000*, 59–72. Amsterdam: John Benjamins.

Cetnarowska, Bożena. 2002b. Unaccusativity mismatches and unaccusativity diagnostics from derivational morphology. In Paul Boucher (ed.), *Many morphologies*, 48–81. Somerville, MA: Cascadilla Press.

Chomsky, Noam. 1993. A minimalist program for linguistic theory. In Kenneth Hale & Samuel J. Keyser (eds.), *The view from Building 20: Essays in linguistics in honor of Sylvain Bromberger*, 1–52. Cambridge, MA: MIT Press.

Chomsky, Noam. 2000. Minimalist inquiries: The framework. In Roger Martin, David Michaels & Juan Uriagereka (eds.), *Step by step. Essays on minimalist syntax in honor of Howard Lasnik*, 89–155. Cambridge, MA: MIT Press.

Cinque, Guglielmo. 2010. Mapping spatial PPs: an introduction. In Guglielmo Cinque & Luigi Rizzi (eds.), *Mapping spatial PPs* (The cartography of syntactic structures 6), 3–25. Oxford: Oxford University Press.

Cinque, Guglielmo & Luigi Rizzi. 2008. The cartography of syntactic structures. *CISCL Working Papers, Studies in Linguistics* 2. 42–58.

Collins, Chris. 1994. Economy of derivation and the Generalized Proper Binding Condition. *Linguistic Inquiry* 25(1). 45–61.

Corver, Norber. 2017. Freezing effects. In Martin Everaert & Henk van Riemsdijk (eds.), *The Wiley Blackwell companion to syntax*, 2nd edition, chap. 28, 1–33. John Wiley & Sons. DOI:10.1002/9781118358733.wbsyncom055

Curnow, Timothy. 2006. La interrogación y la negación en Awa Pit. *Amerindia* 29/30. 219–234.

Cysouw, Michael. 2004. Interrogative words: An exercise in lexical typology. Handout for a talk at Bantu grammar: Description and theory workshop, ZAS Berlin, February 13.

Cysouw, Michael. 2005. The typology of content interrogatives. Handout for a talk at the 6th meeting of the Assiociation for Linguistic Typology, Padang, Indonesia.

Czaykowska-Higgins, Ewa. 1988. *Investigations into Polish morphology and phonology*. MIT dissertation.

De Clercq, Karen. 2013. *A unified syntax of negation*. University of Ghent dissertation.

De Clercq, Karen. 2018. Syncretisms and the morphosyntax of negation. In Lena Baunaz, Karen De Clercq, Liliane Haegeman & Eric Lander (eds.), *Exploring Nanosyntax*, 180–204. New York: Oxford University Press.

de Swart, Henriette. 1998. *Introduction to natural language semantics*. Stanford, CA: CSLI Publications.

Declerck, Renaat. 1979. Aspect and the bounded/unbounded (telic/atelic) distinction. *Linguistics* 17(9–10). 761–794. DOI:10.1515/ling.1979.17.9-10.761

den Dikken, Marcel. 2010. On the functional structure of directional and locative PPs. In Guglielmo Cinque & Luigi Rizzi (eds.), *Mapping spatial PPs* (The cartography of syntactic structures 6), 74–126. Oxford: Oxford University Press.

Dickey, Stephen. 2016. Lexical and grammatical aspect. In Nick Riemer (ed.), *Routledge handbook of semantics*, 338–353. London: Routledge.

Dickey, Stephen & Laura Janda. 2009. *Hohotnul, shitril:* The relationship between semelfactives formed with -nu- and s- in Russian. *Russian Linguistics* 33(3). 229–248. DOI:10.1007/s11185-009-9044-9

Dimmendaal, Gerrit J. 1989. Complementizers in Hausa. In Zygmunt Frajzyngier (ed.), *Current progress in Chadic linguistics: Proceedings of the International Symposium on Chadic Linguistics, Boulder, Colorado, 1-2 May 1987*, 87–110. Amsterdam/Philadelphia: John Benjamins.

DiSciullo, Anna Maria. 2005. *Asymmetry in morphology*. Cambridge, MA: MIT Press.

Dixon, R. M. W. & Alexandra Aikhenvald. 2006. *Complementation: A cross-linguistic typology*. Oxford: Oxford University Press.

Dol, Philomena. 1999. *A grammar of Maybrat: A language of the Bird's Head, Irian Jaya, Indonesia*. Leiden University dissertation.

Dowty, David. 1979. *Word meaning and Montague grammar*. Dordrecht: Kluwer.

Eckert, Rainer, Elvira-Julia Bukevičiute & Friedhelm Hinze. 1994. *Die baltischen Sprachen. Eine Einführung*. Lepzig/Berlin/München: Langenscheidt.

Egg, Markus. 2018. Semelfactives. *Oslo Studies in Language* 10(2). 65–81. https://www.journals.uio.no/index.php/osla.

Embick, David. 2015. *The morpheme: A theoretical introduction*. Boston/Berlin: Mouton de Gruyter.

Embick, David & Rolf Noyer. 2007. Distributed Morphology and the syntax–morphology interface. In Gillian Ramchand & Charles Reiss (eds.), *The Oxford handbook of linguistic interfaces*, 289–324. Oxford: Oxford University Press.

Fábregas, Antonio. 2007. An exhaustive lexicalisation account of directional complements. *Nordlyd* 34(2). 165–199. DOI:10.7557/12.110

Fanselow, Gisbert. 1987. *Konfigurationalität*. Tübingen: Narr.

References

Fennell, Trevor G. & Henry Gelsen. 1980. *A grammar of modern Latvian*. The Hague: Mouton.

Flier, Michael. 1972. On the source of derived imperfectives in Russian. In Dean S. Worth (ed.), *The Slavic word: Proceedings of the International Slavistic Colloquium at UCLA, September 11-16, 1970*, 236–253. The Hague: Mouton.

Friedman, Victor A. 1991. Romani nominal inflection: Cases or postpositions? In *Problemy opisu gramatycznego języków słowiańskich*. (Studia Gramatyczne 11), 57–63. Warszawa: Polish Academy of Sciences.

Goldberg, Adele. 1995. *Constructions: A construction grammar approach to argument structure*. Chicago: University of Chicago Press.

Goldberg, Adele. 2006. *Constructions at work: The nature of generalization in language*. Oxford: Oxford University Press.

Goldberg, Adele & Ray Jackendoff. 2004. The English resultative as a family of constructions. *Language* 80(3). 532–568.

Greenberg, Joseph H. 2000. *Indo-European and its closest relatives. The Euroasiatic language family*. Vol. 1: Grammar. Stanford: Stanford University Press.

Grewendorf, Günther. 1989. *Ergativity in German*. Dordrecht: Foris.

Grosu, Alexander. 2002. Strange relatives at the interface of two millennia. *GLOT International* 6. 145–167.

Grzegorczykowa, Renata. 1997. Nowe spojrzenie na kategorię aspektu w perspektywie semantyki kognitywnej. In Renata Grzegorczykowa & Zofia Zaron (eds.), *Semantyczna struktura słownictwa i wypowiedzi*, 25–38. Warsaw: Warsaw University Press.

Grzegorczykowa, Renata & Jadwiga Puzynina. 1979. *Słowotwórstwo współczesnego języka polskiego*. Warsaw: PWN.

Gussmann, Edmund. 1980. *Studies in abstract phonology*. Cambridge, MA: MIT Press.

Hale, Kenneth & Samuel J. Keyser. 1993. On argument structure and the lexical expression of syntactic relations. In Kenneth Hale & Samuel J. Keyser (eds.), *The view from Building 20. Essays in linguistics in honor of Sylvain Bromberger*, 53–108. Cambridge, MA: MIT Press.

Hale, Kenneth & Samuel J. Keyser. 2002. *Prolegomenon to a theory of argument structure*. Cambridge, MA: MIT Press.

Halle, Morris. 1963. O pravilax russkogo sprjaženija (predvaritel'noe soobščenie). In *American contributions to the Fifth International Congress of Slavicists, Sofia, 1963*, vol. 1, 113–132. The Hague: Mouton.

Halle, Morris. 1997. Distributed morphology: Impoverishment and fission. In Benjamin Bruening, Yoonjung Kang & Martha McGinnis (eds.), *Papers at the in-*

terface (MIT Working Papers in Linguistics 30), 425–449. Cambridge, MA: MITWPL.

Halle, Morris & Alec Marantz. 1993. Distributed Morphology and the pieces of inflection. In *The view from Building 20. Essays in linguistics in honor of Sylvain Bromberger*, 111–176. Cambridge, MA: MIT Press.

Halle, Morris & Alec Marantz. 1994. Some key features of Distributed Morphology. In Andrew Carnie & Heidi Harley (eds.), *Papers on phonology and morphology* (MIT Working Papers in Linguistics 21), 275–288. Cambridge, MA: MITWPL.

Halle, Morris & Andrew Nevins. 2009. Rule application in phonology. In Eric Raimy & Charles Cairns (eds.), *Contemporary views on architecture and representations in phonology*, 355–382. Cambridge, MA: MIT Press.

Hay, Jennifer, Christopher Kennedy & Beth Levin. 1999. Scalar structure underlies telicity in 'degree achievements'. In Tanya Matthews & Devon Strolovitch (eds.), *Proceedings of SALT IX*, 127–144. Ithaca: CLC Publications.

Hoji, Hajime, Satoshi Kinsui, Yukinori Takubo & Ayumi Ueyama. 2003. The demonstratives in modern Japanese. In Yen-hui Audrey Li & Andrew Simpson (eds.), *Functional structure(s), form and interpretation: Perspectives from East Asian languages*, 97–128. London: Routledge.

Holvoet, Axel. 2016. Semantic functions of complementizers in Baltic. In Kasper Boye & Petar Kehayov (eds.), *Complementizer semantics in European Languages*, 225–264. Berlin: Mouton de Gruyter.

Huybregts, M. A. C. 1976. Vragende(r)wijs: Progressieve taalkunde. In Geert Koefoed & Arnold Evers (eds.), *Lijnen van taaltheoretisch ondezoek*, 303–366. Groningen: H. D. Tjeenk Willink.

Hyman, Larry. 2003. Basaá. In Derek Nurse & Gérard Philippson (eds.), *The Bantu languages*, 257–282. New York: Routledge.

Isačenko, Aleksandr V. 1962. *Die russische Sprache der Gegenwart: Formenlehre.* Halle (Saale): Max Niemeyer Verlag.

Jabłońska, Patrycja. 2004. When the prefixes meet the suffixes. *Nordlyd* 32(2). 363–401. DOI:10.7557/12.73

Jabłońska, Patrycja. 2007. *Radical decomposition and argument structure.* CASTL/University of Tromsø dissertation.

Jackendoff, Ray. 2002. *Foundations of language.* Oxford: Oxford University Press.

Jakobson, Roman. 1948. Russian conjugation. *Word* 4(3). 155–167. DOI:10.1080/00437956.1948.11659338

Jenks, Peter, Emmanuel-Moselly Makasso & Larry Hyman. 2017. Accessibility and demonstrative operators in Basaá relative clauses. In Gratien Gualbet

Antindogbe & Rebecca Grollemund (eds.), *Relative clauses in Cameroonian languages*, 17–46. Berlin: Mouton de Gruyter.

Katz, Jerrold & Paul Postal. 1964. *An integrated theory of linguistic descriptions.* Cambridge, MA: MIT Press.

Kayne, Richard. 1994. *The antisymmetry of syntax.* Cambridge, MA: MIT Press.

Kayne, Richard. 2005. Some notes on comparative syntax, with special reference to English and French. In Guglielmo Cinque & Richard Kayne (eds.), *The Oxford handbook of comparative syntax*, 3–69. New York: Oxford University Press.

Kayne, Richard. 2007. A short note on *where* vs. *place*. In Roberta Maschi, Nicoletta Penello & Piera Rizzolatti (eds.), *Miscellanea di studi linguistici offerti a Laura Vanelli da amici e allievi padovani*, 245–257. Udine: Forum.

Kayne, Richard. 2017. Antisymmetry and morphology: Prefixes vs. suffixes. In Clemens Mayr & Edwin Williams (eds.), *11-11-17. Festschrift für Martin Prinzhorn* (Wiener Linguistische Gazette 82), 145–162. Institut für Sprachwissenschaft, Universität Wien.

Kenesei, István, Robert M. Vago & Anna Fenyvesi. 1998. *Hungarian.* London & New York: Routledge.

Kiparsky, Paul. 2018. Outward sensitive allomorphy in Nez Perce? Manuscript, Stanford University.

Klein, Wolfgang. 1994. *Time in language.* London: Routledge.

Komárek, Miroslav. 2006. *Příspěvky k české morfologii.* Olomouc: Periplum.

Koopman, Hilda. 2000. Prepositions, postpositions, circumpositions, and particles. In Hilda Koopman (ed.), *The syntax of specifiers and heads*, 204–260. London: Routledge.

Kracht, Markus. 2002. On the semantics of locatives. *Linguistics and Philosophy* 25(2). 157–232. DOI:10.1023/A:1014646826099

Kuno, Susumu. 1973. *The structure of the Japanese language.* Cambridge, MA: MIT Press.

Lander, Eric & Liliane Haegeman. 2016. The nanosyntax of spatial deixis. *Studia Linguistica* 72(2). 362–427. DOI:10.1111/stul.12061

Laskowski, Roman. 1975. *Studia nad morfonologią współczesnego języka polskiego.* Wrocław: Zakład Narodowy imenia Ossolińskich.

Lasnik, Howard & Mamoru Saito. 1992. *Move α: Conditions on its application and output.* Cambridge, MA: MIT Press.

Lawal, Adenike S. 1991. Yoruba *pé* and *kí*: Verbs or complementizers. *Studies in African Linguistics* 22(1). 73–84.

Leu, Thomas. 2007. These HERE demonstratives. In *U. Penn Working Papers in Linguistics. Proceedings of the 30th annual Penn Linguistics Colloquium*, 141–154. University of Pennsylvania.

Leu, Thomas. 2015. *The architecture of determiners.* New York: Oxford University Press.

Levin, Beth & Malka Rappaport Hovav. 1995. *Unaccusativity: At the syntax-semantics interface.* Cambridge, MA: MIT Press.

Levin, Beth & Malka Rappaport Hovav. 2005. *Argument realization.* Cambridge, UK: Cambridge University Press.

Lightner, Theodore M. 1972. *Problems in the theory of phonology. Vol. 1: Russian phonology and Turkish phonology.* Edmonton: Linguistic Research.

Lohndal, Terje. 2011. Freezing effects and objects. *Journal of Linguistics* 47(1). 163–199. DOI:10.1017/S0022226710000010

Lyons, Christopher. 1999. *Definiteness.* Cambridge, UK: Cambridge University Press.

Makasso, Emmanuel-Moselly. 2010. Processus de relativisation en Bàsaá: de la syntaxe á la prosodie. In Laura Downing, Annie Rialland, Jean-Marc Beltzung, Sophie Manus, Cédric Patin & Kristina Riedel (eds.), *Papers from the Workshop on Bantu relative clauses* (ZAS Papers in Linguistics 53), 145–158. Berlin: ZAS.

Mateu, Jaume. 2002. *Argument structure. Relational construal at the syntax-semantics interface.* Universitat Autònoma de Barcelona dissertation.

Mateu, Jaume. 2014. Argument structure. In Andrew Carnie, Yosuke Sato & Daniel Siddiqi (eds.), *The Routledge handbook of syntax*, 24–41. Oxford/New York: Routledge.

Mathiassen, Terje. 1997. *A short grammar of Latvian.* Columbus, OH: Slavica Publishers, Inc.

McCawley, James. 1968. The role of semantics in a grammar. In Emmon Bach & Robert Harms (eds.), *Universals in linguistic theory*, 124–169. New York: Holt, Rinehart & Winston.

Mihalicek, Vedrana. 2012. *Serbo-Croatian word order: A logical approach.* The Ohio State University dissertation.

Mokrosz, Ewelina. 2014. Exhaustive *to* in Polish: a Minimalist account. In Jacek Witkoś & Sylwester Jaworski (eds.), *New insights into Slavic linguistics*, 269–282. Frankfurt am Main: Peter Lang.

Müller, Gereon. 1998. *Incomplete category fronting: A derivational approach to remnant movement in German.* Dordrecht: Kluwer Academic Publishers.

Müller, Gereon. 2008. Syncretism without Underspecification in Optimality Theory: The role of leading forms. In Fabian Heck, Gereon Müller & Jochen Trommer (eds.), *Varieties of competition* (Linguistische Arbeitsberichte 87). Leipzig University.

Müller, Gereon. 2010. On deriving CED effects from PIC. *Linguistic Inquiry* 41(1). 35–82. DOI:10.1162/ling.2010.41.1.35

References

Mykowiecka, Agnieszka. 2001. Polish relatives with the marker *co*. In Adam Przepiórkowski & Piotr Bański (eds.), *Generative linguistics in Poland: Syntax and morphosyntax*, 149–158. Warsaw: Institute of Computer Science, Polish Academy of Sciences.

Nagórko, Alicja. 1998. *Zarys gramatyki polskiej (ze słowotwórstwem)*. Warsaw: PWN.

Nau, Nicole. 1998. *Latvian*. Munich & Newcastle: Lincom Europa.

Nau, Nicole. 2009. Towards a comprehensive description of Latvian relative clauses. In Sturla Berg-Olsen (ed.), *The Baltic languages and the Nordic countries*, 93–116. Vilnius: Lietuviu kalbos institutas.

Nau, Nicole. 2011. Declension classes in Latvian and Latgalian: Morphomics vs. morphophonology. *Baltic Linguistics* 2. 141–177.

Neeleman, Ad & Krista Szendrői. 2007. Radical pro-drop and the morphology of pronouns. *Linguistic Inquiry* 38(4). 671–714. DOI:10.1162/ling.2007.38.4.671

Ngonyani, Deo. 2001. Evidence for head raising in Kiswahili relative clauses. *Studies in African Linguistics* 30(1). 59–73.

Nichols, Johanna. 1994. Ingush. In Rieks Smeets (ed.), *The indigenous languages of the Caucasus: Northeast Caucasian Languages*, 79–145. Delmar, NY: Caravan Books.

Olsen, Mari Broman. 1994. The semantics and pragmatics of lexical aspect features. *Studies in the Linguistic Sciences* 24(2). 361–375.

Olsen, Mari Broman. 1997. *A semantic and pragmatic model of lexical and grammatical aspect* (Outstanding dissertations in linguistics). New York: Garland Press.

Pantcheva, Marina. 2008. The place of PLACE in Persian. In Anna Asbury, Jakub Dotlačil, Berit Gehrke & Rick Nouwen (eds.), *Syntax and semantics of spatial P*, 305–330. Amsterdam: John Benjamins.

Pantcheva, Marina. 2011. *Decomposing path: The nanosyntax of directional expressions*. CASTL/University of Tromsø dissertation.

Penner, Zvi & Thomas Bader. 1995. Issues in the syntax of subordination: A comparative study of the complementizer system in Germanic, Romance, and Semitic languages with special reference to Bernese Swiss German. In Zvi Penner (ed.), *Topics in Swiss German syntax*, 73–289. Bern: Peter Lang.

Plakendorf, Brigitte. 2007. *Contact in the prehistory of the Sakha (Yakuts). Linguistic and genetic perspectives*. Universiteit Leiden dissertation.

Plank, Frans. 1999. Split morphology: How agglutination and flexion mix. *Linguistic Typology* 3(3). 279–340. DOI:10.1515/lingty-2017-1006

Pokorny, Julius. 1959. *Indogermanisches etymologisches Wörterbuch*. Bern/Munich: A. Francke.

Postal, Paul. 1972. On some rules that are not successive-cyclic. *Linguistic Inquiry* 3(2). 211–222.

Praulinš, Dece. 2012. *Latvian: An essential grammar.* Oxford/New York: Routledge.

Ramchand, Gillian. 2008. *Verb meaning and the lexicon. A first phase syntax.* Cambridge, UK: Cambridge University Press.

Ramchand, Gillian. 2013. Argument structure and argument structure alternations. In Marcel den Dikken (ed.), *The Cambridge handbook of generative syntax*, 265–321. Cambridge, UK: Cambridge University Press.

Richards, Norvin. 2001. An idiomatic argument for lexical decomposition. *Linguistic Inquiry* 32(1). 183–192. DOI:10.1162/002438901554649

Rizzi, Luigi. 2006. On the form of chains: Criterial positions and ECP effects. In Lisa Cheng & Norbert Corver (eds.), *On Wh-movement*, 97–133. Cambridge, MA: MIT Press.

Rizzi, Luigi. 2007. On some properties of Criterial Freezing. In Vincenzo Moscati (ed.), *CISCL Working Papers on Language and Cognition*, 145–158. Università degli studi di Siena.

Rizzi, Luigi & Ur Shlonsky. 2007. Strategies of subject extraction. In Hans-Martin Gärtner & Uli Sauerland (eds.), *Interfaces + recursion = language? Chomsky's minimalism and the view from syntax-semantics*, 115–160. Berlin: Mouton de Gruyter.

Roehrs, Dorian. 2010. Demonstrative-reinforcer constructions. *Journal of Comparative Germanic Linguistics* 13(3). 225–268. DOI:10.1007/s10828-010-9038-4

Rothstein, Susan. 2004. *Structuring events. A study in the semantics of lexical aspect.* Oxford: Blackwell.

Rounds, Carol. 2001. *Hungarian: An essential grammar.* London: Routledge.

Roussou, Anna. 2016. Complement clauses: Case and argumenthood. Manuscript, Univeristy of Patras.

Rubach, Jerzy. 1984. *Cyclic and lexical phonology: The structure of Polish.* Dordrecht: Foris.

Rubach, Jerzy. 1993. *The lexical phonology of Slovak.* Oxford: Oxford University Press.

Salzmann, Martin. 2006. Resumptive pronouns and matching effects in Zürich German relative clauses as distributed deletion. *Leiden Papers in Linguistics* 3(1). 17–50.

Salzmann, Martin. 2017. *Reconstruction and resumption in indirect A′-dependencies. On the syntax of prolepsis and relativization in (Swiss) German and beyond.* Berlin: Mouton de Gruyter.

References

Scheer, Tobias. 2003. The key to Czech vowel length: Templates. In Petr Kosta, Joanna Błaszczak, Jens Frasek, Ljudmila Geist & Marzena Żygis (eds.), *Investigations into formal Slavic linguistics*, 97–118. Frankfurt am Main: Peter Lang.

Scheer, Tobias. 2011. Home-made Western Slavic vowel length. In Roman Sukaè (ed.), *From present to past and back*, 165–187. Frankfurt am Main: Peter Lang.

Schmitt, Rüdiger. 1981. *Grammatik des Klassisch-Armenischen*. Innsbruck: Institut für Sprachwissenschaft der Universität Innsbruck.

Šimík, Radek. 2009. The syntax, semantics, and pragmatics of the focus particle *to* in Czech. In Gerhild Zybatow, Denisa Lenertová, Uwe Junghanns & Petr Biskup (eds.), *Studies in formal Slavic phonology, morphology, syntax, semantics and information structure: Proceedings of FDSL 7, Leipzig 2007*, 327–340. Frankfurt am Main: Peter Lang.

Smith, Carlota. 1997. *The parameter of aspect*. 2nd edition. Dordrecht: Kluwer.

Starke, Michal. 2004. On the inexistence of specifiers and the nature of heads. In Adriana Belletti (ed.), *Structures and beyond* (The cartography of syntactic structures 3), 252–268. New York: Oxford University Press.

Starke, Michal. 2006. The nanosyntax of participles. Lectures at the 13th EGG summer school, Olomouc.

Starke, Michal. 2009. Nanosyntax: A short primer to a new approach to language. *Nordlyd* 36(1). 1–6. DOI:10.7557/12.213

Starke, Michal. 2014a. Cleaning up the lexicon. *Linguistic Analysis* 39(1). 245–256.

Starke, Michal. 2014b. Towards elegant parameters: Language variation reduces to the size of lexically stored trees. In M. Carme Picallo (ed.), *Linguistic variation in the Minimalist framework*, 140–152. Oxford: Oxford University Press.

Starke, Michal. 2017. Resolving (DAT = ACC) ≠ GEN. *Glossa: a journal of general linguistics* 2(1). 104. DOI:10.5334/gjgl.408

Starke, Michal. 2018. Complex left branches, spellout and prefixes. In Lena Baunaz, Karen De Clercq, Liliane Haegeman & Eric Lander (eds.), *Exploring Nanosyntax*, 239–249. New York: Oxford University Press.

Steriade, Donca. 2016. The morphome vs similarity-based syncretism: Latin *t*-stem derivatives. In Ana Luís & Ricardo Bermúdez-Otero (eds.), *The morpheme debate*, 112–172. Oxford: Oxford University Press. DOI:10.1093/acprof:oso/9780198702108.003.0006

Stump, Gregory. 2001. *Inflectional morphology. A theory of paradigm structure*. Cambridge, UK: Cambridge University Press.

Svenonius, Peter. 2004a. Slavic prefixes and morphology: An introduction to the Nordlyd volume. *Nordlyd* 32(2). 177–204. DOI:10.7557/12.67

Svenonius, Peter. 2004b. Slavic prefixes inside and outside the VP. *Nordlyd* 32(2). 205–253. DOI:10.7557/12.68

Svenonius, Peter. 2010. Spatial P in English. In Guglielmo Cinque & Luigi Rizzi (eds.), *Mapping spatial PPs* (The cartography of syntactic structures 6), 127–160. Oxford: Oxford University Press.

Szczegielniak, Adam. 2005. Two types of resumptive pronouns in Polish relative clauses. *Linguistic Variation Yearbook* 5. 165–185. DOI:10.1075/livy.5.06szc

Szpyra, Jolanta. 1989. *The phonology-morphology interface: Cycles, levels, and words.* London & New York: Routledge.

Tajsner, Przemysław. 2008. *Aspects of the grammar of focus. A minimalist perspective.* Frankfurt am Main: Peter Lang.

Tajsner, Przemysław. 2015. On specification predication and the derivation of copular *to*-clauses in Polish. *Studia Anglica Posnaniensia* 50(4). 25–66. DOI:10.1515/stap-2015-0032

Tajsner, Przemysław. 2018. On left-peripheral particle *to* in Polish and Czech: A focus, a topic head, or neither? *Poznań Studies in Contemporary Linguistics* 54(4). 541–572. DOI:10.1515/psicl-2018-0022

Taraldsen Medová, Lucie & Bartosz Wiland. 2018a. Functional sequence zones and Slavic L>T>N participles. In Lena Baunaz, Karen De Clercq, Liliane Haegeman & Eric Lander (eds.), *Exploring Nanosyntax*, 305–328. New York: Oxford University Press.

Taraldsen Medová, Lucie & Bartosz Wiland. 2018b. Semelfactives are bigger than degree achievements. *Natural Language & Linguistic Theory.* DOI:10.1007/s11049-018-9434-z

Taraldsen, Tarald. 2010. The nanosyntax of Nguni noun class prefixes and concords. *Lingua* 120(6). 1522–1548. DOI:10.1016/j.lingua.2009.10.004

Taraldsen, Tarald. 2012. Modeling the Neighborhood Hypothesis for syncretisms. Handout for a talk given at the 43rd annual meeting of the North East Linguistic Society (NELS), The City University of New York, October 19.

Torrego, Esther. 1985. On empty categories in nominals. Manuscript, University of Massachusetts, Boston.

Townsend, Charles & Laura Janda. 1996. *Common and comparative Slavic: Phonology and inflection.* Columbus: Slavica Publishers.

Van den Berg, René. 1989. *A grammar of the Muna language.* Dordrecht: Foris Publication.

van Riemsdijk, Henk. 1989. Swiss relatives. In Dany Jaspers, Wim Klooster, Yvan Putseys & Pieter Seuren (eds.), *Sentential complementation and the lexicon: Studies in honour of Wim De Geest*, 343–354. Dordrecht: Foris.

van Riemsdijk, Henk. 2003. East meets West: Aboutness relatives in Swiss German. In Jan Koster & Henk van Riemsdijk (eds.), *Germania et alia: A linguistic webschrift for Hans den Besten*, 1–20. Groningen: University of Groningen.

References

Vanden Wyngaerd, Guido. 2018a. *Here, there, where*. Paper presented at the Olomouc Linguistics Colloquium (Olinco), Palacký University in Olomouc, June 7–9.

Vanden Wyngaerd, Guido. 2018b. The feature structure of pronouns: A probe into multidimensional paradigms. In Lena Baunaz, Karen De Clercq, Liliane Haegeman & Eric Lander (eds.), *Exploring Nanosyntax*, 277–304. New York: Oxford University Press.

Vangsnes, Øystein. 2013. Syncretism and functional expansion in Germanic wh-expressions. *Language Sciences* 36. 47–65. DOI:10.1016/j.langsci.2012.03.019

Vendler, Zeno. 1967. *Linguistics in philosophy*. Ithaca: Cornell University Press.

Weerman, Fred & Jacqueline Evers-Vermeul. 2002. Pronouns and case. *Lingua* 112(4). 301–338. DOI:10.1016/S0024-3841(01)00049-3

Wexler, Kenneth & Peter Culicover. 1980. *Formal principles of language acquisition*. Cambridge, MA: MIT Press.

Wiland, Bartosz. 2009. *Aspects of order preservation in Polish and English*. Adam Mickiewicz University in Poznań dissertation. http://ling.auf.net/lingbuzz/000906.

Wiland, Bartosz. 2010. Overt evidence from left-branch extraction in Polish for punctuated paths. *Linguistic Inquiry* 41(2). 335–347. DOI:10.1162/ling.2010.41.2.335

Wiland, Bartosz. 2012. Prefix stacking, syncretism, and the syntactic hierarchy. In Mojmir Dočekal & Marketa Ziková (eds.), *Slavic languages in formal grammar* (Proceedings of FDSL 8.5, Brno 2010), 307–324. Berlin/Frankfurt: Peter Lang.

Wiland, Bartosz. 2016. Le charme discret of remnant movement: Crossing and nesting in Polish OVS sentences. *Studies in Polish Linguistics* 11(3). 133–165. DOI:10.4467/23005920SPL.16.007.5881

Wiland, Bartosz. 2018a. A note on lexicalizing 'what' and 'who' in Russian and in Polish. *Poznań Studies in Contemporary Linguistics* 54(4). 573–604. DOI:10.1515/psicl-2018-0023

Wiland, Bartosz. 2018b. Anti-freezing and peeling. In Sherry Hucklebridge & Max Nelson (eds.), *NELS 48: Proceedings of the forty-eighth annual meeting of the North East Linguistic Society*, vol. 3, 235–244. GLSA Publications, University of Massachusetts.

Wiland, Bartosz. 2018c. Ordering paradoxes in a cross-categorial paradigm: On syncretisms with the declarative complementizer. In Pavel Caha, Karen De Clercq & Guido Vanden Wyngaerd (eds.), *The unpublished manuscript. A collection of LingBuzz papers to celebrate Michal Starke's 50th birthday*, 127–147. http://ling.auf.net/lingbuzz/003993.

Willim, Ewa. 2006. *Event, individuation and countability: A study with special reference to English and Polish*. Kraków: Jagiellonian University Press.

Wise, Mary Ruth. 1986. Grammatical characteristics of PreAndine Arawakan languages of Peru. In Desmond C. Derbyshire & Geoffrey K. Pullum (eds.), *Handbook of Amazonian languages*, vol. 1, 567–642. Berlin: Mouton de Gruyter.

Xiao, Zhonghua & Anthony McEnery. 2004. A corpus-based two-level model of situation aspect. *Journal of Linguistics* 40(2). 325–363. DOI:10.1017/S0022226704002543

Žaucer, Rok. 2005. Slovenian inceptive prefix *za-*: a VP internal P. In Claire Gurski (ed.), *Proceedings of the 2005 annual conference of the Canadian Linguistic Association*, 1–12. Department of French, University of Western Ontario.

Zompí, Stanislao. 2017. *Case decomposition meets dependent-case theories*. University of Pisa MA thesis. http://ling.auf.net/lingbuzz/003421.

Zwarts, Joost. 2005. Prepositional aspect and the algebra of paths. *Linguistics and Philosophy* 28(6). 739–779. DOI:10.1007/s10988-005-2466-y

Name index

Abels, Klaus, 34
Acedo Matellán, Víctor, 8
Acquaviva, Paolo, 8
Aikhenvald, Alexandra, 83

Bach, Emmon, 57
Bacz, Barbara, 46, 47
Bader, Thomas, 141
Baerman, Matthew, 16
Bassong, Paul, 141
Baunaz, Lena, 37, 38, 81, 84–86, 89, 90, 99, 102, 106, 112, 115, 116
Bayer, Josef, 140
Beavers, John, 64
Bernstein, Judy, 94
Bianchi, Valentina, 148
Blevins, James, 6
Bobaljik, Jonathan, 1, 10, 14, 16
Boeckx, Cedric, 34
Booij, Gert, 8
Borer, Hagit, 7, 8
Borgman, Donald, 116
Botwinik-Rotem, Irena, 126
Brandner, Ellen, 140
Bräuning, Iris, 140
Browning, M.A., 34
Budina Lazdina, Tereza, 109, 110
Burzio, Luigi, 16

Caha, Pavel, v, 6, 10, 12, 16–18, 21, 24, 25, 32, 33, 35, 63, 78, 98, 122, 126, 135, 136, 152

Campbell, Lyle, 116
Cardinaletti, Anna, 32
Carlson, Greg, 53, 58
Carstens, Vicki, 145
Chomsky, Noam, 13, 33
Cinque, Guglielmo, 7, 127
Collins, Chris, 34
Corver, Norber, 34
Culicover, Peter, 31, 34
Curnow, Timothy, 116
Cysouw, Michael, 106, 115, 116
Czaykowska-Higgins, Ewa, 40, 41, 44

De Clercq, Karen, 16
de Swart, Henriette, 57
Declerck, Renaat, 57
den Dikken, Marcel, 127
Dickey, Stephen, 47, 57
Dimmendaal, Gerrit J., 84
DiSciullo, Anna Maria, 5
Dixon, R. M. W., 83
Dol, Philomena, 6
Dowty, David, 44, 51

Eckert, Rainer, 110
Egg, Markus, 36, 64
Embick, David, 8
Evers-Vermeul, Jacqueline, 9

Fábregas, Antonio, 11
Fanselow, Gisbert, 34
Fennell, Trevor G., 111

Name index

Flier, Michael, 41
Friedman, Victor A., 6

Gelsen, Henry, 111
Goldberg, Adele, 8
Greenberg, Joseph H., 130
Grewendorf, Günther, 34
Grohmann, Kleanthes, 34
Grosu, Alexander, 141
Grzegorczykowa, Renata, 41, 47
Gussmann, Edmund, 15, 44, 66

Haegeman, Liliane, 91, 95, 98, 118, 122
Hale, Kenneth, 8
Halle, Morris, 8, 10, 41, 66
Hay, Jennifer, 44
Hoji, Hajime, 91, 95
Holaj, Richard, v
Holmberg, Anders, v
Holvoet, Axel, 111
Huybregts, M. A. C., 34
Hyman, Larry, 142

Isačenko, Aleksandr V., 41

Jabłońska, Patrycja, 40, 41, 47, 48
Jackendoff, Ray, 8
Jakobson, Roman, 36, 66
Janda, Laura, 40, 41, 47
Jenks, Peter, 142, 144–149

Katz, Jerrold, 126
Kayne, Richard, 5, 7, 13, 34, 126, 145, 146
Kenesei, István, 88
Keyser, Samuel J., 8
Kiparsky, Paul, 75
Klein, Wolfgang, 46
Klimek-Jankowska, Dorota, v

Komárek, Miroslav, 41
Koopman, Hilda, 126
Kopecky, Felix, v
Kracht, Markus, 126
Kuno, Susumu, 95, 141

Lander, Eric, 37, 38, 81, 84–86, 89–91, 95, 98, 99, 102, 106, 112, 115, 116, 118, 122
Laskowski, Roman, 40, 41
Lasnik, Howard, 34
Lawal, Adenike S., 82, 83
Leu, Thomas, 95, 105, 126
Levin, Beth, 8, 54
Lightner, Theodore M., 41, 66
Lohndal, Terje, 34
Lyons, Christopher, 110

Makasso, Emmanuel-Moselly, 142, 144
Marantz, Alec, 8
Mateu, Jaume, 8
Mathiassen, Terje, 110, 120
McEnery, Anthony, 64
McCawley, James, 9
Mihalicek, Vedrana, 89
Mokrosz, Ewelina, 97
Müller, Gereon, 16, 34
Mykowiecka, Agnieszka, 87

Nagórko, Alicja, 97
Nau, Nicole, v, 109, 120, 123
Navicka, Tatjana, v, 123
Neeleman, Ad, 9
Nevins, Andrew, 66
Ngonyani, Deo, 145
Nichols, Johanna, 6
Nordhoff, Sebastian, v
Noyer, Rolf, 8

Name index

Olsen, Mari Broman, 36, 64

Pantcheva, Marina, 14, 16, 24, 25, 29, 71, 126, 127, 135, 136, 152
Penner, Zvi, 141
Plakendorf, Brigitte, 6
Plank, Frans, 6
Pokorny, Julius, 130
Postal, Paul, 34, 126
Praulinš, Dece, 109, 122, 126
Puzynina, Jadwiga, 41

Ramchand, Gillian, 7, 8, 11, 54
Rappaport Hovav, Malka, 8, 54
Richards, Norvin, 49
Rizzi, Luigi, 7, 34
Roehrs, Dorian, 94
Rothstein, Susan, 44, 64
Rounds, Carol, 88
Roussou, Anna, 117
Rubach, Jerzy, 15, 36, 41, 44, 66

Saito, Mamoru, 34
Salzmann, Martin, 140, 148
Scheer, Tobias, v, 74, 75
Schmitt, Rüdiger, 6
Shlonsky, Ur, 34
Šimík, Radek, v, 97
Smith, Carlota, 36, 64
Starke, Michal, v, 1, 2, 7, 10, 12, 16, 18, 22–25, 32, 67, 78, 100, 120, 121, 151
Steriade, Donca, 75
Stump, Gregory, 16
Svenonius, Peter, 41, 63, 127, 128
Szczegielniak, Adam, 87
Szendrői, Krista, 9
Szpyra, Jolanta, 41

Tajsner, Przemysław, 97

Taraldsen Medová, Lucie, v, 16, 18, 44, 45, 47–49, 51, 53, 54, 65, 76, 134
Taraldsen, Tarald, 16, 24, 135
Terzi, Arhonto, 126
Torrego, Esther, 34
Townsend, Charles, 40, 41

Van den Berg, René, 116
Van Riemsdijk, Henk, 140, 141
Vanden Wyngaerd, Guido, 24, 25, 126–128, 136
Vangsnes, Øystein, 16, 115

Weerman, Fred, 9
Wexler, Kenneth, 31, 34
Wiland, Bartosz, v, 15, 16, 18, 32, 34, 44, 45, 47–49, 51, 53, 54, 63, 65, 76, 90, 94, 97, 100, 102, 106, 114, 126, 134
Willim, Ewa, 47, 57
Wise, Mary Ruth, 116
Witkoś, Jacek, v

Xiao, Zhonghua, 64

Ziková, Marketa, 63
Zompí, Stanislao, 16
Zwarts, Joost, 126
Žaucer, Rok, 63

Language index

Afrikaans, 83, 94
Amuecha, 116, 117
Arawakan, 116
Austronesian, 116
Awa Pit, 116, 117

Balkan Romani, *see* Romani
Baltic, 3, 109
Bantu, 3, 139, 145
Barbacoan, 116
Basaá, 1, 3, 139–142, 142^1, 143–145, 147–149
Basque, 83
Bavarian, 140
Bernese dialect, 141

Chukchi, 6^2
Classical Armenian, 6^2
Czech, 1, 2, 39–44, 44^5, 45–48, 48^8, 49–53, 53^{11}, 55–60, 62, 63, 65^{14}, 71, 73–78, 90, 97^5, 122^9, 130, 143

Dutch, 34, 83, 89, 139

English, 6, 16–18, 21, 22, 22^{11}, 23, 25, 26, 32, 34, 47–50, 51^{10}, 52, 53, 58^{13}, 64, 81–86, 89, 90, 93, 94, 103–106, 106^9, 139, 141, 147–149
Estonian, 6^2

Finnish, 6^2, 83

French, 83, 92, 92^3, 93

German, 16, 34, 83, 89, 105^8, 133
Germanic, 94, 95, 105^8, 113, 115^5, 126^{11}
Greek, 117^6, 126^{11}

Hausa, 83, 84
Hebrew, 126^{11}
Hungarian, 88

Indo-European, 114, 130^{15}
Ingush, 6^2
Italian, 81, 83–86, 90, 92, 103

Japanese, 91, 92, 95, 95^4, 96, 141

Karelian, 6^2
Kazakh, 6^2

Latvian, 1, 3, 109–111, 111^2, 112–114, 116–120, 120^8, 121, 122, 122^{10}, 123–126, 128^{13}, 129, 130, 130^{15}, 131–137, 143, 148, 152

Maybrat, 6
Modern Greek, 117^6
Muna, 116, 117

Old Church Slavonic, 41^2

Persian, 126^{11}
Pipil, 116
Pite Saami, 83

Language index

Polish, 1, 2, 5, 6, 6^2, 14^9, 15, 15^9, 16–20, 25, 26, 32–35, 37, 39–41, 41^2, 42, 43, 43^3, 44, 44^4, 44^5, 45, 46, 46^6, 47, 47^7, 48, 48^8, 49, 50, 52, 53, 53^{11}, 54–61, 63, 64, 65^{14}, 77, 78, 86, 87, 90, 91, 93–97, 97^5, 97^6, 98–103, 105, 106^9, 111–113, 114^4, 122^9, 126^{11}, 132–136, 143

Prizren-Timok dialect of Serbian, 6^2

Romance, 94
Romani, 6, 16, 19, 20, 23, 25, 26
Romanian, 81, 83
Russian, 1, 3, 40^1, 41, 41^2, 47^7, 66^{15}, 81, 82, 88–91, 93–96, 97^6, 98, 100–103, 105, 106, 106^9, 107, 109, 111–114, 126^{11}, 133, 136, 143

Sanumá, 116
Serbo-Croatian, 82, 88–90, 100, 112
Shona, 126^{11}
Slavic, 2, 3, 5, 6^2, 14^9, 32, 36^{17}, 37–40, 40^1, 41, 41^2, 43, 52, 63, 66, 66^{15}, 74, 89, 90, 99, 102, 109, 113, 114^4, 133, 137, 151, 152
Spanish, 34
Swiss German, 139–141, 149

Upper German dialects, 140
Uto-Aztecan, 116

West Germanic, 89

Yanomaman, 116
Yiddish, 83
Yoruba, 82, 83

Züritüütsch dialect, 140, 141

Subject index

*ABA, 1, 14, 16, 38, 81, 104, 106, 110, 117, 119, 136, 139, 141–144, 147–149, 152

activity, 41–43, 46, 50^9, 58^{13}, 64, 75
algorithm, *see* spell-out algorithm
allomorphy, 25, 75, 78, 92, 106, 114^4, 131^{16}
argument structure, 7, 8^4, 41, 43, 48, 52, 54, 55, 57, 60, 75

backtracking, 20, 22, 28–31, 36, 37, 40, 66, 71–75, 78, 103, 120, 151

cartography, 7
causative, 43, 51^{10}, 52
complementizer, 1, 3, 5, 21, 22, 37, 38, 81–86, 89, 90, 99^7, 106, 109, 111, 113, 130, 132, 133, 137, 141, 146^2, 152
containment, 1, 6^2, 10, 11, 16, 23, 32^{15}, 33, 37, 38, 49, 62, 68, 69, 79, 81, 82, 86, 88, 89, 95, 107, 109, 113, 115–117, 129, 133, 137, 152
Criterial Freezing, 35
Cyclic Over-ride, 11, 99, 118, 123, 131^{16}

declarative complementizer, *see* complementizer

demonstrative, 1, 22, 37, 38, 81, 82, 84, 86, 88–90, 92^3, 94–96, 98, 102–104, 105^8, 107, 110–112, 114, 118, 120, 123, 126, 129^{14}, 130^{15}, 136, 137, 146–149
Distributed Morphology, 8, 9, 10^6, 10^7

Elsewhere Principle, 10, 11, 11^8
Exhaustive Lexicalization Principle, 11, 23^{12}

feature, 2, 7, 7^3, 8–10, 10^6, 10^7, 11–14, 17, 18, 20, 21, 22^{11}, 23^{12}, 24–26, 30, 33, 35–37, 46, 51, 51^{10}, 55, 56, 58^{13}, 61, 69, 71–73, 79, 85^2, 91, 98, 99, 101, 113, 115, 118–120, 123–125, 131–134, 151
Freezing Condition, 31, 33, 34^{16}, 35
fseq, 2, 14, 16, 17, 22, 26, 33, 98, 100, 101, 104, 106^9, 107, 130, 132, 133, 134^{17}, 135–137, 139, 143, 152
fseq zone, 134^{17}
functional sequence, *see* fseq

glide truncation, 36^{17}, 39, 44^4

interrogative pronoun, *see* wh-pronoun

Subject index

iterative, 1, 2, 25, 35, 36, 39, 43, 50^9, 53, 58, 58^{13}, 59–66, 70, 72–75
iterative alternation, 1, 35, 37, 44, 50^9, 54, 57–61, 70, 71, 73, 74, 76

LCA, 13, 14
lengthening, 73–75
lexicalization, *see* spell-out
light Get, 47–50, 50^9, 51, 51^{10}, 62, 70, 72
light Give, 39, 47–51, 58, 58^{13}, 61, 66, 68
linearization, 7, 12, 14, 19, 151

morpheme, 2, 5–7, 9, 18, 26, 28, 29, 31, 35–37, 39, 40, 42, 44, 45, 48, 50, 58^{13}, 66, 70–72, 85, 91, 96, 107, 114, 120, 126, 135, 142, 143, 151

Nanosyntax, 2, 7–9, 9^5, 10, 11, 18^{10}, 24, 37, 151

paradigm, 1, 10^7, 14, 15, 25, 37, 38, 81, 82, 89, 90, 96, 106, 109, 110, 112, 113, 122^{10}, 124, 130, 131, 133–137, 139–143, 147–149, 152
particle, 2, 21, 23, 97^5
peeling, 32, 32^{15}, 33, 35
phrasal spell-out, *see* spell-out
pointer, 24, 25, 69, 72, 74
preposition, 2, 6, 21, 23, 25, 127, 128, 128^{13}

reduction, 2, 26, 28–31, 35–37, 39, 40, 44, 65, 67, 68, 70, 71, 78, 151, 152

relative clause, 87, 142, 144–146, 146^2, 147–149
relative pronoun, *see* relativizer
relativizer, 1, 22, 38, 81, 84, 86–88, 90, 106, 122, 140, 142, 147–149
root, 5, 6, 8^4, 12, 13, 16–18, 20, 22^{11}, 36, 39–41, 41^2, 42–48, 50, 51, 51^{10}, 55, 58, 63, 66, 68, 71, 73–75, 97, 103, 104, 110

semelfactive, 1, 2, 35, 36, 39, 40, 41^2, 44–47, 47^7, 48, 49, 51–58, 60–67, 71–73, 75, 76, 122^9
semelfactive-iterative alternation, *see* iterative alternation
shortening, 73–75
Shortest Move, 12, 13, 27
shrinking, 69, 71–73
spell-out, 2, 3, 5, 7–14, 16–27, 29, 30, 35–37, 42, 50–52, 55, 56, 61–63, 65–67, 69–71, 73, 74, 78, 79, 84, 90, 99, 100, 107, 109, 118, 119, 122^9, 124, 129, 131^{16}, 132, 135, 137, 151
spell-out algorithm, 2, 16–18, 24, 30, 35, 37, 65, 66, 101, 102, 152
subextraction, 2, 3, 29–31, 34–37, 40, 67, 68, 70, 71, 73, 75, 78, 79, 109^1, 151, 152
Superset Principle, 10, 11, 14, 16, 17, 24, 29, 29^{13}, 50, 68, 84, 92, 118, 136
syncretism, 1, 6^2, 14–17, 21, 25, 38, 48, 79, 81, 82, 88, 89, 106, 109, 115, 117, 123, 135, 137, 139, 141, 143, 144, 147, 152

terminal node, 2, 7^3, 8–10, 13, 21, 86

thematic suffix, 36^{17}, 39–43, 44^4, 44^5, 47^7, 48, 54, 56, 58^{13}, 63, 70, 72, 74, 77, 78, 122^9
theme vowel, *see* thematic suffix

verb, 1–3, 5, 8^4, 25, 32, 36, 39, 40, 40^1, 41, 41^2, 42, 43, 43^3, 44–48, 48^8, 49, 50, 52, 53, 53^{11}, 55, 57, 58^{13}, 60–64, 77, 78, 82, 83, 89, 126–128
vowel truncation, 66, 66^{15}, 125

wh-pronoun, 1, 38, 81, 82, 84, 86, 88, 90, 103, 106, 113, 115, 122, 124, 135, 136